— THIRD EDITION —

# NEW YORK CITY'S
# BEST
## PUBLIC ELEMENTARY SCHOOLS

### A PARENTS' GUIDE

## Clara Hemphill

**with Deborah Apsel, Catherine Man,
and Pamela Wheaton**

TEACHERS
COLLEGE
PRESS

TEACHERS COLLEGE
COLUMBIA UNIVERSITY
NEW YORK

D1301582

Published by Teachers College Press, 1234 Amsterdam Avenue, New York, NY 10027

*Library of Congress Cataloging-in-Publication Data*

Hemphill, Clara, 1953–
    New York City's best public elementary schools : a parents' guide /
Clara Hemphill with Deborah Apsel . . . [et al.] — 3rd ed.
      p.  cm.
    Includes index.
    ISBN 0-8077-4613-4 (pbk. : alk. paper)
        1. Public schools—New York (State)—New York—Directories. 2
    Elementary schools—New York (State)—New York—Directories.  I. Title
    L903.N75N495  2005
    371.01′025747′1—dc22                                    2005041924

ISBN 0-8077-4613-4 (paper)

Printed on acid-free paper
Manufactured in the United States of America

12  11  10  09  08                          8  7  6  5  4  3  2

To my children's teachers:
Isabel, Paula, MaryAnne, Ann Marie,
Jody, Dani, and Caroline

# CONTENTS

# Contents

Contents

# Contents

# PREFACE TO THE THIRD EDITION

This completely updated and revised edition of *New York City's Best Public Elementary Schools* includes more than 70 new school profiles, bringing to 200 the total number of schools reviewed. This 3rd edition includes 112 in-depth school profiles as well as 90 shorter reports on good neighborhood schools, new schools, and established programs that are moving in a new direction. Happily, there are more good elementary schools in New York City than there have been in recent memory.

For this book, the staff of *www.Insideschools.org*, the online guide to New York City public schools sponsored by Advocates for Children, visited nearly 500 of the city's 600 elementary schools. In Brooklyn we found marked improvements in gentrifying neighborhoods in and around Williamsburg, Brooklyn Heights, and Park Slope. We were pleased by the progress we saw in a few poor neighborhoods, such as East New York, as well as in some immigrant communities and middle-class neighborhoods, like Bay Ridge.

In Staten Island, new principals and new teaching techniques have invigorated previously lackluster schools. In some Queens neighborhoods, such as Astoria and Long Island City, schools that had been adequate but a bit dull have found a new sense of excitement and purpose. Even in the South Bronx some of the city's most beleaguered schools have begun to show signs of life.

The gains have been uneven. The well-regarded schools of District 26 in northeast Queens and Manhattan's District 2 (covering the East Side and downtown) have maintained their star quality. But many Upper West Side and Upper Manhattan schools have continued to struggle with uneven leadership. Albany's refusal to substantially increase aid to schools—and City Hall's insistence that the schools can be improved without allocating more city tax revenues to education—have too often forced the school system to choose between much needed remedial education for the neediest children and advanced instruction for the most able.

The 3 years since the 2nd edition of this book was published have been tumultuous ones for the New York City school system. Mayor Mike Bloomberg wrested control of the schools from the discredited Board of Education and set in motion a massive reorganization, ending 30 years of decentralized control.

The mayor and his schools chancellor, Joel Klein, instituted a new, uniform curriculum—an ambitious attempt to offer all the schools in the city the progressive teaching techniques that had previously been the province of middle-class or wealthy neighborhoods such as Manhattan's Upper East Side. Inviting classroom libraries of children's literature and picture books have replaced dull and dusty textbooks. Tables, chairs, and rugs have replaced desks in rows. Teachers have been encouraged to lead class discussions, rather than to offer lectures. Children have begun to write far more frequently and in more depth than had been common in elementary schools.

The mayor, the first in a generation to have direct control of the schools, made missteps at first. His consolidation of 32 districts into 10 regions caused many administrative problems, some of which remain unresolved. Thousands of special education records were misplaced, and thousands of children didn't get the services they needed. Telephones ring unanswered in the new regional offices, and even the "voice mailboxes" are full. In some schools, particularly in Queens, the reforms were presented as a non-negotiable list of new rules to be followed, rather than a creative new approach to teaching. In those schools, not surprisingly, principals and staff rebelled at what they called micromanagement by the central administration.

The mayor and his chancellor—neither of whom had experience in education—alienated some of the school system's most seasoned and competent senior administrators with ill-considered directives and arrogant attitudes that were dismissive of their many accomplishments. Dozens of the city's best principals and administrators left, depriving the school system of much their needed leadership.

In the middle of the mayor's first term, however, the hemorrhaging of talent slowed and there were even signs of improvement, at least in the elementary schools. The chancellor appointed a knowledgeable deputy chancellor for instruction, Carmen Fariña, former principal for PS 6 in Manhattan and superintendent of District 15 in Brooklyn. While not universally loved, Farina is widely respected, and she carried out Bloomberg and Klein's program of reform with considerably more grace and competence than her predecessor, who left in a patronage scandal. If the recent gains are consolidated—and if Albany and City Hall can be persuaded to make the financial commitment that the schools so desperately need—the future looks promising.

# ACKNOWLEDGMENTS

Even more than previous editions, this book was a collaborative effort. It could not have been completed without the backing of the nonprofit organization for which I work, Advocates for Children. AFC executive director Jill Chaifetz gave me precious time off from my other duties to research and write the book. The entire staff of Insideschools.org, AFC's free online guide to New York City public schools, contributed to the book. Melanie Acevedo, Deborah Apsel, Judith Baum, Marcia Biederman, Carolina Gonzalez, Vicki Henderson, Tom Huser, Elizabeth Kiem, Catherine Man, John Thomas, Jacqueline Wayans, Pamela Wheaton, Vanessa Witenko, Helon Zelon, and Laura Zingmond visited many of the schools listed here (and many more which we decided not to include). Alex Ruano compiled the Department of Education data. Vanessa Witenko meticulously checked the facts in the manuscript.

The Alfred P. Sloan Foundation, the David L. Klein Foundation, and the Starr Foundation provided financial support for our research at *Insideschools.org*. My editor at Teachers College Press, Brian Ellerbeck, and publisher Carole Saltz, both public school parents, were enthusiastic backers of the project. The TC Press production staff, particularly Karl Nyberg, put the book out in record time, while the marketing and publicity staff worked hard to promote it.

The generosity of Department of Education officials, principals, and teachers cannot be overstated. They opened their doors to us, allowed us to sit in on classes and to write candidly about everything we saw, the good and the bad.

My husband, Robert Snyder, and children, Max and Allison, tolerated months of my distracted attention as I struggled to complete the project which has come to be know in our house as The Book That Never Ends. They are, as always, my greatest love and inspiration.

—Clara Hemphill

# New York City Department of Education
## Map of Instructional Divisions

# INTRODUCTION

Your daughter is 4, and you're trying to decide where to send her to kindergarten. Or you have an older son, and you're unhappy with his school. Or you're just moving to the city, and you're trying to decide where to live. What do you do? You've heard stories about New York City schools where kids beat each other up and almost no one learns to read. You've also heard that the city's public schools produce more winners of the prestigious Intel Science Talent Search prize than just about any other place in the country. How do you avoid the horror shows and get your child into the best school? And what is the "best" anyway?

Finding a good public elementary school among the more than 600 in New York City can challenge even the most intrepid parent. Although New York City has long had the largest system of school choice in the country—and dozens of schools accept children from outside their immediate neighborhood—finding out about the good schools and wrangling admission for your child can be a major chore. The Department of Education is in the midst of the most radical reorganization of public schools in a generation, and rules on admission change from year to year—or even, it seems, from month to month. Each person you telephone at a school or Department of Education office, it seems, will put you on hold, then forward you to someone else who will tell you the opposite of what the first person said. (That is, if you make it through their voice mail system.)

But don't despair. New York City has a surprising number of excellent public elementary schools—and you may have one just a few blocks from your home. New schools are opening all the time, and strong leadership can transform a mediocre school into a good one in just a few years.

Our favorites are included here. We picked them based on our visits and interviews with parents, teachers, and administrators. We chose not only schools with the highest test scores, but also those with strong leadership, lively classes, and a sense of community. We also included some schools we believe are poised to make gains in the coming years. We particularly sought out schools that admit children from outside their immediate neighborhood. We concentrated on neighborhoods, particularly in Manhattan and Brooklyn, in which parents shop around for schools. At the same time, we tried to make the guide useful to all parents in the city, not just those living in the richest neighborhoods: You don't have to live on Park Avenue to get a good education for your child (although living in a posh neighborhood generally helps).

You've read in the newspapers about crumbling school buildings, serious overcrowding, and chronic budget woes. The problems are real. But what makes a good school good isn't the beauty of its physical plant, but the quality of its principal and its teachers. Good principals attract private grant money to make up for shrinking tax revenues. They recruit and train the best teachers. They set the tone, create the atmosphere, and define the philosophy of the school.

Far too many New York City public schools are grim, depressing places, where the teachers are overwhelmed and demoralized, the students are alienated, and the administration is weak and ineffectual. The very best public schools in New York City, however, compete successfully for students with the very best private schools. Their teachers are drawn from some of the best teaching colleges in the country. New York is a magnet for talent, and the schools attract professionals from other fields who choose teaching as a second career or who volunteer part-time: stockbrokers and artists, dancers and scientists. Some of the city's most energetic and highly qualified teachers seek out the public schools—partly because they pay better than private or parochial schools.

Unfortunately, the city loses many talented teachers to the suburbs, because salaries are higher and working conditions easier in Westchester and Nassau counties than they are in the city. Nonetheless, during the course of writing this book, I came across half a dozen teachers who moved *to* New York City *from* jobs in the suburbs, willing to take a pay cut to be part of the spirit of innovation that characterizes the best New York City public schools. Much more than in the suburbs, teachers at New York City's best public schools have an opportunity to draw on new research and best practices developed at some of the nation's top schools of education: Bank Street College of Education and Teachers College, Columbia University, as well as important work being conducted at New York University, Fordham University, and Queens College. Administrators at one well-regarded suburban school, for example, boasted to me that one of their teachers had taken a summer school course with writing guru Lucy Calkins at Teachers College. In many New York City schools, the entire faculty has had such training. A teacher who moved to New York from a well-regarded school in a Washington suburb told me the city was 5 years ahead of practices there. Several parents who moved to the city from the suburbs—and who were lucky enough to land their children in good public schools—told me they were pleasantly surprised by the contrast. They found that the city schools had more creative teachers and a more rigorous curriculum than the suburban schools to which they had been accustomed.

Private schools in New York City promote their beautiful facilities and small class size to prospective parents. Public schools, on the other hand, starved for money for decades, tend to have stark physical plants and class sizes that are larger than ideal. But according to parents who have had experience with both, the quality of teaching is comparable in good private and good public schools. Catherine Hausman, co-author of *The Manhattan Family Guide to Private Schools*, switched her children from private schools to PS 6 on the Upper East Side where, she said, the teaching is superior. Parents at successful public schools aggressively raise extra money to support their budgets; in rich neighborhoods the PTA budgets top $250,000 a year. Principals at successful public schools are skilled in seeking extra funds from private foundations, corporations, and individuals. In addition, they aggressively court volunteers to help out in the classrooms, in the office, and in the lunchroom.

Some well-off parents choose public schools because they want to shield their children from what they consider the rampant materialism and competition over fancy clothes and expensive vacations that exist at some private schools. Moreover, they want their children to be exposed to people of different races and cultures. There are schools in Queens where 40 languages are spoken. Children learn about the Chinese New Year and Ramadan, Chanukah, and Kwanzaa—not from a book, but from other children's celebrations. Children learn respect and tolerance for others that serve them well whatever they do.

Race relations are as complicated in the schools as they are in the city as a whole, and everyone, it seems, feels like an aggrieved minority at one time or another. The school system is 40% Hispanic, 33% black, 14% white, and 13% Asian. Some of the schools are as segregated as the neighborhoods they serve; others are racially mixed.

But parents who are willing to enroll their children in a school in which they're in the minority sometimes have a better chance of getting into a sought-after program. Many schools value diversity and give special consideration in admission to children of a race or ethnic group that's underrepresented.

At the turn of the twentieth century, philosopher John Dewey wrote that schools must teach children to be "social beings," trained for leadership as well as obedience, trained to be voting citizens in a multiethnic democracy, not passive subjects. Teaching them to be social beings without letting them mingle with other children, Dewey wrote, is like teaching them to swim without letting them go in the water. In a city that's often divided by race, class, and religion, there's no better place to learn to live together than the New York City public schools.

# Getting Started

Every school-aged child is entitled to attend his or her "zoned" or neighborhood school. (In cases of severe overcrowding, your child may be bused to another school.) To find out the school for which your child is zoned, call the City of New York at 311 or (212) NEW-YORK.

Children may start kindergarten the year they turn 5, although school isn't compulsory until a child is 6. Any child whose 5th birthday falls before December 31st the year he or she starts school is entitled to attend kindergarten. Kindergarten classes last from 8:30 a.m. to 3 p.m. each day.

The city has hundreds of free prekindergarten programs for 4-year-olds, most of which last half a day, either 3 hours in the morning or 3 hours in the afternoon. Some of these prekindergarten programs are in ordinary public schools; some are housed in day care centers or nursery schools. There aren't enough seats for all the 4-year-olds in the city, and there is no automatic entitlement to prekindergarten. Many prekindergarten programs operate on a first-come, first-served basis. Call your regional office and ask the "pre-K coordinator" for a list of prekindergarten programs in your neighborhood, or check out the list on *www.insideschools.org*, a 2,000-page website sponsored by the nonprofit Advocates for Children of New York.

The vast majority of elementary school children attend their "zoned" or neighborhood school. So start by investigating your neighborhood school. If it isn't included in this book, check it out at *www.insideschools.org,* which has profiles of every school in the city as well as comments from parents and staff. You also can look at the Department of Education website, *www.nycenet.edu/daa*, to find an 8-page "annual school report card" on each school's performance.

It's important to visit a school to get a sense of its atmosphere, tone, and philosophy. Find out if tours are available for prospective parents. See if you can attend a school fair, a musical performance, or a social event to get a feel for the school. Talk to parents dropping their children off in the morning or picking them up in the afternoon. Try to attend a meeting of the Parent–Teacher Association. You'll get a good idea of parents' concerns and worries.

If your neighborhood school is satisfactory, you can relax. All you need to do is register your child in the spring before he or she starts school. Be sure to bring proof of residence (a lease or electric bill), your child's birth certificate, and immunization records. But if you're unhappy with your neighborhood school, you'll need to investigate other possibilities.

# Figuring Out Your Options

If your neighborhood school is unsatisfactory, or if you want your child to have a crack at the dozens of alternative schools or specialized programs that accept children from outside their immediate neighborhoods, or if you're just one of those obsessive parents (like me) who needs to visit a couple dozen schools before deciding, you should start your search a full year before your child enters school. Many Manhattan schools offer tours for prospective parents in October, and some have application deadlines as early as November or December. Schools in Brooklyn and Queens tend to start the application process later. Many have their tours in January, and applications are due in February or March. Each district—sometimes even each school—has a different procedure. Deadlines change constantly, so telephone to confirm the information listed here.

Neighborhood schools accept all children who live in the neighborhood or zone. All you need is proof of address to attend. But there are dozens of New York City public schools that are unzoned—and that accept kids by lottery, or a test, or other admissions criteria. Moreover, some neighborhood schools will give special permission, called a **variance**, to children who live outside the zone—if room is available. Even if room is limited, some neighborhood schools will consider a hardship case for a child from outside the zone if, for example, the parent works in the neighborhood or the child's neighborhood school is a threat to his or her health or safety. Children attending low-performing schools may be eligible for a transfer to a better school under federal legislation known as No Child Left Behind.

Options for school choice are more limited than they were a number of years ago. Many of the most desirable schools have become very popular and simply have no room for extra kids. Moreover, principals who once had authority to admit children to their schools now must submit all approvals for "variances" to regional superintendents, appointed by the newly centralized Department of Education. Principals say the regional officials—hoping to encourage children to stay in their neighborhood schools—increasingly overrule their recommendations. Still, there are some possibilities.

**Unzoned schools** or "schools of choice" accept children from a wide geographical area—a whole district or, in a few cases, the whole city. Some, like Manhattan School for Children in District 3 or Midtown West in District 2, both in Manhattan, require parents to fill out an application expressing their support of the school's philosophy. Others, like the Children's School in Brooklyn's District 15, conduct a

5

lottery. Still others accept children on a first-come, first-served basis. At PS 251 in District 29 in Queens, parents have been known to camp outside the school to be the first in line when kindergarten registration begins. Unzoned schools sometimes are called "option" schools or "alternative schools." There are a handful of **charter schools** in the city as well. These are tuition-free schools that operate independently of the Department of Education. Admission is by lottery. For a list of charter schools, see the Department of Education website, *www. nycenet.edu/charterschools,* or *www.insideschools.org.*

**Gifted and talented** programs generally admit children based on their scores on an IQ test or an interview. Some restrict admission to children living in the neighborhood or the district; others accept children from the whole borough or even from the entire city. The Special Music School of America in Manhattan looks for children with musical talent and accepts children from all five boroughs.

**Magnet schools** receive special federal or state grants for the purpose of racial integration. These schools have special programs in, say, music, art, or law, and are designed to attract children from outside their immediate neighborhoods. These schools attempt to draw nonwhites to mostly white schools and whites to mostly nonwhite schools. Call your regional office to ask about any magnet programs that might allow your child to attend a school outside your neighborhood. The schools with magnet programs change from year to year—as grants run out or are renewed.

## Weighing What's Important to You

Okay, so you have a list of schools you want to consider. You have a stack of "school report cards," and you've asked the schools you're interested in for any publicity brochures they might have. Now what?

You'll really need to visit the schools. But, before you do, think a bit about what's important to you. No school is perfect, and it's easier to weigh the pluses and minuses of any particular program if you've sorted out in your mind what your child needs the most.

Don't think there is some "best school" out there that your child *must* attend no matter what. A school that's great for one child might be awful for another. An active child might go berserk in a school without a playground or organized sports—no matter how challenging the academics. Some children are happiest in a highly structured school, where they know exactly what's expected of them; others flourish when given the freedom to follow their own interests. Some thrive on competition; others hate to be ranked and sorted.

Think about your values as well. Do you believe childhood is a time to enjoy life and to make friends? Or do you believe too much play means a child won't be prepared for the rigors of high school and college? Do you believe children need to learn to follow rules and accept authority? Or is it more important for them to challenge authority and think for themselves? There are no right or wrong answers to these questions, but you will be happiest with a school that shares most of your own values.

Consider whether you prefer a **traditional** or a **progressive** school. There are good schools in both camps. Some of the best incorporate elements of each.

**Traditional schools** emphasize basic skills of reading and arithmetic. Good penmanship is prized, and quick recall of facts is encouraged. Teachers may rely on textbooks to ensure that all children cover the same material. Children may be grouped by ability in "honors," general, and remedial tracks. The teacher may stand at the front of the class and give lessons to all the children at once, and the children are expected to absorb the information they are given. Although very few elementary schools still have desks in rows, traditional schools are unlikely to have kids sprawled on the floor. Parents often appreciate the order and discipline of good traditional schools. Traditional schools often emphasize their pupils' scores on standardized tests, and many traditional schools listed here have high test scores.

**Progressive schools** encourage children to work at their own pace, to follow their own interests, and to do independent research. Progressive schools may have no assigned desks at all; children work on the floor or at small tables. Each child might be involved in a different activity: reading a book of his or her own choosing, or caring for a class pet, or figuring out a problem in multiplication using wooden blocks put together in rows. Progressive schools shy away from textbooks, encouraging children instead to read novels, science discovery books, or biographies. The content of children's written work is considered more important than the handwriting. Children of different abilities are placed in the same class, and each child may read a different book. Parents appreciate the fact that a bright child can work ahead of peers and that a child who is having trouble can get individual attention. Advocates of progressive education say it's more important to learn how to gather and interpret information than to memorize facts.

There are strengths and weaknesses to each philosophy. A bad traditional school can be oppressive; a bad progressive school, chaotic. Parents at some traditional schools say their children know the facts—dates in history or the multiplication tables—but don't know what to do with them. Parents at some progressive schools say their children understand big concepts—such as trends in history or how to go about solving a math problem—but don't know basic facts. The best schools, of course, insist children learn facts and concepts; they teach basic skills and encourage children to think for themselves. The combination is crucial, whatever the school's philosophy.

In recent years, the line between progressive and traditional has been blurring. Many traditional schools have abandoned desks-in-rows and heavy reliance on textbooks, while many progressive schools, bowing to the national mania for standardized testing, have reined in their freewheeling curriculums. Carol Stock, the principal of PS 199 on the Upper West Side, says the old categories of "progressive" and "traditional" are changing, just as the political categories of "left" and "right" have been evolving.

Under the 2003 reorganization of the school system, Schools Chancellor Joel Klein introduced a uniform curriculum for all but 209 high-achieving "exempt" schools. The curriculum, solidly in the progressive camp, calls for children to learn to read from picture books and children's literature rather than textbooks and to understand the underlying concepts of mathematics rather than learn arithmetic facts by rote. Before centralization of the Department of Education under the mayor, each school had leeway to choose its own teaching methods. Now, schools are under pressure to conform to the mandates of the central bureaucracy. That means the traditional schools increasingly are introducing progressive methods, while the progressive schools are paying more attention to basic skills.

## Things to Think About Before You Visit

**Location**. The closer to home, the better. One thing good schools have in common is a sense of community. That's a lot easier to achieve if most children walk to school, if parents are welcome to drop in when they have a spare minute, if it's easy for children to get together and play after school. If your neighborhood school is fine, but not quite as good as one further away, consider whether the time spent schlepping your child to another zone or district could be better used improving your neighborhood school.

**Size**. All other things being equal, small is better. Schools with 300 or 400 pupils are very cozy; and even those with 500 or 600 children are quite manageable. Teachers and staff know everyone and children don't get lost. The principal isn't overwhelmed with the mechanics of crowd control—and therefore has time to concentrate on curriculum and instruction. A school with 1,000 pupils may have 60 teachers—a very large number for a principal to supervise effectively.

Good schools have a sense of community, and that's easier to build in a small school. On the other hand, there are sometimes advantages to a large school. Some large schools have more extensive special education services. Large schools may have better facilities, such as a fully equipped gym and auditorium. Some schools are as large as they are because they are seen as super-desirable, and parents move into the neighborhood just to send their kids there. For that reason, a large school may be superior to a smaller (half-empty) school nearby.

**Safety**. All the schools included here are safe places for children. Every school has a school safety officer stationed at the front door. Everyone who enters a school must show identification and sign a register. The incidents of violence you read about in the press mostly take place in junior and senior high schools. Parents at a few schools did complain to me about occasional fights on the playground. (I've noted places where supervision at recess could be improved.) If you're concerned, attend a PTA meeting or talk to other parents about safety. Even a brief visit will give you a sense of whether a school is orderly or out-of-control.

**"Gifted" classes versus classes of mixed abilities**. Don't immediately jump to get your child into a "gifted" class, even if he or she is very intelligent; some of the best schools in the city refuse to group children by ability, and manage to bring all children to a high level of achievement. Sometimes a "gifted" program creates an unpleasant atmosphere, dividing the school into the privileged "haves" and the neglected "have-nots." And sometimes "gifted" programs have unrealistic expectations for children, such as an oppressively heavy homework load or unhealthy competition among the kids.

The important question to ask a principal or teacher is: How do you deal with a range of abilities in a class? How do you challenge children at the top? How do you help children who are having trouble? Most schools claim to "individualize" or "differentiate" instruction, but it's worth asking for examples of how they do it. My son's kindergarten teacher, for example, had puzzles of different degrees of difficulty. When my son finished a 100-piece puzzle, she pulled down a 200-piece puzzle for him to work on.

Schools with desks in rows and the teacher standing at the front tend to focus on "whole-group instruction." In these classes, if everyone reads the same book, it's going to be too hard for some kids, and too easy for others.

But schools in which the classrooms are organized to accommodate a range of abilities are more likely to challenge the high achievers. In these schools, children work individually or in small groups, and each child reads a different book or works on a different project.

One child may write an essay of a few sentences, while others write several pages.

What about the super-intelligent child? Won't he or she be bored in a regular class? It depends. Ellen Winner, author of *Gifted Children: Myths and Realities,* says that if a school has high standards for everyone, all but the most exceptional children are better off in regular classes. Gifted education in segregated classes, she argues, should be reserved for the true child prodigies—for the 3-year-old who's teaching himself algebra, for example. (They exist; she's interviewed them.)

Unfortunately, we live in the real world, and most of us don't have a choice between a high-performing neighborhood school with classes of mixed abilities and a gifted program 10 blocks away. If your neighborhood school is uninspiring and there are no other good choices nearby, a "gifted" class may well be your best bet, if your child is one who scores well on tests.

Try not to feel bad if your child is refused admission to a gifted program. Most experts are dubious about whether tests given to 4-year-olds can predict future academic achievement. A shy child, or one who doesn't separate from you easily, or one who is just learning English may do poorly on an IQ or other test at the age of 4—and may still be an academic star by 3rd grade.

**Test scores**. I've given each school one to five stars on two different scales. The first, reading scores, shows what proportion of the school's students in grades 3 and above met the state standards for reading and writing on the 2004 city reading test and state English language arts test, which includes reading and writing. I gave one star to schools in which 0–19% of children met the state standard; two stars to those in which 20–39% met the standard; three stars for 40–59%; four stars for 60–79%; and five stars to those with more than 80% meeting the state standard.

The second scale, math scores, shows what proportion of children met the state standards on the 2004 state math test. (I believe the math tests are not sufficiently challenging. For example, state standards require children to know their multiplication tables only at the end of 4th grade. But the test results are the only objective data I had with which to compare schools.)

Test scores are a useful guide, but they can be deceptive and shouldn't be the only criteria by which you make a decision. For example, schools with a large proportion of children receiving special education services may have scores that are deceptively low—that is, the children in general education do well, but those with special needs don't score well on tests. Schools with a "gifted" program may have scores that are deceptively high—that is, the children in the "gifted" program do well, but the others do not. In schools with a large immigrant population, children sometimes score poorly in the lower grades, but improve as they get older. Some alternative schools welcome children who are struggling elsewhere. The quality of teaching may be very good and your child may flourish, even if the test scores are mediocre. Some schools with very high test scores drive their students very hard, with tons of homework, no recess, and lots of tedious test preparation. You may decide you would prefer a school with more time for play and more emphasis on, say, the arts or creative projects.

When a new principal improves a school dramatically, it takes a few years for the changes to be reflected in the test scores. To be fair, you should look at the scores after the principal has been in a school for at least 4 years, because children who started kindergarten under that new principal will be tested for the first time in 3rd grade. If you want a grade-by-grade breakdown of test scores, or a comparison of test scores over a 3-year period, or a comparison of a school with others with similar demographics, check the Department of Education website at *www.nycenet.edu/daa.*

**Free lunch**. In each profile, I include the percentage of children qualifying for the federal lunch program for children from low-income families. The citywide average is 70.3%. Some working families qualify for free hot lunch. Schools with a high free-lunch rate qualify for federal anti-poverty money for remedial reading and other extra academic help. Some schools with very high poverty rates function well, but many of the best schools have a core of middle-class parents who are able to volunteer and raise money that offsets budget cuts and pays for special programs.

**Ethnicity**. The Department of Education classifies children according to race and ethnicity: white, black, Hispanic, and Asian. I've listed the percentage of each group represented at each school. Even schools that are racially homogeneous have more diversity than you might imagine: An all-black school might have African-Americans, children from various Caribbean islands, and new arrivals from Africa. A mostly white school might have Arab and Israeli children, new arrivals from Russia, and Irish-Americans and Italian-Americans who've lived in New York for generations.

## Deciphering the Jargon

You'll hear a lot of incomprehensible jargon on your tours. You can safely tune out a lot of it. You'll be better off looking for yourself to see if the kids are happy and engaged than trying to decipher what principals mean when they say their schools are "totally child-centered, with activity-based instruction and a process-oriented approach" or that they have "effectively implemented a Renzulli enrichment program." (If you care, the first is a progressive school, the second an approach to "gifted" education.)

But some of the unfamiliar terms you hear are important. They describe significant trends, teaching methods, and philosophies of education. Understanding them will better help you choose the right school for your child.

**Whole-language, phonics, and balanced literacy**. Whole-language is a philosophy of instruction that swept the schools in the 1980s. It's based on the notion that children don't learn to read merely by sounding out letters in textbooks. Rather, the whole-language instructors maintain, children learn to read new words by putting together a whole series of clues. A picture in a book, or the rhyme at the end of a line of poetry, may give a child a hint of what a word might be. A child may guess the word in context. The octagonal shape of a stop sign may help a child identify the word "stop." Whole-language schools abandoned "basal readers," in which children read short passages written with a limited vocabulary, and replaced them with "whole" texts, easy-to-read "little books" or picture books for younger children and "chapter books" or novels for older children.

There is one great benefit to the whole-language approach: Children have easier access to interesting and fun-to-read works of literature, rather than the often dry basal readers. Children who choose from a wide variety of books tend to be more engaged and excited about reading. But there is also one great drawback: Some whole-language purists stopped teaching phonics, or how to sound out words phonetically. In schools where the study of phonics was abandoned, some children simply never learned to read.

Most schools now say they offer **balanced literacy**, or an approach that mixes "whole-language" with phonics. In plain English, that means they allow different children in the same class to read different books, rather than have them move together, lock-step, in the same textbook. They also teach children that "th" sounds like "th" or that the final "e" makes a vowel long. **Balanced Literacy** (with a capital *B* and a capital *L*) also refers to a method of instruction developed in Australia that exposes children to different kinds of reading (and writing) experiences each day. Teachers may read a difficult text outloud to the whole class, offer small-group instruction for part of the day, encourage children to read "independently," and "share" a text by having kids all recite a poem or song. In 2003, Schools Chancellor Joel Klein introduced a uniform curriculum of balanced literacy in the city's public schools. Although several hundred high-achieving schools were permitted to choose their own teaching methods, most of these have adopted balanced literacy as well.

If you find these explanations confusing, you're not alone. Rather than try to sort out the theories, look at what the kids are reading when you visit a school. If most of the kids are reading challenging books, it's probably a good school. If most are stuck on very easy-to-read books, even in the upper grades, watch out.

**The Writing Process.** Lucy Calkins and others at Teachers College, Columbia University, transformed the teaching of writing in the public schools with the method called the Writing Process. With it, children learn to write, even before they learn to read, by stringing together whatever letters they know to approximate words. A kindergartner might write BTN to stand for "button" or HSPTL to stand for "hospital." These early efforts at writing, sometimes called **invented spelling**, allow children to express complicated and interesting ideas from the very beginning, at a time when other children their age are merely tracing lines of letters. These techniques also help children learn to read as they begin to make a correspondence between a sound and a written letter. (By 2nd grade, children are expected to use "dictionary spelling," not their own approximations.)

I'm always impressed with the quality of writing when I visit schools whose teachers are well trained in the Writing Process. Children learn sophisticated elements of a writer's craft at a young age. They develop a voice; they learn to write evocative descriptions of sights, sounds, and smells; and they learn to use dialogue effectively and understand metaphors. Children learn, as adult writers know, that each piece of writing must be revised many times before it is "published."

Occasionally parents complain that teachers who use the Writing Process don't place enough emphasis on spelling, grammar, and penmanship. While that complaint may be justified in a few instances, the most expert teachers insist on good form as well as content. What the Writing Process gives children is the excitement of expressing themselves in print at a very young age—and a reason for wanting to write well.

**TERC math, Chicago math, constructivist math.** While a truce has been declared in the "reading wars" (and just about everyone agrees that balanced literacy is the way to go), battles still wage in the "math wars." The first salvo was launched in a 1989 manifesto of the National Council of Teachers of Mathematics (NCTM) that declared the old math, with arithmetic drills and rote memorization of formulas, had sapped the enthusiasm of generations of students and left children without an understanding of underlying concepts of mathematics. Math instruction, the NCTM declared, should not consist merely of computation—simple addition, subtraction, multiplication, and division—but also should introduce children to elements of logic, probability, statistics, geometry, and algebra. Young children, moreover, can best capture the excitement and beauty of mathematics if they learn to solve problems on their own in concrete ways, rather than being given a formula for solving them by the teacher, the NCTM declared.

Many schools quickly adopted math curriculums in line with the NCTM standards, including TERC math, a program developed in Cambridge, MA, and Everyday Math, also called Chicago Math, developed at the University of Chicago. Schools Chancellor Klein threw the weight of the Department of Education behind the new math when he introduced Everyday Math as the city's uniform curriculum in 2003.

The new math is similar in many respects to the wave of math reform of the early 1960s, then called the "new math." Sometimes you'll hear people refer to the latest reforms as "the new new math." Out went the textbooks. In came "manipulatives"—small plastic blocks the children put together in rows to study multiplication, or bags of coins they used to make change and study addition and subtraction. Children were taught there is more than one way to solve a problem; they were expected to "construct" their own solution— hence the term "constructivist." Children were no longer taught, for example, to add 29 and 34 by putting the numbers in rows, adding 9 and 4 and "carrying" the 1 to the 10s column. Rather, one child might round 29 up to 30 to make a "friendly" or easy-to-add number, then add 30 and 34 to make 64, then take one away to make 63. Another child might add the two numbers on a number line. And a third might use coins to add the numbers. Children were expected to "show their work"—write a sentence describing how they solved a problem.

The new methods sparked a storm of controversy. Critics dubbed the programs "fuzzy math," because children often were praised for their attempts at solving a problem rather than for getting the right answer. Children often learned concepts at the expense of proficiency. They could, for example, laboriously add $7 + 7 + 7 + 7$ to get 28, but they couldn't automatically say $7 \times 4 = 28$. Many students reached middle school unable to divide large numbers. New immigrants with limited command of English were baffled by the new curriculum's heavy reliance on word problems and by the teachers' insistence that they write English sentences explaining their work.

The NCTM modified its standards somewhat to address some of these concerns, and individual schools have supplemented their curriculums to include more drills of math facts and more use of formulas or "algorithms." Deputy Schools Chancellor Carmen Fariña coined the expression "balanced math" to reflect her attempts to blend the old and the new. But the debate between old and new is still raging in most of the city.

I have no nostalgia for the old math, which I believe alienated generations of students (particularly girls) and left many adults without even basic competency in arithmetic. In my visits to classrooms that have adopted the new standards, I've seen some strokes of genius. In one 2nd-grade class, for example, kids rolled two dice repeatedly, added the two numbers, and graphed the number of times each number came up. A bell curve emerged—an important lesson in probability, combined with an arithmetic drill in simple addition. With the new math, I believe, kids feel more competent and are much less likely to feel "dumb." Math is taught as a series of games and, believe it or not, kids can get excited about something as mundane as adding fractions.

But there are drawbacks. In too many schools, the curriculum moves at a glacial pace. And while it's important to show children there's more than one way to solve a problem, the tendency of some teachers to withhold the "algorithm" or formula leaves too many kids reinventing the wheel. Further, children often don't get the drills they need to make computation automatic. The schools that teach math the best (and there are very few of them) ensure that bright children can move ahead of their peers—either by working on more complex problems with paper and pencil, or by working independently on math websites—rather than insisting they wait while their classmates finish a problem. These teachers don't withhold the algorithm from students, and ensure that children have enough arithmetic drills that basic facts become automatic.

**Tracking.** Some traditional schools group children by ability, with "slow" children in one class, average in another, and "bright" in a third. Proponents of "tracking" say the narrower the range of abilities in one class, the easier for the teacher to prepare lessons. This also is called **homogeneous grouping**. Progressive schools avoid tracking, saying it hurts children in the bottom classes without significantly helping those in the top classes. These schools mix children of various abilities in one class, which, they say, forces the teacher to individualize instruction. The best teachers, they say, can handle a wide range of abilities in one class. This is also called **heterogeneous grouping**.

Some schools compromise, grouping children by ability for reading and math, but keeping them with children of other abilities for other subjects. This is sometimes called **streaming**.

Some progressive schools have **bridge classes** with, say, 1st and 2nd graders in one class, and 3rd and 4th graders in another. Children stay with one teacher for 2 years and have the opportunity to be both the youngest and the oldest child in a class. Many teachers complain that it's extremely difficult to teach a class of 30 or more children with such a wide range of ages and abilities. Others enjoy the challenge. Some schools **loop** their classes, or have teachers move up with the same pupils. A teacher then stays with the same children for 2 years. This gives the advantage of continuity offered by bridge classes without the disadvantage of trying to reach children of different ages and abilities.

Children who don't speak English may be placed in a **bilingual class** or a class in **English as a Second Language**. In a bilingual class, teachers attempt to maintain and perfect a child's knowledge of his or her native language, while teaching English. Both languages are used in class. In English as a Second Language, or ESL, classes, teachers concentrate on English only.

A few schools have classes in **dual-language immersion**. In these classes, half the pupils are native English speakers, and half speak another language, usually Spanish. Classes are taught in each language on alternate days or weeks, and children are expected to become fluent in both.

## What to Look for When You Visit

Once you've thought about what you want in a school, start visiting the ones that interest you. Many of the schools listed here offer tours for parents in the fall or winter. It's better to visit during the day, when classes are in session, but evening tours also can tell you a lot if you know what to look for. Schools that don't offer tours might let you visit during "open school week" in November, when parents and members of the community are invited to see the school in action. Each school now has a "parent coordinator"—a full-time position created as a liaison between the administration and parents. The parent coordinator may organize the tours. If not, see if someone from the PTA can show you around. If the school never allows visitors, I'd be wary.

You want a school where children love to spend their days. The nicest schools make you slightly envious of your child. You'll wish you were 5 years old again so you could start kindergarten. The physical look of a classroom will tell you a lot. And so will the sounds.

You don't want anarchy, and you don't want a police state. You don't want total silence, and you don't want an incessant din. Look for classrooms in which kids are focused and engaged in their work—not staring out the window or wandering aimlessly. Look for children's work (not decorations made by the teacher or provided by a textbook company) displayed on the bulletin boards and walls, preferably not identical shapes cut from construction paper, but work that shows individual thought and creativity.

You want a place where parents are welcome. Fresh paint and general cleanliness are a plus, but the school doesn't have to be fancy to be good. Don't look for expensive equipment; what you really want is a good principal who hires good teachers. (The teachers' contract limits principals' ability to hire, and jobs at most schools are allocated according to seniority. A good principal, however, knows how to bend the rules to get the best staff. Ask if a staff has voted to be a "school-based option" school. That is a provision of the teachers' contract that allows a panel of administrators, teachers, and parents to interview and hire teachers, superseding rules that assign teachers according to seniority.)

The best schools have a coherent **philosophy**, articulated by a strong principal and carried out by a unified staff. The philosophy may be traditional, progressive, or a mixture of the two, but the best schools have teachers and a principal with similar goals and a common vision of how to reach them. Avoid schools with warring factions, or a mishmash of ideologies where teachers shift for themselves.

The **principal** is the most important person in the building. A good principal can transform a mediocre school into a gem in just a few

---

### Questions to Ask on a Tour

- How do you handle the transition to kindergarten?
- How much homework do you think is appropriate?
- What do children do during recess on rainy days?
- How often do children have physical education?
- How do you handle discipline problems?
- Where do most of your graduates go to middle school?
- Do you hire teachers according to the seniority provision of the teachers' contract, or are you able to interview them first?

years. A bad principal can dismantle good programs and demoralize a competent staff just as quickly. Not all good principals are personable, and some who are charming as people aren't great as educators. What good principals have in common is an abiding respect for the pupils in their care—a respect that is obvious even on a brief tour. It's fine to be strict, but watch out for principals who yell at kids or who regularly use a bullhorn to keep order. A principal should be not merely an administrator, but an educational leader who can articulate his or her vision for the school and help the staff carry it out. A principal should spend time in classrooms regularly and shouldn't be holed up in the office pushing paper. Ideally, the principal knows the name of every child in the school—not just the stars and the troublemakers.

**Class size** is important. Under the contract with the United Federation of Teachers, most New York City public schools have a maximum of 25 children in kindergarten, 28 in grades 1–3, and 32 in grades 4–6. That's too big, in my opinion, but a skillful principal will bring those numbers down, at least for part of the day, by getting extra grown-ups in the classroom. Parent volunteers, retired people from the neighborhood, or student teachers can work with small groups of children while the teacher concentrates on the others. A visiting musician or artist can work with half the class while the teacher helps the others. The skill of the classroom teacher is more important than the size of the class. Better to be in a big class with a good teacher than in a small class with a bad one. In general, though, small is better.

Many schools in recent years have received federal and state funds available for **class size reduction.** In these, classes have been reduced to 20 in kindergarten through 2nd grade. Smaller classes make a big difference for children and teachers. However, some of the best schools have been unable to reduce class size, precisely because they are so popular and parents move into the zone simply to enroll their children. Research shows that small class size is critical for poor children and those "at risk" of educational failure. Middle-class children, on the other hand, often can weather a large class with fewer problems.

**Look for interesting, fun-to-read books**. Good schools, whether traditional or progressive, don't rely exclusively on textbooks to teach reading, math, history, and science. The more progressive schools have no textbooks at all, but teach all subjects from "real" books that you might read for pleasure. Other good schools use textbooks to make sure everyone gets the basics of how to read, but move quickly to picture books, novels, books about historical events, biographies, and science discovery books. Good schools have a rich class library in each classroom, and each child may well be reading a different book, depending on his or her ability and interest. If everyone in a class spends most of the day reading the same textbook, I'd be worried that a lot of kids are bored.

You should see examples of **children's writing** in the very youngest grades. Good schools ask children to keep journals and to write their own stories using their experiences and their imagination. Watch out for schools where most of the writing is material copied from the blackboard.

Good schools have plenty of **things children can touch and feel in math and science**. Again, beware of heavy reliance on textbooks. Science textbooks are particularly deadly: Look for classrooms with live animals, plants, fish tanks, and materials such as magnets and electric motors.

Little kids (and a lot of adults) have trouble with the abstract concepts of mathematics. They need something concrete they can see and hold. That's why so many kids count on their fingers. Good schools encourage children to use their fingers to calculate. They also provide children with small objects to count with, called **manipulatives**, such as tongue depressors or buttons, or specially designed small blocks or rods. Little kids use them to learn how to add and subtract; older kids use them to calculate decimals or multiply fractions.

**Trips** are an important part of the curriculum. Concerts, museums, the zoo, the beach—all can be incorporated into what children are studying in the classroom. Trips expand children's general knowledge of the world, build their vocabularies by showing them new things, and indirectly improve their reading skills. One school in Harlem, the Family Academy, discovered that kids did better on a standardized test after a trip to an airport, where they learned specialized vocabulary words that were on the citywide reading exam.

Many schools that are good in other respects give up the **cafeteria and playground** as lost causes. The cafeteria food is terrible, the din is deafening, and the playground is chaotic. Those that refuse to acknowledge defeat manage to rein in the bedlam. Some have children eat family-style in their classrooms, or have someone read aloud in the cafeteria. Recess can be a time for organized circle games. These schools believe every minute of the day can be used for instruction.

Very few schools manage this, so don't get frazzled trying to find one. And perhaps noisy lunchrooms are preferable to the gloomy silent lunches that a few schools insist upon.

Many schools have **after-school programs** to provide care for children whose parents work. Alas, these programs vary in quality as much as the schools themselves. Many have fallen victim to budget cuts. Some after-school programs are first-rate, taught by regular classroom teachers or outside experts in music, art, drama, or chess. Others are marginally acceptable, with neighborhood high school students or other low-wage employees hired to supervise the kids. Most charge a fee. Some after-school programs are on school grounds. Others are at nearby community organizations or houses of worship. The members of the community organizations generally pick up children up at their schools and walk them to a nearby after-school center. Child Care Inc., a nonprofit advocacy and referral agency, has a list of after-school programs. Call (212) 929-7604, extension 3035, or look at *www.childcareinc. org*. See also The After School Corporation (*www.tascorp.org/programs*) or the Department of Education website, *www.nycenet.edu/administration/offices/youthdev/community/networksAfterschool/default/htm*.

A few schools receive special grants to have free classes year-round, on Saturday mornings or in the late afternoon. I've mentioned some of these academic **extended-day programs** in the school profiles that follow.

## Getting In

This is where the craziness begins. If you're lucky enough to have a good neighborhood school, you'll do fine. But otherwise, get ready for major-league frustration. The whole process is exasperating because procedures vary tremendously from year to year, and nobody, it seems, can give you a straight answer. Getting information from the Department of Education is like nailing Jell-O to the wall. Plan to spend hours on hold on the telephone. Assume that everyone who eventually answers the telephone will give you a slightly different answer to a seemingly simple question like, "How can I apply to a school outside my neighborhood?"

In overcrowded districts, school choice doesn't really exist; unless you're zoned for a school, forget about getting in. In districts where there's a lot of shopping around, the best schools are often oversubscribed.

Try not to panic. Remember, you need only one seat for one child at a time. You have more options than you realize. Some good schools in District 1 on the Lower East Side and District 4 in East Harlem, for example, generally have space for kids outside the neighborhood. Even in overcrowded districts, individual schools sometimes have space. And even the super-hard-to-get-into schools sometimes find that they have one empty spot in September, after neighborhood kids have registered. So keep your chin up.

There are three ways to get into schools: (1) follow the rules; (2) lie; (3) stretch the truth, cajole, and pull strings. Start by following the rules. Look at your neighborhood school. Have your child take the test for a "gifted" program, if one appeals to you. Fill out an application for an "option" school. Try a lottery for a charter school.

Each entry in this book lists **admissions** criteria. A neighborhood school automatically accepts children living within its zone, and accepts others only if space is available.

Call the school to arrange a tour. In Manhattan, tours mostly are held in the fall and early winter. In Brooklyn, tours mostly are held in the winter. In the Bronx, Queens, and Staten Island, schools may not have regularly scheduled tours and you may have to improvise. Call the parent coordinator or the PTA. Tours fill up quickly, particularly in Manhattan, so call early. Alas, admissions procedures for children from outside the school's immediate neighborhood vary from year to year, depending on available space. There's no substitute for calling the school and the regional office directly.

Even something as straightforward as **kindergarten registration** for your neighborhood school can be a chore. Most districts start registering kindergartners in March. All accept registrations the last week of August and in September, just as school begins. But if you wait that long in an overcrowded district, your child may be bused out to another school.

When you apply to a school outside your immediate neighborhood, remember that many principals are looking at you, the parent, rather than your child. The schools want and need the volunteer labor that parents can provide. Can you read out-loud to kids? Make costumes for the class play? Help rebuild a playground on weekends? Photocopy worksheets at your office? Write the school newsletter?

A lesbian couple I know promised not one but two active PTA moms. Their child got into every school to which she applied. I met an unemployed father who volunteered as a school security guard, a father who worked nights and wrote the school newsletter during the day, and a mother who decided it made more sense to quit her job and work full-time in the PTA than to pay private school tuition. You say you simply can't volunteer your own time? Volunteer your mother-in-law's.

Even more than sweat equity, principals are looking for parents who share their vision and philosophy of the school. Running a New York City public school is difficult in the best of circumstances. Having parents who constantly challenge the principal's authority only makes it worse. So if you want your child to go to a school, don't whine about the math curriculum on your tour.

Make friends with the principal or the head of the PTA. Tell them their school is your absolute first choice (if it is). These tactics won't help your child get in on a lottery, but if a principal has any wiggle room—say, if one seat becomes available when a child moves out of town—it will put your child on the top of the waiting list. (Alas, most decisions on admission now are handled by the regional offices, not the principal, so don't count on any of these tactics working.)

Principals are very busy and hard to reach by telephone, particularly during school hours. Every school has a parent coordinator, a new position created by the chancellor in 2003. This person is the liaison between the administration and parents and is often the best person to call.

It's an open secret that some parents lie about their address to get into a school they like. I don't recommend it. At the very least, your child may be embarrassed when he or she has to write those inevitable essays about his or her neighborhood. And what if the school calls you at your phony address during a real emergency? However, some parents feel that desperate situations call for desperate measures. If lying is really, truly your only option, the charade involves putting your name on a friend's Con Ed bill, buying a phony lease at a stationery store, or making up a persuasive story about how your child really lives with an aunt across the street from the school. A lot of schools check addresses carefully, so don't count on these ploys working. Some schools even send "attendance teachers" (formerly known as truant officers) to see if you actually live where you say you do. Expect the attendance teacher to look in closets for clothes and toys and other evidence of a lived-in apartment.

Short of out-and-out lies, which can lead to trouble, you may consider stretching the truth. Even overcrowded districts will give "variances"—special permission to attend a school—to protect a child's health and safety; if you can demonstrate your neighborhood school is dangerous, you've got a chance. If your child has asthma and a construction project at the school stirs up a lot of dust, you may have a chance. Some parents use what I call "the babysitter ploy." If your babysitter picks up your child from school, you sometimes can get a variance for your child to attend the school near the sitter's house.

Some parents say political connections help, and they ask their city council member or state assembly representative to intercede with the district superintendent on their behalf. Politicians' children, they insist, are disproportionately represented in some desirable schools, and the politicians can help you get in. Even if you don't want an elected official to open doors for you, it doesn't hurt to call them for advice. Many are very knowledgeable about schools in their district. But I don't think most of them are the fixers they are cracked up to be.

If all this seems like an enormous hassle, you're right. In many cases, you'd be better off if you used the energy it takes to get a variance to improve your neighborhood school instead. But if your neighborhood school seems beyond repair, take heart. In my experience, the parents who persevere generally get their child into a good school—even if they have to wait until the first week of September for a spot to open up.

The best public schools have all the brains, variety, and excitement of the city itself. They help make this complicated, multiracial city work, by teaching people of different backgrounds to live together. Neighborhood by neighborhood, they build communities of people who care about one another. And they'll give your child a first-rate education—for free.

## If Your Child Needs Extra Help: Special Education

Parents of children with disabilities face enormous hurdles in their search for a good education. It's important to know your rights and to find someone to help you navigate the bureaucracy. The Advocates for Children (AFC) website, *www.advocatesforchildren.org*, is a good place to start. An organization called the Least Restrictive Environment Coalition, led by AFC, has a useful list of noteworthy special education programs on its website, *www.lrecoalition.org*. Another website sponsored by AFC, *www.Insideschools.org*, also has pertinent information.

Children with disabilities are entitled by law to "free and appropriate" education. They may receive special services to allow them to stay in a regular classroom, or they may be placed in a separate class especially for children with special needs.

A wide range of services is available (at least in theory): smaller classes for part of the day, speech therapy, psychological counseling, and individual attention from a specially trained teacher in a regular classroom for a few hours each day. Visually impaired students may have extra-large computer keyboards and screens. Partially deaf children may participate in a regular class in which the teacher wears a microphone with an FM radio unit that transmits to a child's hearing aid. An impulsive child may be assigned an aide to help him learn to control his behavior. A child with unusually bad handwriting may receive occupational therapy to learn to hold a pencil and form letters better. A dyslexic child may receive tutoring from a specialist.

But getting these services for your child can be a chore of major proportions. If finding an appropriate school for a typical child is difficult, finding a good match for a child with special needs can be a nightmare. If things get complicated, you may need a lawyer to assert your child's rights. AFC represents a small number of low-income families for free and refers other families to attorneys in private practice. Call (212) 947-9779, Tuesdays and Thursdays from 10:30 A.M. to 1 P.M.

If you think your child has a disability, your first step it to have him or her evaluated. Your region's Committee on Special Education will conduct an evaluation, but you may prefer to have a private evaluation first. If the evaluators determine that the child needs special services, a team that includes the parents will draw up an Individual Educational Plan, or IEP. The services may be available at your neighborhood school or at a specialized program elsewhere in your district. Children with severe disabilities are referred to District 75, an administrative entity that supervises highly specialized programs. Some District 75 programs are contained within regular schools. Some have their own school buildings.

The quality of special education programs varies tremendously from school to school. Some excellent programs manage to give children with complicated special needs the extra help that allows them to participate fully in regular classrooms. Others consign disabled children to dingy, segregated classrooms in a school basement—even if their learning problems are fairly mild.

Special education in New York City is in great flux. For years, a large proportion of disabled children were segregated in what are called **self-contained classes** where they had little contact with the general population. Now, under pressure from federal laws that ensure the rights of the disabled, the city has launched what it calls a **new continuum** to place children in the **least restrictive environment**—often in their neighborhood school with specially trained teachers or aides assigned to help them. In theory, the new continuum means that most disabled children may receive the help they need in a regular classroom close to home. In practice, however, some children with special needs are placed in regular classes inappropriately and don't receive the support they need. It's impossible to generalize, because some schools are integrating children with special needs very well while others are doing a terrible job. Be sure to visit the class before enrolling your child, and ask as many questions as you can about the program. We've described noteworthy special education programs in the school profiles that follow.

Many schools have launched **inclusion** classes to integrate disabled children with their peers in general education. In some, the child may be assigned a full-time teacher's aide. In others, a specially trained teacher may spend an hour or two a day in a child's regular class and advise the classroom teacher on strategies that might help.

In other inclusion classes, two thirds of the pupils are in general education and one third receive special services. In these, two teachers—at least one of whom is certified in special education—team teach. This approach, called **collaborative team teaching**, or **CTT**, seems to work well when class sizes are kept small and when the two teachers are enthusiastic about working together as a team. I am skeptical, however, about the effectiveness of inclusion classes that are too large or that have teachers who aren't committed to inclusion. One program that works particularly well is District 15's Children's School in the Park Slope section of Brooklyn. Listed at the back of the book are special education programs that we believe show promise.

If, because of the severity of your child's disability, a self-contained or segregated special education classroom is your best option, look for one in which your child will take part in the life of the school. Disabled children should be included in class trips, assemblies, and sports. Their classrooms should be indistinguishable from others except for their smaller class size; if the general education classes have fish tanks, colorful bulletin boards, and beautiful class libraries, the special education classes should too. The best schools are proud of all their children, including those in special education.

Ask what happens when your child is too old for the program to which he or she initially is assigned. Some pleasant programs for little kids feed into horrible programs for older children. Ask what proportion of children graduate to general education programs (or check yourself on the school report card: *www.nycenet.edu/daa*). Of course, some disabilities are lifelong—you wouldn't expect a deaf child, for example, to stop needing services. But many good programs are proud that their graduates can cope in regular classrooms without continuing extra help.

Ask how a school gauges a child's progress. Even if your child is severely disabled, you want a school that expects your child to advance academically, not one that only gives custodial care. Ask whether your child will follow the general education curriculum and whether he or she will eventually be eligible for a high school diploma.

For advice about your child's rights, call the **Advocates for Children** hotline Tuesdays and Thursdays from 10 a.m. to 1 p.m.: (212) 947-9779. For help navigating the byzantine special education bureaucracy, you also can call **Resources for Children with Special Needs**, a nonprofit advocacy and referral agency: (212) 677-4650. For parent-to-parent advice and hand-holding, call Ellen McHugh at **Parent-to-Parent** at (800) 405-8818. She will put you in contact with a parent whose child has a disability similar to yours. For a $100 annual membership fee, **The Parents League** at (212) 737-7385 (*www.parentsleague.org*) will give advice about private schools, including those that may accept children with special needs. Good luck.

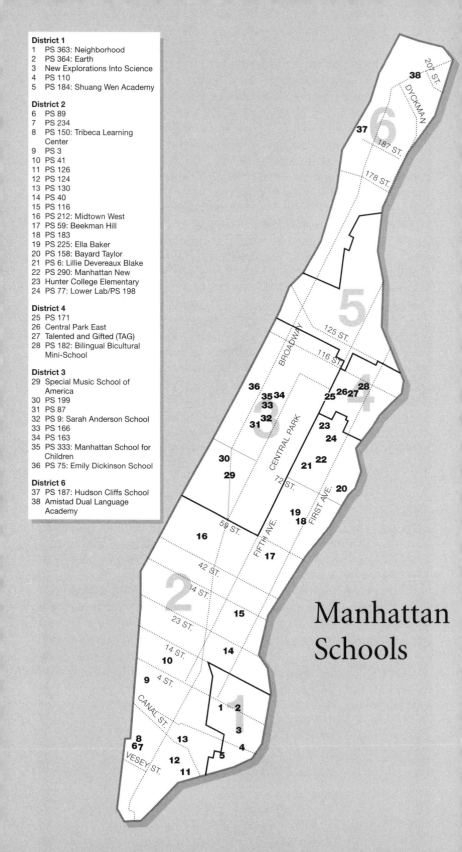

**District 1**
1. PS 363: Neighborhood
2. PS 364: Earth
3. New Explorations Into Science
4. PS 110
5. PS 184: Shuang Wen Academy

**District 2**
6. PS 89
7. PS 234
8. PS 150: Tribeca Learning Center
9. PS 3
10. PS 41
11. PS 126
12. PS 124
13. PS 130
14. PS 40
15. PS 116
16. PS 212: Midtown West
17. PS 59: Beekman Hill
18. PS 183
19. PS 225: Ella Baker
20. PS 158: Bayard Taylor
21. PS 6: Lillie Devereaux Blake
22. PS 290: Manhattan New
23. Hunter College Elementary
24. PS 77: Lower Lab/PS 198

**District 4**
25. PS 171
26. Central Park East
27. Talented and Gifted (TAG)
28. PS 182: Bilingual Bicultural Mini-School

**District 3**
29. Special Music School of America
30. PS 199
31. PS 87
32. PS 9: Sarah Anderson School
33. PS 166
34. PS 163
35. PS 333: Manhattan School for Children
36. PS 75: Emily Dickinson School

**District 6**
37. PS 187: Hudson Cliffs School
38. Amistad Dual Language Academy

Manhattan
Schools

# MANHATTAN

The real estate mantra "location, location, location" applies doubly to public schools in Manhattan. The quality of education your child receives depends a lot on where you live, and the gap between good and bad is dramatic. Although there are some opportunities for "school choice," most children attend their zoned neighborhood schools. So choose carefully when you rent or buy an apartment.

Manhattan is divided into six school districts. Of these, District 2, serving the Upper East Side, midtown, and downtown, has the most consistently strong leadership and the most successful schools. While not every school in the district is a gem, overall the quality is high.

Sky-high real estate prices, of course, mean that most families can't afford to move into District 2. Parents priced out of the high-rent districts will find good schools in less expensive neighborhoods as well. District 1, serving the Lower East Side, and District 4, serving East Harlem, have a long history of school choice and welcome children from outside their borders. District 3 on the Upper West Side also has some good schools.

There are other options as well. Charter schools—tuition-free schools that operate independently of the Department of Education—admit children by lottery. And unzoned or "option schools"—schools with no defined attendance zones—accept children who apply directly to them. In addition, there are a number of "gifted and talented" programs open to children from across the city, as well as some whose admission is limited to children living in a particular district. Admission to these programs is determined by a test or an interview.

Under Mayor Michael Bloomberg's reorganization of schools, the three districts serving pupils from downtown, midtown, and the East Side of Manhattan were consolidated into one region, Region 9, at 333 7th Avenue, (212) 356-7500. The three districts serving the Upper West Side and upper Manhattan were consolidated in another region, Region 10, with offices at 4360 Broadway, (917) 521-3700. However, for the purposes of school choice, parents generally apply to schools within the boundaries of the old districts (see map on p. xiv). You may go in person to the district or regional offices with any problems or questions you may have. Be prepared for a frustrating visit: The offices are inadequately staffed and not every employee is knowledgeable or helpful.

# Region 9—Downtown, Midtown, and East Side

**District 1** on Manhattan's Lower East Side has an unusual number of alternative schools with small classes and room for children from outside the neighborhood. The schools vary in philosophy and program, from ultra-progressive to quite traditional. A few are top-notch in quality—and many are not-ready-for-prime-time. So it pays to shop around.

The schools have tours for prospective parents in the fall and winter. The school district office is at 80 Montgomery Street, New York, NY 10002, (212) 602-9767. You may have better luck reaching the regional school choice coordinator at (212) 356-3788.

Many of the school buildings, just a block or two apart from each another, were constructed to serve the teeming immigrant population at the turn of the twentieth century. Not long after they were built, new subway lines to the Bronx allowed people to move to less congested areas. The school buildings built for another era remain, and many are still half-vacant. The luxury of space has allowed the district to experiment. New schools include one for the study of ecology, one where both English and Chinese are taught, and one designed to serve children in kindergarten through 12th grade. The luxury of space also means class size tends to be smaller than average for the city—with 20 kids in the lower grades and 25 in grades 4 and 5. Many schools have free prekindergarten programs.

For years, parts of the Lower East Side had the desolate feel of an abandoned boomtown, with squatters in vacant buildings and shanty-towns built on vacant lots. In recent years, however, the neighborhood has become more gentrified, with trendy bars and boutiques and a sprinkling of luxury apartments. The area north of Houston Street has been renamed the East Village—a name more befitting the high rents now being charged. The public school parents represent a funky and eclectic mix of working-class Puerto Ricans; new immigrants from India, Bangladesh, and China; artists; bohemians with tattoos and pierced noses; and a few accountants and lawyers. A few schools are also popular among parents from Williamsburg, just across the East River in Brooklyn.

**District 2** includes some of the most expensive real estate on the planet: the Upper East Side, Sutton Place, Gramercy Park, Greenwich Village, and Tribeca, as well as some more modestly priced neighborhoods in Chinatown and Hell's Kitchen.

District 2 schools have long been nationally recognized models of urban education, studied and debated by academics and visited by researchers from other cities. The schools are a magnet for talent, and teachers come from across the country (even a handful from better-paying suburban districts) to learn their craft from masters.

Unfortunately, these schools rarely have room for children living outside the district. (A few children may transfer in from failing schools under the provisions of the federal legislation called No Child Left Behind [NCLB]. See *www.insideschools.org* or contact your regional office.)

Tours are offered in the fall. The regional choice coordinator is at 333 7th Avenue, New York, NY 10001, (212) 356-3788.

The schools face the chronic budget woes common to all New York City public schools. However, many of the schools have formidable PTAs that raise hundreds of thousands of dollars annually for books, supplies, and assistant teachers.

The district's great strength has been the teaching of writing—not just book reports or essays on "How I Spent My Summer Vacation," but lively, engaging poetry and prose that give children a sense of power and a voice. Children learn to write for a purpose, for a response, for a real audience beyond the classroom. In kindergarten a child might write to the school custodian telling him a coat hook is broken. By 5th grade, a child might write to the President about her fears that her grandmother's Social Security will be cut, or to *The New York Times* to complain that a rental lease excludes pets. Children learn that writing is not something you do just because your teacher tells you to, but something you want to do because it gives you a sense of confidence and control over your world.

The former district superintendent, Shelley Harwayne, was one of the founders of the Reading and Writing Project at Teachers College, Columbia University, where, with Lucy Calkins and others, she helped transform the way writing is taught to children. The district has continued its close collaboration with Teachers College, where many teachers are trained in the Writing Process, and its principles are deeply ingrained in nearly every school's practices. Schools all over the city have adopted many of these practices in recent years, but District 2 schools have the longest and deepest experience with these methods.

The district is in the forefront of a national movement to reform the teaching of mathematics in line with guidelines put forth by the National Council of Teachers of Mathematics. In a 1989 document that is still hotly debated, the NCTM proposed that mathematics instruction should not concentrate on "computation"—that is, learning the standard rules of addition, subtraction, multiplication, and division. Rather, the NCTM said young children should learn the concepts underlying arithmetic and also should learn elements of algebra, logic, probability, and statistics. Most significant, children should create their own strategies for solving problems, rather than merely learning to manipulate formulas given to them by their teachers.

The National Science Foundation awarded District 2 a grant to implement a math curriculum called TERC. The curriculum has a raft of detractors—and dozens of parents have logged countless hours at PTA and local school board meetings denouncing the new math—but the new math as its defenders as well. Proponents say their children develop a great "number sense," a feel for how numbers work, and an ability to tackle unfamiliar problems. They say children understand math more deeply than they would if they were required merely to memorize the multiplication tables. Detractors say the new math fails to prepare children adequately for the rigors of middle school and high school; that whatever the strength of the new math, children still need to add, subtract, multiply, and divide large numbers quickly and efficiently—without a calculator.

In my experience, the new math offers a solid foundation for the youngest children, and, by making math concrete and fun, it engages children who aren't naturally drawn to it. I saw a lesson at PS 198 on East 95th Street where the children were positively gleeful at the prospect of adding fractions. At the Lab School, also on 95th Street, children were happily cutting strips of graph paper to learn factors; 1,000 might be expressed in a rectangle 10 squares by 100, or in a long strip 1 square wide and 1,000 squares long. Keeping kids interested and engaged is no small accomplishment.

The classes I visited, however, generally moved at a glacial pace. That's not entirely bad. One principal said TERC is like a local train: It makes lots of stops, but it picks everyone up and gets them to the destination. Indeed, the district scores on standardized tests are well above the city average. But, unfortunately, some bright kids are bored. And, as a group, District 2 children don't seem to be getting enough practice in the traditional skills 4th and 5th graders used to have, such as long division.

One recent improvement: Under the mayor's reorganization, each school has a "math coach," a senior teacher assigned to help classroom teachers develop their skills at teaching math. This new focus on math has gone a long way toward improving instruction.

District 2 has gifted and talented (G&T) programs at PS 124 and PS 130, both in Chinatown; PS 11 in Chelsea; PS 116 in Murray Hill; and the Lab School (PS 77) on the Upper East Side. But many parents of high-achieving children are quite content with their neighborhood schools and don't apply to the G&T programs.

**District 4** in East Harlem includes public-housing blocks and run-down buildings as well as some posh Fifth Avenue apartments near

Mt. Sinai Hospital. It also includes Spanish Harlem and a tiny Italian-American enclave. An uncrowded district, it was one of the first in the country to allow parents to choose their child's public school, and there are some important and interesting schools here.

Philosophies vary a great deal from school to school. Some are firmly in the progressive camp—where kids call teachers by first names and sprawl on rugs or sofas—and others are firmly in the traditional camp—with kids in uniforms and a formal tone.

Unfortunately, the district's 30-year history shows that "choice" is not a cure-all for failing public schools. Many schools in the district still have very low levels of achievement, and the system of choice may have exacerbated the gaps between the best and the worst. The district accepts applications from children who live outside its boundaries. The district office is at 319 East 117th Street, New York, NY 10035, (212) 828-3509. Or try the regional school choice coordinator at (212) 356-3788.

# Region 10—
# Upper West Side, Harlem, and Washington Heights

Searching for a good elementary school has long been an obsession for West Side parents—and with good reason. **District 3**, which covers the West Side of Manhattan from 59th Street to 122nd Street, has schools that vary tremendously in philosophy and quality. The district has some of the highest-performing schools in the city, as well as some of the lowest. Many of the best schools accept children from outside their immediate neighborhood, and, unfortunately, some of the neighborhood schools are to be avoided. So be prepared to spend the fall before your child enters kindergarten with dozens of other anxious parents trooping from one school tour to another.

You may have to put your child through the ordeal of testing for a gifted and talented program. You may decide to promote yourself as the world's greatest fund-raiser and most active member of the Parent–Teacher Association. You will, undoubtedly, chew your fingernails while waiting for a response—which may come in April, and may not come until school actually begins in September. It's an idiotic system and I make no apologies for it. But it's also true that most parents who have slogged their way through the agonizing application process have, eventually, found a spot for their children at an acceptable or even a good school.

The admissions procedures for elementary schools are under review, so be sure to contact the school choice coordinator, Nicky Kram Rosen, at the regional office, 4360 Broadway, (917) 521-3730, for updated information. You also may try the district office of school choice at 154 West 93rd Street, New York, NY 10025, (212) 678-2885, or check out *www.insideschools.org*. But the region has also promised to make the admissions process to all schools more rational and clear-cut.

In the past, the oversubscribed schools maintained waiting lists, and children not admitted on the first round often were accepted later in the spring or summer. If a school is your first choice, call or write the principal saying so, and dream up ways you can be every principal's favorite parent. Don't lay it on too thick. Most principals are put off by overly aggressive parents. But they want active, helpful parents. One caveat: In the past, principals had discretion about who was admitted to their school. But recently Department of Education officials have been overruling those decisions, and out-of-district applications are being discouraged.

**District 5**, in Central Harlem, has long had some of the lowest-performing and most poorly managed schools in the city. The district office is at 425 West 123rd Street, New York, NY 10027, (212) 769-7500. District 5 parents who were eager to get a better education for their children once applied to better-regarded elementary schools downtown in District 3, but parents say the Department of Education now seems to have limited those options. Instead, the district has created its own new gifted and talented programs in an attempt to curtail the brain drain downtown. For updated information, contact the school choice coordinator, Nicky Kram Rosen, at the regional office, 4360 Broadway, (917) 521-3730.

**District 6**, serving northern Harlem, Washington Heights, and Inwood, is one of the most crowded districts in the city. School construction didn't keep pace with the waves of immigrants who moved to the neighborhood in the 1980s and 1990s, and hundreds of pupils are bused to less crowded schools downtown and in the Bronx.

Several small alternative schools have opened in recent years at the urging of activist parents. In addition, the district has opened some gifted and talented programs. For information, contact the school choice coordinator, Nicky Kram Rosen, at the regional office, 4360 Broadway, (917) 521-3730.

Over the years, upper Manhattan has changed from mostly Irish and Jewish to predominantly Dominican. Recently, Russian immigrants have moved to the area, along with artists and musicians escaping sky-high rents downtown. The most prosperous families live in large co-op apartments surrounded by formal gardens on Cabrini Boulevard and in Castle Hill Village overlooking the Hudson River. But most of the district consists of poor and working-class families living in rental apartment buildings. The district office is at 4360 Broadway, 4th Floor, New York, NY 10033, (917) 521-3713.

# PS 363: Neighborhood School
## 121 East 3rd Street
## New York, NY 10009
## (212) 387-0195
*www.theneighborhoodschool.org*

**Admissions:** District 1 priority
**Grade levels:** PK–6
**Enrollment:** 250
**Class size:** K: 18; 6: 28

**Reading scores:** ★★★★
**Math scores:** ★★★
**Ethnicity:** 32%W 19%B 33%H 16%A
**Free lunch:** 68%

"Purple hair! Just like your Mom!" director Judith Foster said admiringly as she greeted a girl in this very hip, very East Village school off Avenue A. The Neighborhood School attracts an eclectic mix of children of professionals, artists, and hippies, along with working-class people and families receiving public assistance. There are a few Bengali girls, dressed in the traditional head scarves and long dresses, a few Japanese students, and the usual New York mix of white, black, and Latino.

Learning is never passive at the Neighborhood School. On one of our visits, the irresistible smell of fresh bread wafted through the air as one class set up its own bakery. Students made butter, measured ingredients, baked the bread, then priced it and sold it to classmates and teachers—practicing arithmetic in the process. Even spoiled ingredients served a purpose. Students observed stages of decomposition and charted mold growth.

In another class, students designed computer-driven "robots" from Lego pieces. In yet another class, students put on a theater production—with help from a professional acting instructor.

Singing is a school-wide passion. Everyone in the school sings together regularly, and students and staff published a songbook filled with tunes in English and Spanish.

Foster says one of the books that most influenced her thinking about education is *I Learn from Children*, by Caroline Pratt, the founder of the City and Country School in Greenwich Village, one of the oldest progressive schools in the United States. The Neighborhood School is filled with Pratt's ideas, from the elaborate block villages that stay up for a week to the wooden cars and trucks built by 4th and 5th graders. Children learn elementary geometry when they cut angles with a miter box; they learn elementary physics by timing how fast the cars go down an inclined plane.

"The school is very academic, but based on concrete experiences that are interesting to children," says Foster.

"What I want this school to be is a safe, special place for children," she adds. Too often, she says, schools send the message that kids are good at some things and not other things. "School should be an opening up, not a closing off."

Classrooms are laid back, and there is an informality and collaborative feeling to the place. In a 3/4th-grade class students were working on independent writing. Some were sprawled on their stomachs on the rug, perched on benches, and tucked against the wall among hats and coats in an open closet—wherever they felt most comfortable. All classes have an "open work" time for a few periods each week, during which kids have unstructured time to work on projects or do explorations. In a 1/2nd-grade classroom during open work time, some students were playing with Legos, others were making puppets and drawing with Crayolas, and still others were playing with the class' pet snake.

The school has strong teachers, and lessons we observed encourage kids to think independently and to voice their views. "The curriculum is a molding of teachers' ideas and students' ideas," says Foster.

In one 5/6th-grade classroom, students were gathered on a rug in front of the teacher, engaged in a very sophisticated lesson about communism, dictatorships, and voting. "Was the Soviet Union a communist country?" one boy asked. "How do countries that have monarchies or dictatorships turn into democracies?" asked another girl. In response, a boy offered: "There's a lot of chaos at first." The teacher wove the discussion together, allowing the kids to ask questions and encouraging all the kids to participate.

The children don't receive report cards, but the teachers write letters to parents twice a year describing the children's progress. The children, too, write home at the end of the year, listing their accomplishments. A 4-year-old boy wrote his own report card with drawings of the school. "i LOVE LEGOS," he wrote. "like Bloks."

Parents say the school teaches children to work together in teams, to work independently, and to be active participants in their education—rather than passive recipients. It also teaches them to get along with people of different ethnic groups.

"Students here are taught not just to take what they are given, but to find out things themselves," said one mother. "There's a liveliness, a mix of ideas," said another.

And parents say the school offers a place where they can have a real say in their child's education. "In private school, if you don't like something, you can go somewhere else," explained one mother, who transferred her child from a private school. "Here, parents have input. There's an ability to contribute and change."

The school shares a building with PS 63, a neighborhood school that serves many kids from the housing projects on Avenue D and the tenements on the Lower East Side. The Neighborhood School does not have any self-contained special education classes, and students with special education needs are mainstreamed into regular classrooms.

The school has a fantastic new library that was designed by a father who is an architect. There is a weather station where kids learn to record humidity, wind speed, and other factors. Every child receives instruction in Spanish, physical education, art, music, and technology.

Tours are offered twice a month from October to February. Admission is by lottery. There is an after-school program that includes clubs like modern dance, French, and Capuera.

# PS 364: Earth School

## 600 East 6th Street
## New York, NY 10009
## (212) 477-1735
### *www.theearthschool.org*

**Admissions:** District 1 priority
**Grade levels:** PK–6
**Enrollment:** 290
**Class size:** K: 18; 6: 27

**Reading scores:** ****
**Math scores:** ****
**Ethnicity:** 38%W 18%B 33%H 11%A
**Free lunch:** 68%

"Look at the worms!" a 3rd-grade boy said as he hefted a pitch-fork to turn the dirt in a narrow strip of a garden in back of the Earth School, a small, progressive school dedicated to the study of ecology. A girl in prekindergarten looked on intently.

"I see some ants!" she said.

"Wanna see some more?" the boy asked.

"We found worms!" she said, and grabbed a magnifying glass for a closer look.

Kids at the Earth School dig in the dirt, plant in the outside herb garden, collect compost from classrooms, and study recycling—all part of a curriculum designed to engage them and to make them good citizens. The nearby Tompkins Square Park is used as a living laboratory.

It's an egalitarian place, where children call teachers by their first names and teachers make decisions together with the director. Parent volunteers help set up art projects, work in the office, lead tours, and escort their children to class. Founded in 1991, the school has flourished under the strong and consistent leadership of director Michelle Harring, who has led the school since the late 1990s. The school also benefits from an unusually talented and dedicated staff. The student body is diverse and includes the children of artists and professionals, as well as working-class people and families receiving public assistance.

The school has a focus on science and unusually strong social studies instruction as well. Students are encouraged to make discoveries through their own experiences, and they are taught to learn from the world outside their classroom. "The wonderful thing about science is to look at the world outside and see how it's working, and learn how to test your ideas," explains Harring.

Students take field trips in order to do hands-on science learning. Fifth and sixth graders spend a whole week in Frost Valley, an environmental education center in the Catskills, where they study the idea of water systems and water sheds. Students also take \[...\] to learn about ecology closer to home: in Inwood Park, Forest \[...\] Queens, or the Marshlands in New Jersey.

The school clearly cares about the social and emotional needs \[...\] students, and lessons seem to genuinely focus on process as much as results. In one hallway, drawings that 3rd graders did of microscopes were displayed in a row: Students were asked to draw them before they actually could use them. "We want them to slow down and learn how to care for them and learn how they work," said the principal. "And looking at a drawing can tell us a lot about a child." She pointed to one that was deflated and uncertain-looking. "For example," she said, "this child is very spatially challenged." Pointing to another one, she said, "This one's messy, but comprehensive. It's a lot more sophisticated."

Students are encouraged to work independently and many lessons are interdisciplinary. Lessons are creative, and many weave literacy and science into creative, artistic projects. In an art class, 2nd graders had come up with book ideas, had written stories, and were working on making pop-up books. In 5th- and 6th-grade classrooms, students were absorbed with putting the finishing touches on board games they were creating. Each child had researched an endangered species and designed a board game around the animal: They created the boards, the research-based questions, and the game pieces. One boy, Jackson, designed a sophisticated game around the grizzly bear: The aim was to get the grizzly bear to the wildlife sanctuary in the middle of the board. He had a stack of index cards full of questions about the grizzly, which he would pose to the class the next week, when students were scheduled to play one another's games.

The school has an after-school program that offers homework help, Spanish, knitting, a fund-raising club, and chess. Plus, it offers "time to relax," says Herring. "There's a real need for kids to have downtime." Students also get "community open time," or "COW time," during the school week, which gives them a chance to play, learn and explore in a less structured classroom setting.

All classes mix two grades, so students typically stay with the same teacher for 2 years in a row. There are three full-day, mixed-grade pre-K/kindergarten classes. The school does not have any self-contained special education classes, and students with special needs are integrated into regular classrooms and provided with extra help. The Earth School, which shares its building with two other schools—PS 64 and Tompkins Square Middle School—is housed in a big brick building that spans two city blocks. The school has a new, spacious play area with basketball court.

# plorations Into Science,
# ogy & Math (NEST+M)

11 Columbia Street
ew York, NY 10002
(212) 677-5190
*www.newexplorations.org*

**Admissions:** citywide
**Grade levels:** K –12
**Enrollment:** 920
**Class size:** 20-25

**Reading scores:** * * * * *
**Math scores:** * * * * *
**Ethnicity:** 46%W 9%B 28%H 17%A
**Free lunch:** 42%

New Explorations Into Science, Technology & Math—NEST+M for short—is a school designed to blend progressive and traditional teaching philosophies and to serve children in kindergarten through 12th grade. Designated as a gifted and talented school in 2004, admission has become highly competitive. Some children arrive by taxi from the Upper East Side, and some parents have chosen NEST+M over private schools.

The school's motto is, "A public school with a private school mission." Principal Celenia Chevere says that means, "We serve a public school population as well as a private school or better."

NEST+M has child-friendly furniture, "commons" for the older children, and small classes—20 in kindergarten and 25 in middle and high school. Students call teachers by their first names. Beginning in the 3rd grade, students wear khaki pants and polo shirts of various colors bearing the school insignia. They are required to wear sneakers to navigate what one parent called the "humongous maze of a school."

The newly renovated building, constructed in 1959, is flooded with light. It has brightly painted white classrooms, new furniture, and a "dining hall" with round tables designed to encourage conversation and civility. The halls gleam, and the building is unusually clean. There is a large gym and a pleasant playground.

The kindergarten classrooms are large and inviting, with a huge rug and gathering area in one corner, elaborate block structures, and children moving noisily from one "center" to another. Some of the projects, like the apple study, are typical of progressive schools. Kids go on an apple-picking trip upstate, count and tally apples, make applesauce, and write stories about apples. But kindergarten at NEST+M is more academic than at most other schools. Vocabulary "word walls" are up and children are expected to be able to read and write before they enter 1st grade. Reading is taught using a mix of phonics and "shared reading," in which the teacher talks about the words in a poem or other brief piece of writing with the children. Kindergartners write and illustrate their own stories using the model of the Writers Workshop developed by Teachers College, Columbia University.

Rather than use the progressive math programs now typical in city schools, NEST+M has adopted what is called "Singapore Math," a program that includes more drill and emphasis on basic skills. "Ready, go, sprint!" a teacher shouted as children scrambled to see how many addition problems they could complete in a minute. The teacher then shouted out the answers, and the children chanted "Yes" in unison for each correct reply. "63!" "Yes!" "74!" "Yes!" "40!" "Yes!"

In a music class, children sang scales, followed by a rendition of "America the Beautiful" in harmony. Private violin lessons are available during the day. In an art class, children made lush landscapes with Craypas, studying how to make objects appear close or far away and how to use warm or cool colors to create a mood.

One of the great draws of NEST+M is the fact that it is a K–12 school (although children must reapply for the middle school and high school, and admission is not guaranteed). In the middle school and high school, boys and girls are separated for math and science. Chevere says that helps girls develop confidence in subjects in which boys traditionally have dominated. Small class size, an accelerated curriculum, and a good college office have contributed to NEST's success. The administration says graduates have been admitted to Yale, Wesleyan, and the University of Pennsylvania. (For more on the middle and high schools, see *New York City's Best Public Middle Schools* and *New York City's Best Public High Schools*.)

A mother said she chose NEST+M over private schools (or the well-regarded District 2 schools where she lives) because it had both the small class size and continuity from elementary to high school that successful private schools have, and the mix of families of different backgrounds that good public schools have. "I finally found one that brought together the best of all the schools," said the mother. "The kids really love it. They're so excited, so thrilled. That's what's really important."

Another mother said she was impressed by the way children were taught to work independently. "From the earliest grades, you are taught focus and organization. You are responsible for yourself," she said. Homework is assigned everyday, even in the youngest grades.

Other parents have been disappointed by what they consider the school's unnecessarily punitive reaction to minor behavior problems, by the principal's reluctance to make appointments to meet with them, and by the daunting admissions process. Parents say the school offers little help to children who are struggling, and children who cannot keep up with the workload may be asked to leave. Chevere makes no apologies for her leadership style. She says the school has high standards for academic achievement as well as behavior. She says her job is to be in the classrooms overseeing instruction—not to be always available to parents. And the admissions process is designed to ensure that only students who are willing and able to keep up with the work are admitted.

More than 500 children apply for 94 seats in kindergarten. Tours of the elementary school begin in December and continue through February. Parents submit an application that includes a letter of reference from the child's preschool. About 300 of the applicants are invited for an interview. Parents are expected to be active in the school and to be willing to work nightly with their children on homework. At the interview, children may be asked to put together puzzles, to identify letters and numbers, or to perform other tasks that assess their readiness for kindergarten.

Unlike Hunter College Elementary School and the Anderson program at PS 9, NEST+M does not ask children to take an IQ test. "We use more of a performance assessment," said Chevere. She says a bright but quiet child, or one who speaks a language other than English at home, will tend to do poorly on an IQ test. In the interview, the school looks for perseverance, children who do not give up easily on a task, and children who work well with other children and work independently. A child who has difficulty separating from a parent at the interview would not be a good candidate, she said. Applications are accepted from all five boroughs, although most students come from Manhattan.

NEST+M has no after-school program. Special education services are very limited. A very active PTA raises a substantial amount of money for the school, and requests that each family contribute $500. Despite the straight-arrow image of the school, the parent body includes a number of punk rock musicians who staged a fund-raiser at the club CBGBs.

# PS 110: Florence Nightingale School

## 285 Delancey Street
## New York, NY 10002
## (212) 674-2690
*http://schools.nycnet.edu/Region9/ps110*

**Admissions:** neighborhood school
**Grade levels:** PK–8
**Enrollment:** 530
**Class size:** K: 24; 5: 29

**Reading scores:** ★★★★
**Math scores:** ★★★★
**Ethnicity:** 5%W 16%B 63%H 16%A
**Free lunch:** 73%

Renovating a 103-year-old building is no easy task, but the teachers and students at PS 110 all pitched in. According to assistant principal Brian Culot, the school raised enough money to give the building a professional facial on the outside—a new brick façade. More professional work is needed to set up rooms for air conditioners, but on the inside, parents are replacing old school furniture, and kids are making things pretty.

The school has an architecture program, led by a retired teacher and the Henry Street Settlement, which works on projects that are slowly infiltrating throughout the building. Stylized, geometric wooden portals bearing bugs and flowers painted the colors of spring mask the classroom doors. Furniture in the main office, the school store, and even the security guard's desk flaunt the club's signature designs.

The architecture program is not new; the Henry Street Settlement has been working with the school for about 20 years. In addition, PS 110 is able to fund other arts programs for students, such as instrumental music and a drama club.

Perhaps it is this affection for the arts that has smoothed the school's transition into a new era of progressive instruction. Classrooms are well decorated with learning aids, such as colorful bulletin boards with vocabulary words. Students are engaged here, either gathered on a rug to play a spelling game or discussing a recent apple-picking trip where they discovered a deer carcass in a field. In the Sunrise Science program, students work on science projects before school with a former parent who is also a scientist. Students also take an overnight trip to the Taconic outdoor education center in upstate New York.

The tone at PS 110 continues to be traditional, though, with test scores that are among the highest in the district. The school interviews and hires its teachers (rather than relying on seniority transfers or hiring halls), and Principal Irene Quvus says her teachers are "experts at figuring out what kids need" in order to do well. There are high expectations for both students and parents. Parents are kept up-to-date on what's happening in the classroom, and teachers call home if a child doesn't complete his or her homework.

"When people talk about PS 110 they say, 'Oh, you have to be prepared to do your work,'" said Quvus. "This is not a school for students to slack off [—or for parents either]. Our parents are committed to doing what it takes for their child to achieve."

The school mixes high-achieving children and those who are struggling in the same class for most of the day. However, children are grouped by ability for reading and math. Students receiving special education services are integrated into regular classes whenever possible.

Out-of-zone children are admitted on a first-come, first-served basis, except for prekindergarten, which admits children by lottery. Applications are given out on tours, which are held from October to April. Call the parent coordinator to schedule an appointment.

# PS 184: Shuang Wen Academy
### 293 East Broadway
### New York, NY 10002
### (212) 529-5025

**Admissions:** District 1 priority
**Grade levels:** PK–8
**Enrollment:** 359
**Class size:** K: 20; 6: 28

**Reading scores:** *****
**Math scores:** *****
**Ethnicity:** 5%W 9%B 4%H 82%A
**Free lunch:** 61%

The Shuang Wen Academy, opened in 1998, is a small experimental school designed to teach children to be fluent in both Chinese and English. It attracts both English-speaking families who want their children to learn Chinese and Chinese-speaking families who want to ensure that their children are literate in Chinese.

One mother is a fourth-generation Chinese-American who wants to maintain a cultural connection to China. A second wants her adopted daughter from China to speak her native language. The third wants to give her child the advantage of acquiring another language. All agree that a second language is important in an increasingly interconnected world—and that it's best to learn young if you want the best results.

More than half of the pupils speak Chinese at home, but many of those speak dialects other than Mandarin, which is taught at the school. Others are of Chinese ancestry, but don't speak Chinese. About one fifth are white, black, or Latino children attracted by the high standards of the school and the opportunity to learn another language.

Shuang Wen shares a building with PS 134. The dual-language school is expanding to include 6th, 7th, and 8th grades, to be housed at nearby PS 137. Class sizes are becoming larger due to increasing popularity among parents. A long day is necessary to learn two languages, particularly because learning to read and write in Chinese is so difficult. Neither space nor time is wasted here; students attend from 8:30 a.m. to 5:30 p.m., they work on portable word processors in lieu of a computer lab, and principal Ling-Ling Chou serves lunch to her kids in order to ensure a smooth and efficient lunch period.

Morning instruction is taught mainly in English, while Mandarin predominates in the afternoon. Classrooms have unusually large libraries for readers of many levels (currently most of the books are printed in English, although the school plans to purchase more Chinese literature) and children seem to enjoy their reading time. They also write and revise their own essays, following the Teachers College Writers Workshop program. After 3 p.m., the regular classroom teachers are replaced by a group of teachers who specialize in the Chinese language. Students are immersed in Mandarin and learn to write short compositions with traditional Chinese characters. Work is neatly displayed on bulletins boards titled "Composition Playground" in Chinese.

"We stress two things: academics and conduct," said Chou. "Work hard and be nice. There are no shortcuts on the road to success."

The school is very demanding, but parents say the long hours and hard work are worth it. "When I first heard about [the extended school day], I almost cried," one mother said. "I thought, 'When will I see my daughter?' But I realized that to be literate in Chinese takes so much extra time."

In 2003, parents saw the "work hard" philosophy pay off in other ways. The school's first standardized test scores were released, confirming that an impressive 97.2% of 4th graders passed the state math exam, while 96.8% passed the reading.

The school chooses to hire its own teachers and Chou looks for strong dedication to children. "Skills—they can be picked up, but dedication is part of one's personality and character." Not surprisingly, the teachers who are hired radiate warmth and affection when they communicate with students. Children wave "hi" to former teachers in the hallways, and some say they have a lot of fun while learning. A pleasant music teacher who visits classes throughout the day taught kindergartners to sing in Mandarin. Children just beginning to learn Chinese danced happily with their classmates even when they couldn't keep up with the lyrics.

Space constraints have led to some tensions between the schools in the building over the use of common facilities, such as the computer room and gymnasium. But the staff seems to play up the intimacy of their situation by inviting other adults into classrooms. There are student teachers in some rooms, and senior volunteers in others. These "grandparent" figures from the community help keep classrooms orderly and watch over little ones in the cafeteria—not to mention open milk cartons when needed. Also, parents are required to volunteer 4 hours per month. To support parents who do not speak Chinese, the school holds weekend workshops and has produced videotapes for students to watch at home.

Priority is given to District 1 students, siblings of children already in the program, and non-Asians. Tours are scheduled for the fall. Call the parent coordinator for details.

# PS 89

## 201 Warren Street
## New York, NY 10282
## (212) 571-5659
## *www.ps89.org*

**Admissions:** neighborhood school
**Grade levels:** PK–5
**Enrollment:** 450
**Class size:** K: 29; 5: 22

**Reading scores:** *****
**Math scores:** *****
**Ethnicity:** 55%W 10%B 13%H 22%A
**Free lunch:** 15%

This beautiful school building with commanding views of New York Harbor at the southernmost tip of Manhattan opened in 1998 after a speedy 18 months of construction. Built by the Battery Park City Authority (rather than the notoriously inefficient School Construction Authority), this combined elementary and middle school is unusual in that the architects consulted with administrators, teachers, and members of the community about what they thought an ideal school should look like.

The result is a building that has nooks in the hall for children to work individually or in groups, spaces for community meetings, and large, sunny classrooms designed so children can move easily from activity to activity. Each classroom has a space for children to sit on a rug as a group and listen to the teacher, as well as tables for them to work in small groups or individually. In the wide corridors, there are carpeted steps where children may sit and talk to one another, put on a small theatrical production, or meet with a teacher.

In a 4th-grade class, children wrote their own poetry, adapting a metaphor or the rhythm of a poem written by an established poet they admired. "Do you want it to breathe more, so people can think more about each piece?" the teacher said to a boy, encouraging him to break his poem, titled *Life,* into shorter lines. "This is powerful by itself!" she said of one line. "Try it a couple of ways and see which way you like it best!"

In the weeks before the citywide standardized reading tests are administered in the spring, many schools are obsessed with test preparation. But PS 89 uses fewer practice workbooks with fill-in-the-bubble queries than other schools.

"Good teaching helps them do well on the test," said a 3rd-grade teacher. For example, she read a biography of Thomas Edison outloud, and encouraged students to synthesize and take notes on what they heard—a skill that would help them on the test, but that also was part of the regular curriculum. Principal Veronica Najjar added that there is some test prep, and children who need extra help are encouraged to attend special after-school sessions to prepare for the test.

The children are used to seeing the principal in their classroom, where she chats with individual children about their work or demonstrates lessons for other staffers. Teachers and even the principal are called by their first names, and there is a friendly rapport between grown-ups and kids.

"It's not a top-down learning environment where the teacher lectures to the class," said Najjar.

"Hi, Ronnie. How's your snake?" one child asked the principal as she visited a class.

"Mmm. Not so good," she replied.

"I hope he's not dead," said another child.

"No, he's just shedding," Najjar replied.

Social studies is a focus at PS 89 because "children need to learn about the world outside of school," said Najjar. "They need to learn how people lived and worked in different cultures and different periods of history." Themes include Mayan and Incan civilizations, the Middle Ages, a map of New York City, and New Amsterdam.

One year, 2nd graders studied bookstores: how publishers acquire books, how bookstores order and stock books, and how a bookstore serves a community. They visited various bookstores in lower Manhattan, interviewed employees, and compared different kinds of bookstores, independent or chain, used or specialized. At the end of the project, they set up their own bookstore in the school.

Even the youngest children are encouraged to study the writer's craft. The day I visited, 1st graders were encouraged to "add details" in second drafts of the pieces they had written about their first memories.

PS 89 has invested time, energy, and money in training teachers in the new math curriculum called TERC that was adopted by the district. Several staffers are as passionate about teaching math as they are about teaching reading and writing and are constantly experimenting with ways to make children feel confident manipulating numbers. Rather than teaching long division as most of today's parents learned it, for example, they teach 5th graders to break large numbers into their factors. "They learn to divide big numbers by breaking them into little numbers," a teacher said. "That's what mathematicians do."

PS 89 has a building that's more luxurious than most other public school buildings. The interior walls are a gray stone. Kindergarten classrooms are particularly ample, with large windows and lots of room to play. There is a big gym and an auditorium. The building is air-conditioned and wheelchair accessible.

Children work on special projects in the corridors, or sit and read on the carpeted steps. In one wide corridor, a speech therapist worked individually with a boy with Downs Syndrome, who tossed a ball to a plastic bin she held as she gave him directions to throw it to her "over the bucket" or "under the bucket."

The school serves children with speech, language, and developmental delays in "collaborative team teaching" classes. In these, children with special needs are taught in the same class as general education pupils, with two teachers, one of whom is certified in special education, and a teacher's aide.

PS 89 is a neighborhood school and children living in Battery Park City are eligible to attend. Tours are offered from December through February.

# PS 234

## 292 Greenwich Street
## New York, NY 10007
## (212) 233-6034
*www.ps234.org*

**Admissions:** neighborhood school   **Reading scores:** * * * * *
**Grade levels:** K–5                 **Math scores:** * * * * *
**Enrollment:** 701                   **Ethnicity:** 67%W 11%B 8%H 14%A
**Class size:** K: 25; 5: 34          **Free lunch:** 10%

Kindergartners grind wheat in a stone mill to make flour, measure ingredients, mix dough, and bake bread in an oven in the classroom. Then they eat it! They learn about the different kinds of bread from around the world, read books about bread—a nonfiction title such as *Tortilla Factory* or a folktale such as *The Gingerbread Man*—and visit a bakery to learn what different jobs grown-ups have. They write stories about bread. They build a vast make-believe bakery from wooden blocks—with little bits of dough to represent bagels and baguettes, wooden people at work, and wooden toy trucks to cart the "bread" to stores.

The bread study is part of PS 234's social studies curriculum, designed to teach children how their world is organized and how the different people of the world meet the common challenges of finding food, clothing, and shelter. Each grade has several social studies units each year: First graders make their own (felt) shoes and visit shoe stores; 2nd graders explore the world of birds; 3rd graders build a model long house or wigwam used by Native Americans; and 5th graders study the ancient Greeks and make pottery vases.

At PS 234, teachers believe children learn best by doing things with their hands, by visiting interesting places, and by researching the answers to questions that interest them. There's plenty of time for more formal lessons in reading and math—and PS 234's test scores are among the highest in the city. But there is also a firm belief that children need unstructured time to explore by themselves.

"Kids need to learn how to learn," says Sandra Bridges, a former teacher and assistant principal at the school, who became principal in Spring 2003. "They need to gain the ability to generalize. I want students to learn how to approach topics that are unfamiliar."

Most other schools have corners filled with wooden blocks only in kindergarten and 1st grade. At PS 234, even 3rd graders are encouraged to build with blocks. Most other schools have "center" time—free time to put together Lego pieces or play a board game—only for the littlest children. At PS 234, even 5th graders have "center" time once a week.

The more academic lessons also are based on a spirit of inquiry. In a science class—a pleasant room filled with plants, fish tanks, and the chirping of birds in cages—3rd graders tested what materials carried sound best. One child struck a tuning fork and touched it first to a wooden yardstick, then to a stretched-out piece of string, and then to a long strip of foil. Another child listened at the other end.

Kids get engrossed in the subject matter they are studying. A tiny 1st-grade boy showed us his seven pages of work, each with a drawing and a good chunk of writing below. "This is a picture of a fish showing the dorsal fin," he said. "And this is a picture of a good filter [on a fish tank] and a bad filter."

In math class, students were working in groups, counting by the number 105 and recording their answers on long scrolls of paper, in order to discover patterns.

A school with no textbooks and no workbooks means children do original research from the very earliest ages. Teachers often build class trips into the curriculum, to allow for hands-on learning opportunities. One class, doing a unit on Central Park, made four separate visits to the park. Kindergartners take a trip to a restaurant to learn how food is prepared, read books about restaurants, then prepare food such as fruit salad and sell it.

PS 234, with one of the most pleasant public school buildings in the city, has large, sunny rooms, light oak tables and chairs, brightly lit corridors, and floors with shiny beige tiles. The school is air-conditioned and wheelchair accessible.

The school has an active PTA that raises more than $160,000 a year. The PTA pays for a music program: children in kindergarten through 3rd grade study rhythm, movement, and percussion. Fourth and 5th graders study strings, brass, and woodwinds.

Children receiving special education services are placed in regular classes and offered extra help. The school doesn't use the inclusion model, in which one class combines general education and special education pupils with two teachers, one of whom is trained in special education. Rather, the children receiving special services are scattered throughout the building, and a specially trained teacher spends time in their classes and offers tips to the classroom teacher on how best to reach them. Children also may receive services such as speech therapy and occupational therapy outside of class.

PS 234 began life in 1977 as a tiny alternative school tucked into an apartment building in Tribeca, a neighborhood that then had more empty warehouses than children. The school had three teachers and 57 children—mostly the offspring of artists and bohemians in downtown lofts. As the neighborhood grew and gentrified, the school did as well. A modern and well-equipped building, with a beautiful library, auditorium, and gym, opened in 1988 and the parent body increasingly included Wall Street bankers and lawyers.

The school is located just three blocks north of where the World Trade Center stood, and a flurry of residential developments in the area in the wake of the September 11, 2001, attacks has created a surge in the school's enrollment. There is talk of building an annex, rezoning, or creating a new school in the area in coming years to address the overflow of students.

Most of the children who attend PS 234 live in the school zone, south of Canal Street and east of West Street. A handful of variances are granted each year, for siblings of current students. Open houses are held in the fall and winter. Call in October for a schedule.

# PS 150: Tribeca Learning Center
## 334 Greenwich Street
## New York, NY 10013
## (212) 732-4392
## *www.ps150.net*

**Admissions:** District 2
**Grade levels:** PK–5
**Enrollment:** 182
**Class size:** K: 28; 5: 28

**Reading scores:** * * * * *
**Math scores:** * * * * *
**Ethnicity:** 52%W 23%B 15%H 10%A
**Free lunch:** 26%

Tribeca Learning Center, also called PS 150, is an intimate, enchanting place, hidden away from the street, off an open brick patio in a modern apartment complex. The atmosphere is cheery and informal—children call teachers by first names—the classrooms are well equipped and brightly lit, and the staff is energetic and talented. Most classes are served by two or three grown-ups, thanks to parent volunteers, high school students, and college student teachers. Parents are not only welcome; they are expected to take part in the day-to-day life of the school.

"If you decide to come here, you have to be involved," said Principal Alyssa Polack, who exudes seriousness and competence. "We ask for a strong commitment to your child's education and to the school." Parents write the school newsletter, help teachers hang children's artwork in the corridors, and organize the annual school auction. The Parents' Association raises a considerable sum for blocks, books, musical instruments, and science equipment. Parent fund-raising allowed the school to hire classroom aides in kindergarten and 1st-grade classrooms, so students in the younger grades get extra individual attention.

The small size of the school, with only seven classrooms and a capacity of 200 children, makes the transition from home or nursery school easy for the smallest children. PS 150 has a morning and an afternoon prekindergarten class. The principal and staff aren't bogged down with the mechanics of crowd control and can spend plenty of time planning lessons together.

"I get to know each and every child," says Polack. "I have 25 first graders at the school. There is one class in each grade. I can wrap my hands around the whole thing. I can see the growth of every child."

"Because it's so small, it's very nurturing," said Andrea Pedersen, a teacher and former PS 150 parent. "It's like a family." The size and the rich ratio of grown-ups to children allow teachers to deal with minor discipline problems in a low-key, gentle way. In an art class, a little boy was a bit goofy as the other kids, dressed in giant white T-shirts, painted with primary colors on big sheets of paper. The teacher, rather than scold, pulled the boy onto her lap and said softly: "What are you doing?"

Teachers are passionate about their craft. Even playtime is an opportunity for learning. When kids play dress-up, teachers encourage them to talk about their fantasies and stretch their imaginations—and their vocabularies.

Children study their community in kindergarten, their neighborhood in 1st grade, and Central Park in 2nd grade. They participate in dance, music, and art every week, and also visit the library. Except for prekindergarten, every classroom has two computers.

Children learn to write critically about the books they read, even in the early grades. Second graders, for example, responded to a biography of the poet Langston Hughes with comments such as: "I learned if you are poor on the outside you still can be rich," and, "If you keep trying your dreams can come true."

Math lessons strive to combine the excitement of discovery with the nuts and bolts of arithmetic drills. In one class, 3rd graders discovered factors with plastic cubes and graph paper, making rectangles with an area of 120. One rectangle had 10 cubes by 12 cubes; another, 6 by 20; a third, 5 by 22. In another class, 4th graders made bar graphs charting their own heights and compared them with younger children's heights. Fifth graders played a card game designed to teach equivalent fractions and decimals, matching a card inscribed *one-fifth* with one saying *.20*, for example.

If there were a prize for the best school lunch in the city, this school would win. Children eat lunch family-style in the classroom, rather than in a huge lunchroom. The school serves homemade food with fresh fruit and freshly made sandwiches or hot meals cooked on the premises, rather than the typical tepid lunches from a centralized kitchen. (Tours for prospective parents include a stop at the kitchen, and the cook is as well loved and respected as the teaching staff.) The children's bathrooms—the low point of most public schools—are clean and cheery, with shiny pastel tiles and plenty of paper towels and soap.

The school has a small media center, lined with books, an aquarium, and a few computers, where kids learn about computer science and library. One drawback is the lack of outside space. The school has no gym or playground. The physical education teacher (who also teaches computer classes) organizes games such as relay races around orange plastic cones on the enclosed brick plaza outside the school.

For recess, children jump rope or play with balls on the plaza, use a playground at the nearby Borough of Manhattan Community College, or play in Washington Square Market Park.

Special education services are limited. Occupational therapy and speech therapy are available several days a week, and children who have trouble with reading or writing may be assigned to a specialist for extra help. But there are no self-contained or inclusion classes for special education.

PS 150 is an option school, and children need not live in the immediate neighborhood to attend. Priority is given to children zoned for PS 234, PS 89, PS 3, and PS 41. In recent years the school has been able to accommodate any District 2 child. Free busing is available for children who live more than 1½ miles from the school. In the past, children from Brooklyn have been admitted.

# PS 3

**490 Hudson Street**
**New York, NY 10014**
**(212) 691-1183**
*www.ps3nyc.org*

**Admissions:** neighborhood school     **Reading scores:** ****
**Grade levels:** PK–5                    **Math scores:** ****
**Enrollment:** 547                      **Ethnicity:** 50%W 25%B 18%H 7%A
**Class size:** K: 18; 5: 28          **Free lunch:** 17%

Walk into PS 3, and you know right away you're in Greenwich Village. Kids are dancing to Calypso music, or organizing a baby shower for a lesbian teacher's pregnant partner, or making pancakes in a classroom kitchen. Mothers and fathers in blue jeans hang out in the parents' room, and toddlers—the preschool siblings of PS 3 pupils—sit in the corridors and put together Duplo bricks. The school is laid back, creative, a little noisy, and very welcoming.

"There's structure here, but it's not the usual structure," says Principal Lisa Siegman, former teacher at Manhattan New School on the Upper East Side, who took over as principal in 2001. The school has a creative spirit, but manages to maintain its own brand of order. Children may not run through the hallways—instead, they are encouraged to skip. Classrooms are noisy, but busy and productive.

The pluses are many: The teachers are unusually hard-working and imaginative. The parents are involved and clearly feel they are partners in their children's education. The children really love coming to school. The curriculum stresses original research over rote learning, so the children learn how to study and how to find out what they want to know. The school is a welcoming, fun place to be.

"There's a fluidity and spirit to the place you feel the minute you walk in," said Jack Tchen, a father whose daughter is a recent graduate. "There is a culture between teachers and parents that's wonderful. And there are some real master teachers."

Shino Tanikawa, co-president of the PTA, adds: "It may seem unstructured or chaotic at times, but the kids are really learning. Everything is really individualized. The school doesn't put a cookie-cutter on kids."

PS 3 was founded in 1971 by parents who wanted an alternative to what was then the very traditional education offered by PS 41, a Greenwich Village school nearby. Since its beginning, PS 3 has attracted an eclectic group of artists, bohemians, and counter-cultural parents from as far away as Brooklyn. It's welcoming to nontraditional families, particularly to gay and lesbian parents.

PS 3 is also a haven for some very capable teachers who are put off by what they see as a cookie-cutter approach to education, who want to put their own imprint and personality into their classes. And, in a district in which notions of progressive education sometimes become their own orthodoxy, that pride in individuality can have some ironic results: Of all the schools I visited in District 2, PS 3 was the only one in which long division was being taught the old-fashioned way—although the new math was in evidence as well. (Elsewhere in the district, the "new math" rules, and children discover many different ways of solving arithmetic problems and sometimes are not taught the tried-and-true methods called algorithms.)

Classes at PS 3 mix different ages and abilities, and children generally stay with the same teacher for 2 years. Every classroom looks different, and the personalities of both the teacher and the children are apparent in how the rooms are decorated. In one 3/4th-grade class, students were rapt as they watched their dynamic teacher, Otis, grimace as he tried to squeeze his foot into a tiny shoe as part of a math lesson about long division. He was giving students a metaphor for how some numbers don't divide, or "fit," into other numbers comfortably. In one K/1 classroom, the teacher, a talented musician, had her students write lyrics and record a CD to raise money for the victims of the December 2004 tsunami in Southeast Asia.

Everyone is on a first-name basis. Parents bring children right to the classroom and often hang out to talk with teachers or other parents in the parents' lounge. The principal's office is always open, and children often wander in just to chat. As the principal walks through the halls, kids run up, hug her, and share their latest discoveries. "Lisa, did you know an aardvark's a mammal?" Classrooms have high ceilings and giant windows, and class size is manageable. In a movement class, 4th and 5th graders swing to Calypso rhythms in dances they choreograph themselves. Kids are encouraged to have opinions, and voice them, and there is a palpable feeling of social consciousness at the school. Older students take field trips to Albany for "lobby day" and write essays about civics. Teachers and parents fund raise for social causes. And on one bulletin board, 4th-grade persuasive essays were titled everything from "Don't eat meat" to "The brain killer" (an anti-T.V. essay).

PS 3 has a half-day prekindergarten program. The school accepts applications from outside the zone. Tours start in October.

# PS 41

**116 West 11th Street**
**New York, NY 10011**
**(212) 675-2756**
*http://ps41.com*

**Admissions:** neighborhood school     **Reading scores:** * * * * *
**Grade levels:** PK–5                              **Math scores:** * * * *
**Enrollment:** 718                                  **Ethnicity:** 69%W 8%B 14%H 9%A
**Class size:** K: 21; 5: 28                        **Free lunch:** 16%

In the heart of Greenwich Village, PS 41 attracts the children of professors from New York University and artists from the West Village. While solidly in the progressive camp for academics, PS 41 is a bit more traditional in tone than its Greenwich Village neighbor, PS 3. Parents who live in the PS 41 zone may choose either school.

"It's not at all a free-form school," one PS 41 mother said. "It's pretty artsy. But it's also very structured." She said Principal Lois Weiswasser has "assembled a very competent staff" and "runs a tight ship." Self-discipline and respect are required of all children (as well as school staff), and rules such as "help people" and "be nice" are illustrated on the walls of kindergarten classrooms. Students exude a sense of productivity and purpose.

Different teachers have different styles, and a parent probably could find either a progressive or a traditional teacher here to best suit a particular child's way of learning. One kindergarten teacher with a love for music found many ways to work songs and poems into her lessons and onto the walls of her room.

Like other District 2 schools, PS 41 strives to spark children's interest in writing, partly by surrounding them with inspirational examples. It's not only student work that is proudly displayed. The school's walls are used as a canvas for the entire community, even the principal, to share personal experiences through their writing. Teachers contributed pieces, with photographs of themselves, titled "the most important thing I learned in school." Parents wrote about how their children's names were chosen, presented alongside their children's responses. One mother said she was thrilled that her 5th-grade daughter had decided, with a group of friends, to put out their own newspaper—not as a school project, but just because they loved to write. Similarly, the daughter read voraciously for pleasure—not just the minimum required.

While some parents complained there isn't enough emphasis on spelling, grammar, and penmanship, others said it was far more important for children to concentrate on developing the content of their papers and to worry about the form later—particularly given the fact that computers now have "spell checks."

The school has a strong art program, with four art teachers with different areas of expertise. A local graffiti artist painted the 1st-floor hallway with the students' favorite literary characters. The project was so successful that the artist returned to do a mural on the building next door. PS 41 also invites artists from respected organizations such as Lincoln Center for the Arts and the Geoffrey Ballet to provide instruction in dance.

While parents are generally enthusiastic about their children's teachers, several complained that the principal is unresponsive, particularly in cases in which children need special education services. One father said the principal refused to return repeated calls and didn't even respond to certified letters about his son's learning disability. Weiswasser said her secretaries sometimes refer calls to the appropriate party, such as the guidance counselor.

Despite these concerns, PS 41 has a warm sense of community. Third graders read to 1st graders in classrooms, spilling out into hallways to do so. Fathers of former students created a local "alumni dads" basketball team. "It's like living in Mayberry," one mother said. "We walk to school, kids bike to school. Parents are really involved." PS 41 has a pleasant, well-lit school building with a large playground. In the past, PS 41 has had children from outside the zone, including some children from Brooklyn. Check with the school for its current admissions policy and tour schedule.

# PS 126

## 80 Catherine Street
## New York, NY 10038
## (212) 962-2188

**Admissions:** neighborhood school    **Reading scores:** ****
**Grade levels:** PK–8    **Math scores:** ****
**Enrollment:** 707    **Ethnicity:** 4%W 19%B 34%H 43%A
**Class size:** K: 20; 8: 30    **Free lunch:** 78%

PS 126 is a rare gem. A school that serves mostly poor children, PS 126 has managed to close the academic gap between children from stable middle-class families and those who struggle with poverty and a raft of social problems such as homelessness or family violence. Children who start school speaking only Spanish or Chinese soon catch up with their English-speaking peers. So successful has the school become that middle-class families from outside the school zone are now requesting admission, even though more than 80% of the school's population is poor enough to qualify for free lunch.

The secret to success is exemplary teaching—not just good teaching, but consistently excellent teaching in every classroom. Strong leadership, small class size, ample books and supplies, and strong guidance from the regional office have made PS 126 a model of urban education. Teachers from other parts of the city regularly visit the school to pick up tips on how to make their own classrooms work better.

The ratio of children to teachers, aides, and other grown-ups is enviable. We saw no classes with only one adult, and paraprofessionals and student teachers from Fordham and New York University are abundant. The generous number of adults means that teachers can work with students in small groups for a good part of the day.

The building, constructed in the 1970s, has wide, shiny corridors; clean, white walls; and doors trimmed in bright, cheerful colors: red, yellow, blue, and lavender, green, purple. A large gym and an indoor play area give children a much-needed place to have recess during cold or rainy weather. A climbing wall (with fake rocks jutting out for children to climb on) has been built in the back of the stage in the auditorium—giving children another indoor place to get exercise.

The art program is unusually good, and children learn to work in various mediums—pastels and oils, charcoal and pencil, collage and sculpture. Self-portraits, landscape drawings, and still life pictures fill the halls. Music, too, seems strong.

The writing program is similar to others in District 2, of which PS 126 is a part. Children write from their own experiences, revising and editing several drafts until a piece is ready to be "published"—presented to the rest of the class or to a parent to read. What makes the writing stand out at PS 126 is that the quality is on a par with schools that serve a more prosperous population, while the stories reflect the trials of the children's lives. One child described how police officers took her father away in handcuffs after he had a fight with her mother. Another described how her parents sent her to live with relatives in the United States while they stayed behind in China to work. A third recounted how her cousins were taken from their home and placed in foster care.

On the border between Chinatown and the Lower East Side, PS 126 serves children from nearby housing projects as well as a homeless shelter that's just on the other side of the school's playground.

PS 126 has been designated as a PK–8 school, but the middle school, called the Manhattan Academy of Technology, has a distinct feel to it. Children are not automatically admitted to the middle school, but must apply. After a recent turnover of leadership, the middle school seems to have stabilized. The children seem happy and engaged and the quality of the teaching is good.

PS 126 has benefited from the strong staff development, or teacher training, for which District 2 has long been known. Daria Rigney, who was principal from 1999 to 2003 and is largely credited with its turnaround, now serves as a "local instructional superintendent" in the new Region 9, which consolidates District 2 with two other districts in Manhattan and one in the Bronx. The new principal, Kerry Decker, was assistant principal at MS 51 in the Park Slope section of Brooklyn and was largely responsible for that school's revival.

The elementary school is a neighborhood school that only occasionally has space for a handful of children from outside the zone.

# PS 124

### 40 Division Street
### New York, NY 10002
### (212) 966-7237
### *www.ps124.org*

**Admissions:** neighborhood school/gifted program
**Grade levels:** PK–5          **Reading scores:** * * * * *
**Enrollment:** 1,015           **Math scores:** * * * * *
**Class size:** K: 25; 5: 33    **Ethnicity:** 2%W 2%B 3%H 93%A
                                **Free lunch:** 70%

A little way from the chronically congested streets in Chinatown lies a school marked by order and structure. Parents drop off children at the door, and little time is wasted getting kids to where they should be. It is not a cold and unfeeling place, however; children may muse at the tall Christmas tree in the small lobby and listen to the steady stream of holiday music. PTA parents undertake the task of decorating the building for the winter holidays, hanging garlands from the furthest corners of the tall ceilings to bring a little bit of magic to children who might not celebrate Christmas at home.

"We celebrate different cultures and holidays here," says the PTA president. Fourth and 5th graders take lessons in Afro-Caribbean dancing, exposing the students—most of whom are of Chinese ancestry—to another culture. Parent activism is the hallmark of PS 124, a well-run, long-respected neighborhood school that also attracts children from Brooklyn and Queens. Parents at PS 124 successfully sought funds from their state senator and a private foundation to build a new playground. Through the "school leadership team," they allocated money for an "extended-day" program—late afternoon classes to provide extra academic help as well as child care for children of working parents.

Built in 1976, PS 124 is well kept and brightly lit, with wide corridors, shiny white floors, a large gymnasium, and a pleasant interior courtyard equipped with a climbing frame and soft rubber surface. The school's main library was redone with brand-new computers and books, and low shelves to better accommodate smaller children; the old books were displayed on shelves in an alcove, available for parents to take home. Children seem happy and attentive, and move smoothly and quickly from one class to another. Each class has a rich classroom library. Children are encouraged to select "just right" books—those that are not too hard and not too easy—from bins kept in easy reach. Class size is larger than at some other schools in the district—ranging from 25 to 28 in kindergarten through 3rd grade, and from 25 to 32 in grades 4 and 5. But work-study students and "America Reads" volunteers from New York University give children extra attention. The school has a gifted program open to students from across the district and, when space is available, to those from outside the district.

In general, teachers are conscientious and ambitious. Teachers actively look for possible partnerships or connections with cultural organizations, such as museums. The result is that children get to visit the Museum of Natural History, Jewish Museum, or Morgan Library often for projects. Some teachers were starting a project to compile binders of creative lessons and activities (that were already road tested) that would be available for others to leaf through, on one condition: that each person who used the binders also contributed something to them. "We want to build a community of teachers who take risks," says one 3rd-grade teacher.

The school is particularly skilled at teaching English to children who speak only Chinese at home. All teachers and support staff receive training in teaching English as a Second Language. Children meet with a teacher in groups of four for intensive English language instruction. Teachers read out-loud frequently and give children many chances to speak. Children may listen with earphones to books-on-tape as they follow along in the text. In addition to the "Reading Recovery" program, which provides one-on-one tutoring for struggling 1st graders, an after-school program offers new immigrants help improving their reading and writing skills. Students take trips throughout the city, and then read and write about their experiences.

A mother whose daughter is in the gifted program said the school's strengths include its "well-informed, enthusiastic parents"; a hard-working staff that "really likes children"; and an "amazing music and dance program" with classes in tap, ballroom, jazz, and ballet. The biggest drawback, she said, is the school's size. With more than 1,000 students and 60 teachers, it's very hard for the school administration to work closely with teachers.

A mother whose child receives special education services said she was thrilled with the individual attention he received. For example, a teacher equipped her son, a bouncy boy diagnosed with attention deficit disorder, with a weighted vest that helped him calm down. The teacher also helped him organize his homework assignments with color-coded folders and different-colored pens for each subject.

Children from outside the district may apply to the general education classes as well as to the gifted program. Applications for the gifted program are available in October and due in December. Tours are held from September through December.

# PS 130

## 143 Baxter Street
## New York, NY 10013
## (212) 226-8072

**Admissions:** neighborhood school/gifted program
**Grade levels:** PK–5          **Reading scores:** * * * *
**Enrollment:** 1098           **Math scores:** * * * * *
**Class size:** K: 16; 5: 36    **Ethnicity:** 4%W 2%B 5%H 89%A
                                **Free lunch:** 77%

On a crooked, narrow Chinatown street lined with walk-up tenement flats and exposed fire escapes lies a large, lavishly remodeled
public school with wide, brightly lit corridors; black wrought-iron
stair rails decorated with delicate cutout designs of animals; a rooftop
playground; an art studio equipped with a kiln; and large classrooms
with high ceilings, wooden reading lofts, and plenty of books.

A $30-million makeover, an unusually capable principal, and an
attentive, hard-working staff have transformed PS 130 from one of the
most neglected and rundown schools in the city—where teachers say
they used to put potted plants on a ladder to catch the drips from a
hole in the ceiling "big enough to see the sky"—into one that parents
from other boroughs fight to get their children enrolled in. "I was on
line at 5 a.m.," one parent enrolling her daughter, recalled, "but it is
worth it. She has just finished prekindergarten with some of the best
teachers around."

PS 130, which has long served the children of garment workers
and restaurant employees, is now beginning to attract more prosperous families as well. The students are predominantly of Chinese heritage, but in recent years more non-Asians have come, particularly in
the popular gifted program, and students from Brooklyn families eager to have their children enrolled in a District 2 school.

In some respects the school is very traditional. Children recite the
*Pledge of Allegiance* each morning and wear crisp blue and white uniforms. Good penmanship is prized, and children always call grown-
ups by their last names. Academics are introduced early, and many
children learn to read in kindergarten. The tone is serious, and parents
say there is a lot of homework, even over holidays.

But Lily Woo, who has been principal since 1990, has incorporated
key elements of progressive education as well. Desks are not in rows,
but arranged in groups. Children may move about the classrooms.

Gone are the basal readers—the reading textbooks favored a generation ago—and in their place are bins of picture books arranged by "levels" or level of difficulty—allowing children to choose books that both interest them and are suitably challenging. Teachers frequently read aloud to the whole class. For math, teachers use a combination of the Everyday Math and TERC programs; both teach children there is more than one way to solve a problem and encourage them to find their own solutions, rather than waiting for the teacher to show them the "right" way.

Drama, dance, art, and music classes leaven the academics. "We do try to build in movement and joy," said Woo. To ensure that there is something for everyone, she has developed an amazingly comprehensive arts curriculum where outside organizations come to work with students in each grade. Midori and Friends, a nonprofit organization founded by the violinist to bring music education programs to underprivileged children, exposes 1st graders to instrumental music. City Lights, a theater group, teaches 2nd graders to write and perform fairy tales. The Third St. Music School Settlement provides violin lessons for 3rd and 4th graders. Fourth graders take weekly dance lessons with the National Dance Institute. Fifth graders put on their own theater, and go to Broadway shows, with the help of Rosie O' Donnell's Broadway Kids. They also study ballroom dancing. The school also has full-time art and music teachers with their own classrooms. All this helps to make up for the school's lack of a regularly scheduled recess (teachers must sign up to bring their classes to a limited-capacity rooftop playground.)

Woo, the Chinese-speaking daughter of a restaurant employee and a pieceworker, came from Hong Kong when she was 2½ and knows how to help new immigrants become acclimated. The school offers English classes for parents four mornings a week (a convenient time for people who work in restaurants). Teachers show parents how to read subway maps, and invite them on trips to museums, children's plays, and libraries as a way to make them less isolated in their community.

Most impressive is the school's skill in teaching English to children who speak only Chinese at home. All of the kindergarten teachers are also certified as specialists in English as a Second Language. A teacher may work with a small group of four children, giving them plenty of time to speak as well as listen. Some teachers also speak Chinese and are certified as bilingual instructors, but the emphasis is on learning English rather than maintaining Chinese. Although the majority of children enter school speaking only Chinese (a handful speak Spanish), nearly all pass the exam that shows that they have adequate command of English within a few years.

Successful as the school is at teaching English, Woo continues to think up ways to further improve instruction. In addition to providing movement and fun for all students, Woo's arts curriculum serves a dual purpose for some; it helps shy children who don't speak English at home to feel comfortable speaking or performing in front of others. "These art programs help them develop speaking skills and learn the language through songs and plays, in nonthreatening ways. This levels the playing field for second-language learners," says Woo, when it comes time to interview for special schools and programs. "It also gives at-risk children a place to shine. Achievement goes up because kids feel successful."

Regular tours of the school are offered in the fall, many led by the personable Woo herself. Children are admitted to the gifted program in kindergarten based on an interview and test given by the district office. Applications are accepted in November.

# PS 40

### 319 East 19th Street
### New York, NY 10003
### (212) 475-5500

**Admissions:** neighborhood school
**Grade levels:** PK–5
**Enrollment:** 530
**Class size:** K: 18; 4: 28

**Reading scores:** * * * * *
**Math scores:** * * * * *
**Ethnicity:** 57%W 11%B 16%H 16%A
**Free lunch:** 19%

PS 40 is a gentle, cozy neighborhood school where a love of reading and writing is combined with an appreciation of the importance of play. Small class size (and a fairly small enrollment overall), a welcoming attitude toward parents, and a young and energetic staff make the school both lively and manageable.

Built in the 1920s, PS 40 has shining floors, high ceilings, and large classrooms with original oak trim and oak coat closets. Most classrooms have rocking chairs and rugs, and some have sofas. The school has an inviting rooftop playground, protected by a rubber mat cut in the shape of Manhattan and equipped with a climbing frame with large recognizable replicas of Manhattan's most famous skyscrapers: the Chrysler Building, Woolworth Building, and Empire State Building.

Principal Susan Felder writes a letter to the children over the summer and asks them to reply. Their responses are posted in the corridor, along with colorful self-portraits of the children. It's a way for the principal to get to know new students and for students to share their thoughts over the long school vacation.

Parents give the principal high marks for her willingness to meet with them and for spending enough time in the classrooms that she gets to know each child. Teachers speak to children in a quiet, respectful way, and the children respond in kind. It's a school in which both the kids and the grown-ups seem happy to be there. "It's a cohesive staff," said Felder. "The teachers go to Broadway shows together, have dinner together, go away on weekends together."

Teachers at PS 40 have a passion for teaching writing, which shows in the quality of children's work. In a 2nd-grade class, some kids were seated and others were kneeling at low hexagonal tables, absorbed in writing essays about their personal memories: the day a baby brother was born, a family vacation to Virginia, or a trip to Grandma's house. The teacher had begun the lesson by reading aloud from picture books such as *When I Was Young in the Mountains* by Charlotte Zolotow and

*At Grandma's When I Was Young* by Cynthia Rylant, books that use what the teacher called "repetition and beautiful language" to recall times past. The children, using the texts as a model, wrote their own "books" in poetic and evocative language.

The school, like others in District 2, uses the so-called TERC curriculum for math, in which children create their own different ways to solve arithmetic problems, rather than relying on grown-ups to teach them one "right" way. In the past, some parents complained that the math program wasn't challenging enough and that children weren't learning basic skills. The administration responded by putting more emphasis on the teaching of basic arithmetic facts, offering more explicit instruction in how to use formulas to solve problems, and offering more-advanced students the chance to move ahead of the rest of their class.

Kindergarten is a time when kids have trouble letting go of parents—and parents have trouble letting go of kids. PS 40 eases the transition by allowing parents to bring their child into the classroom each day and read out-loud for 15 minutes until the child is settled. Parents bring older children to the cafeteria in the morning; it's a time for parents to chat with one another and the staff.

The school has a fledgling 40-piece band, supported with a grant from VH1, and a full-time music teacher. A new "integrated arts" program combines visual and performing arts, including dance and music. A pleasant music room has xylophones and drums purchased by the PTA.

A full-time physical education teacher has developed a system to give kids a real workout in a 45-minute class, without the endless wasted time so typical in gym. "Waiting time—the cardinal sin of PE class—is practically nonexistent," said the teacher, Andrew Bieber.

Just as many elementary classrooms are divided into "learning centers," Bieber divides his gym into "circuits," or stations, with hula hoops, frisbees, or balls in each. Children break up into groups and work on one skill at a time. When Bieber blows the whistle, the children move to the next station; he can circulate or work on an individual child's skills.

While many of the high-performing schools in the district are now predominantly white or Asian, PS 40 has a mix of different ethnic groups. The school rarely admits children from outside the zone. Tours for prospective parents are offered twice a month, October through January.

# PS 116

## 210 East 33rd Street
## New York, NY 10016
## (212) 685-4366
## *www.ps116pta.org*

**Admissions:** neighborhood school/gifted program
**Grade levels:** K–5          **Reading scores:** * * * * *
**Enrollment:** 750          **Math scores:** * * * * *
**Class size:** K: 20; 5: 30          **Ethnicity:** 42%W 16%B 22%H 20%A
                                      **Free lunch:** 26%

"You don't need to use your voice. I can see from your faces when you understand or need help," a 1st-grade teacher reassures the four children sitting around her, who are getting ready to dive into a new book. As they settle into reading silently, a little boy winces at a difficult word.

Surely enough, the teacher responds swiftly and gently to his reaction with assistance. "See? I'm right here."

Such are the interactions you'd find between teachers and students in the classrooms of PS 116. The school is orderly without being rigid and has a gentle hum of children working together. It's a strict place, but the discipline doesn't seem oppressive, perhaps because the children are so happy to be engaged in their work.

Widely recognized for its early adoption of the Writing Process, the method of teaching writing pioneered by Lucy Calkins at Teachers College, Columbia University, PS 116 attracts talented teachers from across the city—and even from out of state—who want to hone their skills. "We look for teachers who embody the same philosophy the school has had," says principal Jane Hsu, a disciple of the former longtime principal who has since become a supervisor of principals in the region. Teachers are provided with ongoing training at the school and are expected to pick things up quickly. In fact, teachers here learn so fast that often the school loses them because they become staff developers. PS 116 is a Teachers College training site for literacy coaches, who visit classes in action. Professors of education conduct research here, and the building also is open to teachers from other schools who want to refine their craft. Examples of model teaching practices from PS 116 are featured in Calkin's book, *The Art of Teaching Writing*.

One beautiful spring morning, kindergartners in a gifted class were sprawled on their bellies on the floor, writing their "memoirs."

67

Paired off in twos, armed with big sheets of newsprint and black markers, the children were deep in concentration.

"Morgan memhwrer," one boy begins. "The HSBOLTOL cad my mom"

"Is this your adoption story? I can't wait to read it," said the teacher, who knows he meant to write: "Morgan's memoir. The hospital called my Mom."

In the Writing Process, children begin to write even before they know how to read, sounding words out and writing whatever letters they can. "Button" might be written "bn" at first, then "btn" then "butn," gradually building up to what the teachers call "dictionary spelling." It gives children the chance to write vivid memories, without being limited to the words they know how to spell.

As the children wrote, the teacher, assisted by a student teacher, "conferenced" with them, praising their work and giving suggestions for spelling and punctuation.

"You did 'brother' in dictionary spelling!"

"Do you want me to show you lowercase Ns? They're the hardest."

"Reread it and find a place for your stop signs [periods]."

The school encourages children to work with one another. In a 5th-grade class, students gathered in a big circle on a rug to discuss their writing projects. One girl shared with her classmates a "seed" idea, a journal entry, that she was interested in developing. Others suggested types of structure—poetic nonfiction for one—she might use to write her story, leading to an impressively mature back-and-forth of ideas between the children.

One mother said the education offered at PS 116 is comparable to that at a private school, although the student body is much more diverse. "I didn't want my child going to school with only the children of stockbrokers and lawyers," she said. At PS 116 there are children of artists, writers, and United Nations diplomats, as well as children living in homeless shelters.

Children receive some arts offerings, including visual arts and music classes, and a dance class in a studio furnished with a keyboard and platform stage for performances. Teaching artists from the Alvin Alley dance company also have worked with the students. The school's PTA offers a wide range of after-school clubs, offering everything from yoga to cooking.

PS 116 has special services for children who are visually impaired as well as for children who have speech and language delays. The school has a gifted and talented program that is open to children from anywhere in the district; admission is based on an interview conducted by the district office. The school has weekly tours for prospective parents, beginning in October.

# PS 212: Midtown West School

**328 West 48th Street**
**New York, NY 10036**
**(212) 247-0208**
*www.midtownwest.net*

**Admissions:** District 2 priority
**Grade levels:** K–5
**Enrollment:** 372
**Class size:** K: 24; 5: 30

**Reading scores:** ****
**Math scores:** *****
**Ethnicity:** 42%W 18%B 27%H 13%A
**Free lunch:** 31%

"Don't skip! Prance!" teacher Ted Pollen shouts as his 4th graders leap across the mirrored dance studio. A tape recorder blasts disco music as he gives instructions to the children, dressed in sweat pants, T-shirts, and stocking feet. "One! Two! Three! Four! Five! Six! Seven! Eight! Even though you're not wearing tight dance clothing, I can see some of you are not using your abdominal muscles!"

Pollen is a former Alvin Ailey dancer who has become a regular 4/5th-grade teacher at Midtown West, a small alternative school founded by parents in 1989. He teaches all subjects with passion and energy, but when he's teaching dance he's positively electric. So are the pupils. Boys and girls, plump children and thin, all are deep in concentration as they move gracefully across the wood floor.

In the heart of the theater district, Midtown West attracts parents and teachers who are looking for an informal, intimate, and welcoming school. "We have all kinds of kids, from shelter kids to people who could easily pay for private schools," a mother said.

Bank Street College of Education sends members of its staff to Midtown West twice a week to help teachers hone their skills. Student teachers from Bank Street receive their training here.

Lessons in reading, writing, science, social studies, and even math are woven into a theme, such as the study of Central Park. Children might take a nature walk in the park, write about it, read books about it, and calculate the number of blocks they traveled. In one class, children built a huge 3-D model of Central Park, almost to scale, and conducted research on Seneca Village, the African-American community that was evicted from the land on which Central Park was built.

The lessons draw on children's imagination and interests. At many schools, a cardboard strip with the alphabet—printed by a textbook company—is posted on the wall. At Midtown West, children draw their own "New York City" alphabet with their own illustrations on sheets of construction paper hung on a cord strung like a clothesline across their classroom: Aa apartments; Bb buildings; Cc Central Park; Dd downtown; Ee Empire State Building; Ff firefighter.

Children stay with the same teacher for 2 years, which provides continuity and gives teachers and children a chance to get to know one another well.

A kindergarten/1st-grade teacher, Carl (a former actor and set designer who went into teaching after his own son attended Midtown West), helped a little girl who was writing a piece based on her "interview" with the school principal about her job. "You told me you couldn't spell the word 'work' and look—you just did," the teacher said, and the girl beamed with pride.

Children with special needs may be placed in a self-contained class or in a collaborative team teaching class. The school is welcoming to gay parents, to interracial families, and to families formed by adoption.

Some downsides: There has been a turnover of staff in recent years, and some administrative bumps in filling vacancies. Liz Saplin, a former teacher at PS 234 in Tribeca and former principal of East Side Middle School on the Upper East Side, became principal in 2004. In her first year, there were some complaints that she was inaccessible, as well as some concerns that she was unaccustomed to the high level of parent involvement for which Midtown West has long been known. Saplin said she has begun greeting parents at the school's entrance every morning as a way of making herself more available to them. And, while she acknowledges that her leadership style may lean more toward accommodating teachers than parents, the school still is far more welcoming to parents than most.

Parents drop off their children in their classrooms in the morning, and many kindergarten parents stay for 20 minutes to read with their children. Parents may chat in the purple-carpeted "family room" equipped with a coffee pot and with crayons and small tables and toys to amuse siblings too young to go to school. Parents are involved in fund-raising and the well-regarded, after-school program.

Midtown West shares a building with a middle school and a high school, but it has separate stairwells, so the little kids don't have much contact with the older students.

The school has weekly tours from October to January. The school has no zone, and prospective parents fill out an application saying why they are interested in having their child attend. There are three times as many applicants as seats available. Applications are accepted in October.

# PS 59: Beekman Hill School

**228 East 57th Street**
**New York, NY 10022**
**(212) 752-2998**

**Admissions:** neighborhood school
**Grade levels:** PK–5
**Enrollment:** 375
**Class size:** K: 24; 5: 28

**Reading scores:** ★★★★
**Math scores:** ★★★★
**Ethnicity:** 46%W 15%B 19%H 20%A
**Free lunch:** 25%

It's only the third week of classes, and the children are already settled in their routines. In one class, the teacher sings, "Stop, look, and listen," and the children respond in unison, "Okay!" and fall silent. In another class, children are sitting on pillows on the floor, or stretched out on a blue sofa, reading to themselves. A smaller group of children are seated in the hall, reading aloud. In a music class, children are composing their own songs for the recorder. Prekindergartners are painting on easels. Children move quickly and quietly from one activity to another. The school has a cohesive feel; teachers seem to share a love of their craft and a common philosophy.

PS 59 attracts teachers from as far away as Texas, New Jersey, and Maryland, drawn to a school in which they can perfect their craft and learn from one another. "The emphasis on professional study is so supportive, so phenomenal, I've learned so much," said a teacher and administrator who came from Denver. "The administration is really good at helping teachers grow professionally."

This is a school that values play as the foundation for learning. In the dress-up area of a prekindergarten class, children invented stories about a make-believe family. "The stories they tell in the housekeeping area are the beginnings of the storytelling we want them to do on paper," Principal Adele Schroeter remarked.

Housed in a three-story, 1960s modern-style building, PS 59 has fewer than 400 children. The school has just two straight corridors (one on each floor, plus the cafeteria on the ground floor) so even the littlest kids can find their way around in their first days of school. Special projects can spill into the halls, still leaving room for children to walk by. There is plenty of space on the playground for children to run around without bumping into one another. Classes have rugs, rich classroom libraries, and cozy reading areas; a few even have sofas. Tables in primary colors have replaced beat-up old desks. As the school has grown, it has taken over a few classrooms in the adjacent

High School of Art and Design, separated from the main PS 59 building by a playground.

Even the lunchroom is civilized. Teachers supervise the kids—although it's not required by their contract—and lunch is more orderly than is generally the case when the less experienced school aides are in charge. Teachers, rather than aides, also supervise the playground.

Parents bring children right to their classrooms in kindergarten and 1st grade, and many stay to read or work on projects for a few minutes.

The United Nations is included in the school zone, and 35 languages are spoken at PS 59. Parents say the children from different countries bring a richness to the school community. "My kids don't think Omar and Fatma and Mohammed are weird names," says Miriam Schneider, whose twin girls attend PS 59. "My daughters went to one birthday party at the Libyan mission and one at the Swedish mission."

An active parents' association brings another kind of wealth. Schneider, who left a job in banking with a six-figure salary when her daughters were born, is one of the parents who volunteer full-time at the school, helping the PTA raise some $150,000 a year. Parents are requested to donate $750 each, and some donate much more.

Like many District 2 schools, PS 59's strength is the way it teaches writing. From the earliest ages, children are encouraged to write from their own experiences on topics that they feel passionately about. The results are vivid. A 2nd grader wrote about the terror she felt when her parents first left her at nursery school: "I thought I would never see my parents again. I felt like I would be locked in an orphanage forever. My heart was beating and I was breathing fast."

The school has collaborative team teaching classes that mix children with special needs and those in general education. These classes have two teachers, one of whom is certified in special education. A mother whose son was diagnosed with attention deficit disorder and hyperactivity said she was thrilled by the way the teachers and administration helped him focus and concentrate.

PS 59 has a particularly good music program. The school has a partnership with the New York Philharmonic. First graders visit the orchestra, and musicians come to the school to prepare them for the visits. Kindergartners study movement and percussion music at the Turtle Bay School of Music. PS 59 has no gym and no auditorium. Admission generally is limited to children who live in the zone.

# PS 183

**419 East 66th Street**
**New York, NY 10021**
**(212) 734-7719**
*www.ps183.org*

**Admissions:** neighborhood school  **Reading scores:** * * * * *
**Grade levels:** K–5  **Math scores:** * * * * *
**Enrollment:** 521  **Ethnicity:** 52% W 13%B 15%H 20%A
**Class size:** K: 22; 5: 27  **Free lunch:** 18%

PS 183 strikes a balance between structure and freedom, hard work and fun. It's challenging academically without being competitive. The teachers share a common vision of progressive education: that children learn best by doing, not by listening to lectures; by working together with children of different abilities, not by competing against one another. The teaching staff is good; the children are attentive; and parents are active and engaged.

More than one third of the parents are research scientists, doctors, or others affiliated with nearby Rockefeller University, Sloan-Kettering Memorial Hospital, and New York Hospital. These institutions draw researchers from around the world for fellowships lasting a year or more, and their children enrich the life of the school. "You get [children of] molecular biologists, brain surgeons, rocket scientists all coming to our school," said a mother who is active in the PTA.

Forty-three languages are spoken at the school. "I like the fact that it's integrated, not just racially but culturally and economically," another mother said. Some teachers take advantage of the diversity in the school's population to teach children about different languages and cultures. Theresa Kubasak's 1st-grade class celebrates Korean Alphabet Day, the holiday that marks the invention of the Korean alphabet. She teaches children to write a few words in Korean and the other languages spoken by children in the class: Chinese, Arabic, Hebrew, Japanese, Russian, and the African languages Bantu and Shumon. "I've got a kid from Beirut writing in Hebrew and a kid from Tel Aviv writing in Arabic and everyone writing in Chinese," Kubasak said.

PS 183 places more emphasis on science than is typical at elementary schools. The PS 183 science coordinator organizes activities such as the robotics competition, in which children design robots from Lego blocks to perform household chores for the handicapped. Kindergartners study the environment at Rockefeller University and animals at the Central Park Zoo. Third graders go on a trip to a mineral mine as part of geology study. Fourth graders sail on the Hudson River in the *Clearwater* ship where they learn to hoist sails, test for oxygen levels in the water, and study zooplankton. Fifth graders take an overnight trip to the Sharpe Environmental Center in Fishkill, NY, where they study life in a pond and track deer.

Like other District 2 schools, PS 183's strong suit is the teaching of reading and writing. In fact, the school attracts teachers from out-of-state who come to be part of District 2's innovative methods.

At first, children string together whatever letters they can to express their ideas. A 5-year-old boy, for example, wrote: "I brt bob home ystrdy mi frnz kam to mi hs." (I brought Bob home yesterday. My friends came to my home.) These approximations of spelling help children learn the relationship between sounds and letters—and help them learn to read. As they get older, they use works of literature as models for their own writing, reading, for example, the memoirs of Patricia Polacco and then writing their own memoirs.

PS 183 kindergarten classrooms are less pressured than many in the city, with lots of blocks, room to play, and a chance to socialize. "There's an extremely easy transition from nursery school to kindergarten," said one mother. Principal Joshua Klaris said, "Our kindergarten teachers have been successful in holding off the push to be 1st grade," a success which one mother attributed to the "absence of Type A parents" at the school.

Klaris, who became principal in 2002, has helped teachers coordinate their lessons with one another, both within a grade and between grades, so the curriculum is ever more coherent. There are occasional complaints from parents, as there are in most District 2 schools, that the math curriculum doesn't emphasize basic skills and that the reading program should have more explicit instruction in phonics. But most parents are enthusiastic about the academic program.

The 5th grade studies dance with the National Dance Institute, in a program that combines jazz and modern forms. The school has a big playground, a small but relatively civilized lunchroom, and a tradition of sending kids out for recess even when it's cold.

The Parents' Association raises nearly $300,000 a year for library books, a librarian, a volunteer coordinator, photocopy machines, teaching assistants, the science coordinator, and art supplies. Parents are asked to contribute $500. Tours of the school are offered monthly from October to March. Admission is limited to children living in the zone.

# PS 225: Ella Baker School
## 317 East 67th Street
## New York, NY 10021
## (212) 717-8809
### *http://Ellabakerschool.org*

**Admissions:** citywide
**Grade levels:** PK–8
**Enrollment:** 275
**Class size:** K: 20; 8: 24

**Reading scores:** \*\*\*
**Math scores:** \*\*\*
**Ethnicity:** 3%W 56%B 35%H 5%A
**Free lunch:** 46%

Ella Baker is a small progressive school housed in the Julia Richman Educational Complex. It shares the building's facilities—including two gyms, a pool, a ballet studio, and a library—with several alternative high schools.

Modeled on Central Park East Elementary School in East Harlem, Ella Baker places two grades of kids in one class, and students have the same teacher for 2 years. Drama, dance, poetry, and art permeate the curriculum, from a puppet show put on by kindergartners to the Ella Baker players, a student musical ensemble. The New York Collegium, a professional ensemble of Baroque musicians, instructs students on a regular basis. Teachers take pride in nurturing children's passions. "When you have a joy for learning and discovery, everything is interesting," said Principal Laura Garcia.

Many schools have center time, when small children play with blocks, dress-up, or draw pictures. Ella Baker has "work time," similar to center time, for older children as well, and kids may study topics ranging from poetry to architecture. "It has the benefits of a small private school but . . . the beauty of a public school being open to everyone," said one parent. "Every child is treated as a gifted and talented child."

Trips are a big part of the curriculum. The younger children go ice-skating every week, and all students explore the city with visits to museums and performances.

The school accepts children from all 5 boroughs. Call to arrange tour. Applications are due in March.

# PS 158: Bayard Taylor School
## 1458 York Avenue
## New York, NY 10021
## (212) 744-6562

**Admissions:** neighborhood school   **Reading scores:** * * * * *
**Grade levels:** PK–5                      **Math scores:** * * * * *
**Enrollment:** 714                          **Ethnicity:** 56%W 9%B 21%H 14%A
**Class size:** K: 17; 5: 34               **Free lunch:** 22%

It's a pleasant fall afternoon, and a dozen East Side mothers—some of whom could afford to send their children to private schools—are gathered in the parents' room at PS 158 to plot strategy. They are among the parents who come to school each day to help out in the lunchroom, organize volunteers to go on field trips, watch children on the playground, and—perhaps most important—raise money for the school.

These are not your basic paper-drive and bake-sale fund-raisers: They raise $300,000 a year. They tap parents, of course, asking each family with a child in the school to contribute $500 a year. They run a magazine drive. They lobby their city councilperson. They drum up grant money. They organize an annual auction. They even sell sweatshirts and baseball caps with the school's motto: "PS 158, Pride of the East Side."

The money goes to pay for assistant teachers in kindergarten, 1st grade, and 5th grade, and to pay for a wide range of programs outside the standard curriculum—chess, classes in circus arts, ballroom dancing, theater arts, and ballet—as well as basics such as kindergarten aides. "It's like running a small business," said a mother who is active in the Parents' Association (PA).

PS 158 has a relaxed and cheerful tone. Principal Darryl Alhadeff spends lots of time in the classrooms and seems to know most of the children by name. She strives to give teachers as much support as they need in order to do their jobs. "I believe you nurture teachers the way you nurture children," she says. Teachers have "common preps," regularly scheduled periods during the day in which they may plan lessons together and ask one another for advice.

"Darryl makes a point of making families know they're welcome," said one mother. The principal is "very personable, very approachable," said another mother.

Housed in a large, well-kept building constructed in 1898, PS 158 has long winding corridors, high ceiling, large windows, and original details such as oak coat closets. It has two gyms and a small but adequate auditorium.

Like other District 2 schools, its strength is its writing program. Even in kindergarten, children write from their own experiences. They learn the correspondence between sounds and letters by writing. One child, for example, wrote, "NI fall i lik to clleckt leafs with my sitr"—her approximation of, "In the fall, I like to collect leaves with my sister." Standard spelling is introduced in 1st and 2nd grades. By 5th grade, a child might pretend she's an immigrant in the days of Ellis Island and write a 1½-page letter to an imaginary friend in her home country recounting her ocean voyage. "They teach you to edit yourself, to rewrite, and to look for all those little errors," said the mother of a 5th grader. Each class has a rich classroom library, so children, with a teacher's help, can choose books that interest them. Kids who need extra help are invited to a "Saturday Academy" in November to prepare for the standardized city and state exams.

The school has an extensive special education program. A staff member offers occupational therapy, physical therapy, and speech services, while visiting teachers offer vision and hearing services and adaptive physical education for the disabled. The school is wheelchair accessible.

The school has several classes that integrate children receiving special education services with those in general education. These collaborative team teaching classes have two teachers, one of whom is certified to teach special education, and an aide. What makes these classes successful is the talent of the teachers—who volunteered to work together—and the class size, kept at a manageable 24 children, eight of whom have special needs. The rich ratio of teachers to children means the classes can accommodate a large range of abilities: One child was reading a novel by Beverly Cleary, while another was reading *Frog and Toad*.

The school's self-contained special education class (i.e., a class exclusively for children with special needs) is one of the best I've seen. Children follow the same curriculum as the rest of the school—whether they are writing their "memoirs" or reading about the Stamp Act—but the teachers adapt the material as needed. One child was able to write a 1½-page autobiography, while another—a multiply handicapped, barely verbal child in a wheelchair—managed to dictate a few short sentences about his lunch at McDonald's. Children use the same "editing checklist" used in mainstream classes, reminding them to check for spelling and punctuation, but also learn social skills that other children might pick up naturally—such as how to make eye contact. The children in this class take part in school-wide enrichment activities, such as ballet and music, with their mainstream peers.

The school has a rich music and art program, thanks in part to the Parents' Association (PA): dance instruction by the National Dance Institute and the Harkness Ballet; classes in "circus arts" such scarf juggling and plate spinning; music and movement offered by Symphony Space. There are mock trials organized by a group called Constitution Works.

The playground is large and well supervised. The PA pays for a program of organized games at recess called "Kids in Game," taught by private coaches. On rainy days, the games are offered in the auditorium or the gym—a welcome relief from the cartoons most school show on rainy days.

There are two half-day pre-K classes and one full-day pre-K class. Tours are offered from October through May. Admission generally is limited to children living in the zone.

# PS 6: Lillie Devereaux Blake School

**45 East 81st Street**
**New York, NY 10028**
**(212) 737-9774**
*http://ps6pta.org*

**Admissions:** neighborhood school
**Grade levels:** K–5
**Enrollment:** 852
**Class size:** K: 27; 5: 28

**Reading scores:** * * * * *
**Math scores:** * * * * *
**Ethnicity:** 77%W 6%B 9%H 8%A
**Free lunch:** 8%

Just off Park Avenue, less than two blocks from the Metropolitan Museum of Art, PS 6 attracts a devoted parent body, many of whom easily could afford private school. Real estate ads for Fifth Avenue apartments tout "PS 6 zone," and one mother described morning drop-off as "pumps and pearls and $150 haircuts."

It's a school where teachers are encouraged to develop their craft; where teaching is seen as an intellectual, even scholarly enterprise. One teacher, a Ph.D. candidate at Teachers College, was conducting research on gender stereotyping in children's books—enlisting her pupils as research assistants.

Children learn about writing not only from talented teachers, but also from a star-studded cast of guest speakers. Retired *Newsday* columnist Jimmy Breslin offered a lesson on journalism. (The kids asked him how he uses punctuation.) Frank McCourt, author of *Angela's Ashes*, spoke about writing memoirs.

The red-brick building, opened in 1957, is clean, well lit, and well maintained. While the architecture is unexceptional, the school has a large auditorium, a nicely kept gym, and a newly renovated library. Each class has its own classroom library and plenty of supplies, and kindergarten room have elaborate block structures. Many classes have sofas and upholstered chairs. A teacher with a hearing-impaired child put tennis balls on chair legs so they didn't make a distracting noise; other teachers liked the idea and implemented it in their rooms as well.

PS 6 has a particularly well-developed writing program, based on the principles outlined by writing guru Lucy Calkins. Teachers College has designated PS 6 as a "mentor school" for its reading and writing project. Teachers and researchers from across the country visit the school on a regular basis to see how it teaches children to write. Not only does each child write about a different topic, but each may write in a different genre as well. By the time they graduate, children have written memoirs, plays, songs, speeches, essays, poetry, and short stories. With each piece, they go through many stages: collecting ideas, picking a "seed" or central theme, planning a first draft, revising, editing, and finally "publishing"—preparing a piece for others to read either in a homemade book or at a "writing celebration" to which family members are invited.

"My daughter knows more about books than I did when I worked at a publishing house," said Catherine Hausman, co-author of *The Manhattan Family Guide to Private Schools*, who chose PS 6 for her child. "She understands the elements of a book—the preface, the index, and so on. They do a fantastic job teaching kids to write like authors and read like scholars. Kids aren't spoon-fed facts. They learn how to find information themselves."

The school uses the TERC math program in which children construct their own answers to problems, rather than applying formulas given to them by their teachers. Many parents say the smallest children learn a love of numbers and an understanding of how numbers work that's hard to beat. Perhaps more than other District 2 schools, PS 6 has blended the new math with the old, giving children a conceptual understanding of math while still allowing them to use the formulas or algorithms that characterize old-fashioned arithmetic lessons.

In addition, PS 6 is complementing the TERC curriculum with extra math exercises from a group at City College called Math in the City, which some parents say helps fill the gaps in the TERC curriculum. Math-loving children may take part in a lunchtime "math team" to prepare for the Continental Math League national competition. Despite these programs, some parents complain that the curriculum doesn't move fast enough, particularly for high achievers in the 4th and 5th grades.

A new science teacher has invigorated the science curriculum with projects drawn from children's questions, such as: "Why do leaves change color?" Kids made a scale model of the solar system. "We made it as far as Saturn, which is as far as we could go in the school yard," said the teacher, Eric Dutt.

Visiting actors conduct a drama program that concludes with a student production of *Macbeth*.

Principal Dan Feigelson has welcomed parents in the life of the school. Parent volunteers on the playground, in the lunchroom, and in classrooms help make the school a more civilized place. One caveat: The office staff can be abrupt, so don't be put off when you telephone.

Teachers take advantage of the Metropolitan Museum of Art and other nearby museums to weave reading, social studies, and art together. Third graders studying Japan read a Japanese novel, look at Japanese art at the Met, and go to the Japanese tea house for a tea ceremony.

The Parent–Teacher Association raises more than $300,000 a year. The PTA pays for assistant teachers in kindergarten and 1st grade, and asks parents in those classes to contribute $600 per child to pay their salaries. In addition, all families are asked to contribute $350 per child per year. The school also has an auction and a magazine drive.

PS 6 has a number of collaborative team teaching (CTT) classes to serve children with special needs. The CTT classes typically have 15 general education pupils and nine students with disabilities, and two teachers, one of whom is certified in special education. On one of my visits, a CTT class had 24 children and five grown-ups: two teachers, an assistant teacher, an aide, and a parent volunteer. "It's the best deal in town," Feigelson said of the rich teacher–student ratio. "I fought to have my daughter in a CTT class." The school also has several self-contained special education classes, designed to serve only special needs kids.

The school limits kindergarten and 1st-grade admission to children who live in the zone. (Exceptions are made for children zoned for the former PS 151, a school that closed indefinitely in 2000.) PS 6 sometimes has room for a handful of students from outside the neighborhood in grades 2–5. "We often don't know if we have space available until late in the year, April, May, or June," said Feigelson. Parents may request an application for admission during parent-led tours, held five times a year from October to May.

# PS 290: Manhattan New School

### 311 East 82nd Street
### New York, NY 10028
### (212) 734-7127
### *www.manhattannewschool.org*

**Admissions:** neighborhood school
**Grade levels:** K–5
**Enrollment:** 680
**Class size:** K: 26; 5: 32

**Reading scores:** * * * * *
**Math scores:** * * * * *
**Ethnicity:** 75%W 5%B 11% 9%A
**Free lunch:** 14%

If children had living rooms, they would look like the classrooms at Manhattan New School. There are comfy sofas and shag rugs, wood bookshelves filled with children's literature, and pretty curtains hung along the windows. Children's self-portraits decorate the walls. Teachers sit in rocking chairs and kids gather around for lessons. Or students sit around tables, in groups, rapt in conversations about writing, or hard at work on interesting projects about history or science or mathematics.

Children are taught that working with one another is important, and that fairness and kindness count. "There's so much work that goes into talking with kids," says Karen Ruzzo, who became principal in 2002, after teaching 2nd grade at the school for many years. "Meanness just isn't tolerated here." The lunchroom tables are round so that students can see one another and carry on conversations as they eat. Kids are taught to accept one another's differences, and teachers take pains to make sure children with special needs are included in regular classroom activities.

Writing is one of the school's major strengths, and children are taught to write well, and creatively, from the very earliest grades. Students are encouraged to find their own voices and write about real-world experiences. First graders conduct interviews of their classmates' parents and write books about what they learn. There are books and essays displayed throughout the school; by the 4th grade, many students are writing moving, textured, and descriptive prose.

Student work is sophisticated. "We have visitors to the school all the time that are just wowed by the level of conversation," says the school's assistant principal Sharon Hill.

"The school teaches kids to be deep, thoughtful thinkers," adds a parent. "The children really feel that they own it. That the school belongs to them."

Kids and teachers alike feel that they have a real say in what goes on at the school: It is a place where their opinions count. Teachers dream up creative lessons, and children are encouraged to come up with their own questions and then explore the answers. Children studying the civil rights movement interview a real-live hero about her experiences: the school's security guard, Ida Chaplin, who integrated the Woolworth lunch counter at a 1960 sit-in in Greensboro, NC. Fifth graders study the First Amendment by reading court cases, writing briefs, and then arguing their positions at a mock trial, which is held at Federal Hall. In technology class, 5th graders learn how to make movies and edit them. One group did a parody of the movie *The Usual Suspects*: The students came up with the project idea and used the school's audio and video equipment to shoot and edit it.

Teachers are unusually creative and dedicated and clearly love what they do. "I wouldn't even call it a job," said Steven Jaffe, the school's technology teacher. The school has many student teachers and parent volunteers, and there are typically several adults in each classroom during the day.

Despite the school's success, and the teachers' experience, there is no sense of complacency at the school. It seems that everyone wants to improve upon what is there. The writing has always been creative at the school, but teachers have added an "interactive writing" component in the younger grades, which focuses on spelling and the mechanics of writing. The administration is focusing on improving the math curriculum and on educating parents about the new progressive math program the school uses.

Founded in 1991 by Shelley Harwayne and a group of teachers who, with Lucy Calkins, founded the Reading and Writing Project at Teachers College, Manhattan New School has the longest and deepest experience implementing the techniques that have transformed the way writing is taught in schools across the city and the nation. The school serves as a laboratory for the teaching of writing, and hundreds of teachers, academic researchers, and policy experts from across the country visit the school each year to observe.

Many Manhattan New School teachers have published books: Karen Ruzzo, the principal, and Mary Anne Sacco, the school's literacy coach, wrote *Significant Studies for Second Grade: Reading and Writing Investigations for Children*. Assistant Principal Sharon Hill and former teacher Judy Davis wrote *The No-Nonsense Guide to Teaching Writing*. Harwayne, now retired, wrote *Going Public*, among other works, about her experiences at Manhattan New School; 1st-grade teacher Paula Rogovin wrote *Why Can't You Behave?* as well as *Classroom Interviews* and *The Research Workshop;* former 3rd-grade teacher Joanne Hindley wrote *In the Company of Children;* and 2nd-grade teacher Sharon Taberski wrote *On Solid Ground: Strategies for Teaching Reading.*

The school has a collaborative team teaching class in every grade, in which special needs children and general education children are placed in the same class with two teachers, one of whom is trained in special education.

The school's building is over 100 years old, and while it is very cheerful, clean, and pleasant, it is cramped and lacks a gymnasium. The small cafeteria, located on the ground floor, doubles as a gym. The building doesn't have a proper library, although many of the school's teachers seem to have a serious addiction to children's literature and have created impressive libraries in their own classrooms. The art room is quite small.

The Parent–Teacher Association raises more than $200,000 a year. In addition to a school auction, the PTA sponsors the Fest with Zest street fair at the end of May, with a flea market, a barbeque, and children's activities.

The school's zone encompasses some of the most coveted real estate in the city, and many students are the children of professionals—doctors, lawyers, novelists, and journalists—who could afford private school tuition, but elect to send their children to Manhattan New School instead. In its early years, the school accepted many children from outside its zone, but in recent years has come to serve almost exclusively children from the immediate neighborhood. While most of the parent body is prosperous, the school still serves some children from modest means, including children of building superintendents and recent immigrants from Turkey, Bosnia, and the former Soviet Union. At the same time, the school lacks the racial diversity that can be found in some other city schools.

There are monthly tours. No children are admitted from outside the zone except in extraordinary circumstances. (Exceptions have been made in the past for children zoned for PS 151, which was closed indefinitely in 2000). The school checks addresses carefully, so don't try to lie. If you say, for example, that you live with a friend and the lease isn't in your name, the school will send someone for a "home visit" to make sure you actually have your clothes, toys, and other belongings there.

# Hunter College Elementary S

## 71 East 94th Street
## New York, NY 10128
## (212) 860-1292
### *http://hces.hunter.cuny.edu*

**Admissions:** Manhattan
**Grade levels:** K–6
**Enrollment:** 350
**Class size:** 24

**Reading scores:** * * * * *
**Math scores:** * * * * *
**Ethnicity:** 60%W 25%B 6%H 9%A
**Free lunch:** 1%

Hunter College Elementary School, part of Hunter College's School of Education, is designed as a laboratory school for the study of "intellectually gifted" children. It's a public school, tuition-free, and supported by tax levies, but it is administered by the college rather than the Department of Education.

Nearly 1,100 children apply for 48 spots in kindergarten each year. Even among children who score above the cutoff point to be considered for admission—which ranges from the 95th percentile to the 98th percentile on the IQ test, depending on the year—the odds are against getting in. Two hundred and fifty children meet the cutoff each year.

So don't set your heart on Hunter, even if your child is very bright. And prepare yourself for a daunting admissions process if you do decide to apply. In August, September, or October, a full year before your child will start school, you must write or e-mail (not call) the school for an application, including your child's name, birthday, and address. The e-mail address is *esadmit@hccs.hunter.cuny.edu*. Starting after Labor Day, the school mails out applications. You may attend an "open house" in the evening, where you can tour empty classrooms and watch a videotape about the school. (One year, the tape showed a 7-year-old Hunter child discussing the complexities of photosynthesis and telling an interviewer he reads 50 books a week.)

The school then gives you a list of approved "testers" who will give your child an IQ test and send the results to Hunter. In recent years, the test has cost $225. A parent whose child scores above the cutoff is then asked to fill out a long application form with open-ended essay questions on the child's special abilities and talents.

Once parents submit the application form, children are called in for a second round of testing. Parents wait nervously outside while a group of children "play" with the grown-ups who decide whether they should be admitted to Hunter Elementary. Notifications are sent in March.

Sound bad? It does set up hundreds of parents and little children or rejection. But the enduring popularity of the school suggests that most parents think it's worth it. And a new admissions director, Tracy Fredericks, has promised to make the whole process less hair-raising.

Before I visited Hunter, I imagined it was a sort of Bronx High School of Science for the nursery set—very competitive, very structured, very academic. In fact, the school leans toward the progressive camp of education, with lots of Lego and other blocks in the early grades, tables and chairs instead of desks, and kids in jeans on the floor messing with crayons and construction paper.

In the upper grades, classes are more structured, with plenty of emphasis on spelling tests and worksheets. Still, children study pottery and woodworking all the way through 6th grade, and independent research is emphasized throughout.

On one of my visits, two kindergartners presented Principal Patricia Manchester with a letter they had written asking (in their little-kid invented spelling) for permission to hold a bake sale to raise money to start an "endangered species club."

"An endangered species club?" Manchester asked.

"Anyone can be in it," the boys replied.

A 1st-grade class was reading a book they had written of "homonym riddles." (What's a bucket that just got scared? A pale pail.) Second graders were practicing three-digit subtractions in a classroom that seemed to emphasize spelling and penmanship, including cursive writing. Children in an art class were making tissue paper collages reminiscent of Ezra Jack Keats or Eric Carle to illustrate homemade books of their poems. A 6th-grade science class was studying cellular respiration, learning how animal cells use oxygen to break down food, and fermentation, how cells get energy without food.

A 4th-grade class studied the Constitutional Convention, with each child taking the part of a delegate. Children researched the role of the delegates; then wrote position papers making the arguments made at the convention, on, for example, giving small states more authority in the new union. In 5th grade, children wrote biographies of famous scientists and mathematicians, in an exercise that combined reading, writing, social studies, math, and science. Math is more accelerated than in other public schools, with children learning elements of algebra beginning in 5th grade.

The homework load varies from year to year and from teacher to teacher. Some children find the work manageable, while others find it overwhelming. A number of parents I spoke to said they hired tutors to help their children keep up.

"There's a tremendous amount of homework," one mother said. "It cuts down on family time, and on extracurricular things. I can't take my daughter shopping in the afternoon, or have a play date. There will be nights when it's her bedtime, and she hasn't finished her homework."

The school has suffered in recent years from a rapid turnover of administrators and staff. Parents have complained that the school lacks a coherent curriculum and that the quality of teaching is uneven. Parents say the teaching ranges from outstanding to mediocre.

"The school doesn't have a cohesive philosophy, and that's hard the on kids," said a mother. "They are like little ping-pong balls. One year it's loosey goosey and 'let's be creative' and the next year it's all spelling and punctuation."

Manchester, formerly assistant principal of the middle school at Trinity School, a private school in Manhattan, was named principal in 2004 and said one of her goals is to bring consistency to the curriculum. The new president of Hunter College, Jennifer Raab, herself a graduate of Hunter College High School, has taken a particular interest in the school, ending years of what some parents considered neglect of the elementary school by the college.

"There are a lot of changes going on," said a mother who is active in the PTA. "The school is taking a very careful look at its curriculum and I'm hopeful that will take care of these concerns."

One of the strongest draws of the school used to be automatic admission to Hunter College High School, widely regarded as one of the best high schools in the city. That policy, however, has changed. Kindergarten parents were informed in 2004 that children who were not making adequate progress would be offered extra help, and that those who still were unable to keep up would be asked in 5th grade to transfer to another school. But Manchester predicted that would affect only a small number of children.

Only Manhattan residents may apply to the elementary school. The school maintains a waiting list of children who applied as 4-year-olds, and may admit children off the waiting list until 3rd grade as vacancies occur. The school does not accept new applications until 7th grade. (For a review of the middle and high schools, see *New York City's Best Public Middle Schools* and *New York City's Best Public High Schools*.)

If your child doesn't get in, take heart. There is a great deal of skepticism among educators—and even among teachers at Hunter—about whether IQ tests given to 4-year-olds can predict academic success. In fact, a study cited in Elizabeth Stone's book, *The Hunter College Campus Schools for the Gifted*, shows that children who were admitted in 7th grade tended to do better in high school than those admitted in elementary school.

# PS 77: Lower Laboratory School
# for Gifted Education / PS 198

## 1700 Third Avenue
## New York, NY 10128
## (212) 427-2798 (Lab) / (212) 289-3702 (198)

**Admissions:** gifted program (Lab) / neighborhood school (198)
**Grade levels:** PK–5          **Reading scores:** ***** (Lab) / *** (198)
**Enrollment:** 350 (lab)/445 (198)    **Math scores:** ***** (Lab) / **** (198)
**Class size:** K: 28; 5: 28 (Lab)    **Ethnicity:** 58%W 9%B 15%H 18%A (Lab)
          K: 21; 5: 27 (198)                18%W 22%B 52%H 10%A (198)
          **Free lunch:** 13% (Lab) / 76% (198)

The low-slung, white-brick building with blue-trimmed windows on 95th Street is divided into two schools: a neighborhood school, PS 198, and a district-wide gifted program called PS 77, or the Lab School for Gifted Education. For years, an atmosphere of "haves-and-have-nots" pervaded the building. The neighborhood school, serving mostly poor children of color, had barely adequate supplies, while the Lab School, serving predominantly middle-class white children, had cheerful classrooms with colorful curtains and plenty of books and equipment.

That's beginning to change, if slowly, and the principals of the two schools are working together to ease the divisions. Joint tours for prospective parents, joint PTA meetings, and joint planning are some steps that PS 198 Principal Sharon Jeffrey-Roebuck and Lab Principal Maria Stile have taken to bring the schools together. "E pluribus unum, Two schools: one community," proclaims an optimistic sign posted in the corridor.

PS 198, once avoided by parents who had a choice, is now attracting some middle-class families, including the children of doctors and researchers at Mt. Sinai School of Medicine. The quality of teaching is strong throughout the building. While the divisions between the schools are still noteworthy—and the Lab School benefits from a PTA that draws on some very well-off families—they are not as stark as they once were.

The Lab School was founded in 1987, at a time when public schools in the neighborhood were still suffering from the doldrums following the fiscal crisis of 1975. PS 198 was half empty. Then-district superintendent Anthony Alvarado, in an attempt to put some life into the building, established the Lab School as a gifted program modeled after two progressive private schools, Manhattan Country School and Bank Street School of Education. The Lab school rapidly gained popularity and drew children from across the city. Kindergarten admission to Lab is now restricted to children living in District 2, although there are sometimes spaces available for out-of-district children in grades 1–5.

The Lab classrooms have cheerful curtains and sofas, donated by the parents. Geraniums in blue plastic pots line a windowsill along a corridor that faces a sunny interior courtyard. The floors are a sparkling blue.

Children call teachers by their first names. Most of the classes have tables—not desks—and children move from one activity to another freely. They sit on rugs, or sprawl on the floor in the hall with a book.

The academics are demanding. Fourth graders may write essays of 750 words. Fifth graders may read classics often read by older children, such as *The Red Badge of Courage*, *The Wizard of Oz*, and *Frankenstein*. Children in grades 3–5 may participate in math competitions throughout the United States. "Some parents feel there is too much homework in the upper grades, but the middle schools love our kids," said Stile, formerly assistant principal at PS 6. Typically, a dozen 5th graders are admitted to Upper Lab, considered the district's most demanding middle school.

A super-active parents' association raises more than $100,000 a year—an astonishing figure considering the school only has 350 pupils. A big source of revenue: The PTA sends out a "direct appeal" to parents, requesting a donation of $900 per child per year. The money goes to pay for assistant teachers in kindergarten and 1st grade, as well as specialists in music, art, and computers.

Lab offers special education services to children who need occupational therapy, physical therapy, or extra help learning to read. And, unlike some other gifted programs in the city, Lab offers struggling pupils extra help rather than asking them to leave. "Once we accept our students, we support them," an administrator said.

The school also has two self-contained special education classes for more-disabled children, who are assigned to them by the regional office.

PS 198, the zoned neighborhood school in the other half of the building, long one of the lowest-performing schools in the city, made a remarkable turnaround in the 1990s and now has test scores that place it in the top quarter of schools citywide. The school's progress is all the more remarkable considering the Lab school continues to draw some of the neighborhood's brightest students.

Jeffrey-Roebuck is an effective, knowledgeable principal (whose own daughter went to Upper Lab, the continuation of Lower Lab, and then to a private girls boarding school in New England). The staff is strong and dedicated. Math is taught with hands-on projects that engage the kids: In one class I visited, kids were positively gleeful about the prospect of adding fractions as part of a board game.

One year, research scientists from Mt. Sinai School of Medicine whose children attend PS 198 organized a 2-week science program. Children grew colonies of bacteria by touching their fingers to jell in glass dishes, then waiting a few days until the growth of bacteria was visible even without a microscope. The head of the comparative neurobiology lab at Mt. Sinai talked to students about how astronauts adjust to "microgravity" in a confined environment.

As PS 198 has attracted more middle-class families (including many African-Americans and people of South Asian ancestry), it also has attracted more parent volunteers. Class size is smaller at PS 198 than at Lab (20, compared with 28). There are plenty of books in the PS 198 classrooms, and children spend lots of time reading with a teacher or volunteer in small groups—a proven way to improve comprehension. The quality of children's writing is good. In one class, 2nd graders wrote imaginative essays on why they might be late to school ("Aliens took me." "A gorilla escaped and tried to eat me." "I was bitten by a radioactive spider.") There seemed to be more explicit instruction in phonics in PS 198 than in Lab.

The administration works hard to accommodate children who are struggling as well as those who are academically advanced. For example, a child who is strong in reading may go to a more advanced grade for literacy, while staying with his peers for other subjects.

The school has collaborative team teaching classes that mix children receiving special education services with those in general education. These classes have two teachers, one of whom is certified to teach special education.

Sadly, the PS 198 classrooms are bare compared with those at Lab. There are no blocks, dress-up boxes, or housekeeping corners for the younger children at PS 198. "Dramatic play is important in kindergarten through 2nd grade," said Jeffrey-Roebuck. "I just don't have the money to pay for it." While Lab has a nice art room, PS 198 has only a rolling cart with art supplies.

PS 198 has a free after-school program.

Any child who is zoned for PS 198 is admitted automatically and needs only to register. Children applying to kindergarten at Lab must live in District 2 and pass a "performance assessment" or screening in January. There are generally 350 applicants for 56 seats. Free bus service is provided for children who don't live within walking distance. There is sometimes room for children from outside the district in the upper grades. Tours are offered in October.

# PS 171: Patrick Henry School

**19 East 103rd Street**
**New York, NY 10029**
**(212) 860-5801**

**Admissions:** neighborhood school/gifted program
**Grade levels:** PK–6      **Reading scores:** ✶✶✶
**Enrollment:** 557      **Math scores:** ✶✶✶✶
**Class size:** K: 25; 6: 28      **Ethnicity:** 2%W 37%B 59%H 2%A
     **Free lunch:** 84%

PS 171 is a spotless, orderly, and highly disciplined school where children are expected to read the minute they step through the front door—literally. They read while eating breakfast in the cafeteria, in the hallways waiting for their teachers, and as a class heading to the bathroom, carrying books that they quietly read while they wait their turn. Children spend every spare minute in the building reading, and even prekindergartners are not exempt from this rule.

"When I was looking for schools for my child and I found out about the reading in the halls, I said to myself, '*Come on, now,*'" a parent of a 5th grader recalls of her disbelief. "But since then I've realized that it's about learning to love reading. The school isn't rigid about it. Children can still talk quietly to each other. And it tones them down in the morning, so they're ready for class."

Although it's become habit for most, this degree of reading is not easy on new students. That's why Principal Dimitres Pantelidis finds ways to encourage children: "You can't just tell them, "Read, read, read!' You have to motivate them." Little slips of paper that say "reading certificate" are given to children who display good reading practices; the certificates enter children in a weekly raffle contest where they can win rewards. Students also receive honor roll medals for other achievements. Different types of literature fill classroom libraries and bins on desks. The school also moved its main library into a larger room recently, decorating it with huge learning blocks and a sectioned-off reading corner.

PS 171 has consistently good test scores and a traditional approach to learning. Pupils wear uniforms and quietly march through the hallways in double lines. Huge charts detailing the school's standards and expectations are hung on the walls of the century-old building, along with bulletin boards filled with children's work. The school also makes use of the walls to exhibit special programs. Children's artwork from Studio in the School, a nonprofit organization that sends artists into schools to teach, and digital pictures of students involved in the Chess in the Schools program line most of the hallways. The school also has an affiliation with the Museum of the City of New York, which is right next door, and the 92nd Street Y, to which students take frequent trips.

Kindergarten classrooms are among the best decorated in the building. You'd think from the painted entrance that you were walking into a large red apple instead of entering one room. Writing begins in kindergarten so huge letter cutouts cover the colorful walls. Large illustrations (with text) of rain, snow, wind, and more hang from the ceiling. Big books for read-alouds neatly line reading areas with rugs for easy access.

PS 171 offers a gifted program that admits children from outside its school zone. Students in these classes are able to work at a faster pace and a year ahead of the standard curriculum for their age level. The school administers its own test for grades K–2 and bases admission to grades 3–6 on the citywide and state exams. Children are tested for the program beginning in February.

# Central Park East School
## 1573 Madison Avenue
## New York, NY 10029
## (212) 860-5871

**Admissions:** citywide
**Grade levels:** PK–6
**Enrollment:** 200
**Class size:** K: 20; 6: 28

**Reading scores:** *** (estimate)
**Math scores:** ** (estimate)
**Ethnicity:** 4%W 44%B 50%H 2%A
**Free lunch:** 57%

Central Park East was founded in 1974 by Deborah Meier, a visionary teacher whose work has had a profound effect on education in New York City and the nation. Her belief that schools should be small, humane, democratic places where children learn how to learn and how to think for themselves helped spark a revival of progressive education in the city and the nation.

Now, when just about every elementary school classroom in the city has a rug and almost no one uses graded readers, it's hard to imagine how revolutionary Central Park East and its two sister schools, Central Park East II and River East, were when they first opened—and how much influence they've had on education in the past 2 decades.

At a time when other schools had desks in rows, Central Park East had tables and sofas. At a time when other schools tracked children into classes for smart kids and dumb kids, Central Park East put kids of different abilities and even different ages into the same class. (More than one third receive special education services.) Instead of accepting racial segregation as a given, Central Park East has always put a premium on enrolling children from different neighborhoods to make the school as racially integrated as possible.

CPE, Central Park East II, and River East have remained true to their roots. They still attract an amazing range of parents and children: lawyers and families on public assistance, high-achieving children who are bored in traditional classrooms, and children who are dyslexic or emotionally troubled. All three have a corps of passionate, articulate, and highly educated parents who are deeply committed to the schools' philosophies.

Even today, the schools represent progressive education in its purest form. Children put together vast cities from wooden blocks, bake pretzels or bagels in kitchens set up in the classrooms, and build covered wagons or puppet theaters with hammers and saws. Even in

6th grade, children play with Lego blocks. They sing in the chorus, play the violin, and paint with gallons of poster paint.

From these activities, the teachers say, children create their own knowledge of the world. Grown-ups help them seek the answers to questions their activities pose. They learn arithmetic from measuring wooden boards that they saw; chemistry from baking; the multiplication tables from putting blocks together.

What the schools offer, parents say, is an unusual attention to children's own interests, and the firm belief that those interests will lead children to explore the world around them in a serious and purposeful way.

Independent work is prized. Even kindergartners are expected to work on their own, whether they're splashing at the water table, writing in their journals, or playing in a toy kitchen. On one of my visits, I saw 4- and 5-year-olds put on their own smocks, take a heavy wooden top off a sand table by themselves, and sweep up spilled sand with a broom—all without the teacher's help or instruction.

The criticism of the CPE schools over the years—and of progressive education in general—has been that too many children fail to master basic skills such as the multiplication tables, dates in history, spelling, and punctuation. The schools have consistently had lower test scores than other schools serving children of similar socioeconomic backgrounds.

Teachers say much of what is taught here isn't measured by multiple-choice tests: the ability to work with others, the ability to find the answers to questions that interest one, the ability to delve into a project for a long period of time.

At least one long-term study suggests that these skills may serve children better in the long run than those taught in traditional urban schools. David Bensman, an educational researcher and professor at Rutgers University and author of *Central Park East and Its Graduates*, found that CPE graduates were more likely to complete high school and attend college than their peers at other New York City public schools. And, while many graduates complained to Bensman that they had weak skills in spelling and math, most said they were able to overcome those weaknesses with extra effort in secondary school.

Unfortunately, CPE has undergone turmoil in recent years. Some teachers have resisted attempts by the regional office to impose the chancellor's new curriculum, which calls for more explicit instruction in reading and more attention to results on standardized tests. The school's leaders have been caught between the dictates of the regional office and the teaching styles of the staff. CPE had four principals in 4 years.

**Central Park East II**, at 19 East 103rd Street, (212) 860-5992, and **River East**, at East 114th Street and the FDR Drive, (212) 860-6033, were both founded in 1982. At Central Park East II, there's a weekly school-wide meeting where all gather together so that each child can have a voice in the larger community. Each day includes "worktime," a CPE II institution in which about an hour is devoted to study or practice inspired by student interests ranging from bugs to woodworking to cooking. "There's a lot of choice here," said art teacher Carlos Velazquez. "We provide materials and guide the students through as they develop their own ideas."

Instead of sending home a report card filled with letter and number grades, teachers at CPE II complete two written reports a year that describe a child's progress, strengths, and challenges. Some teachers also send out their own weekly newsletters, and the school publishes "curriculum letters" to inform parents more thoroughly about what their children are learning. The school is led by a well-regarded principal, Naomi Smith.

Some parents are daunted by River East's remote location: It's as far east as you can get, on FDR Drive. But once inside, they find a welcoming principal's office open to kids, visitors, faculty, and parents, as well as a library furnished with upholstered armchairs and floor pillows. Although the school is firmly in the progressive camp, Director Sid Massey is adapting the curriculum to keep it current with new state standards. More formal phonics and reading instruction have been introduced, and New York University has agreed to conduct an after-school math program. He is introducing approaches from Orton-Gillingham, a teaching method offering kids multisensory ways of understanding. (To learn the alphabet, for example, children might trace letters in sand rather than just see them.)

All three schools have "bridge classes," which combine two grades. Students stay with the same teacher for 2 years. Lessons are adapted to suit each child, so a child might have 3rd-grade reading classes and 4th-grade math classes.

Children come to CPE, CPE II, and River East from Staten Island and Queens, Washington Heights, the West Side, midtown, and the Bronx. Regular bus service is available from upper Manhattan and the Bronx. Parents may request applications for admission in November; in January parents visit the schools. Younger children are asked to spend a half-day at the school. Children in grades 3–5 spend a whole day. Priority goes to siblings of children already in the school and to underrepresented ethnic groups—whites and Asians. Admission is by lottery.

# The Talented and Gifted School (TAG)

## 240 East 109th Street
## New York, NY 10029
## (212) 860-6003

**Admissions:** citywide
**Grade levels:** K–8
**Enrollment:** 430
**Class size:** K: 22; 8: 35

**Reading scores:** * * * * *
**Math scores:** * * * * *
**Ethnicity:** 2%W 55%B 40%H 3%A
**Free lunch:** 67%

The Talented and Gifted School in East Harlem is a competitive and selective school that draws children from as far away as the Bronx and Staten Island. The school ranks near the very top of citywide reading scores, with nearly every child meeting state standards. Children follow an accelerated curriculum that's a year or more ahead of their age level. The school is a formal, no-nonsense kind of place, with uniforms, lots of homework, and a serious, focused student body. Girls wear red plaid jumpers and white shirts. Boys wear navy blue trousers, white shirts, and red plaid neckties.

But the school has a softer side as well: The principal knows nearly every child by name, and chats with kids when they greet her in the hall. Student teachers and Americorps Vista volunteers assist in the classrooms, so children get plenty of attention. "We get to have an extra pair of hands in almost every classroom," said Principal Janette Cesar.

There are more girls than boys: nearly 61% the pupils are female. The student body is mostly black and Hispanic, but, as the neighborhood begins to attract more whites and Asians, a few have joined the school as well. Many of the children are biracial. Administrators say they would welcome more diversity. A white mother (whose children are biracial) said her children are happy and comfortable at the school. "I don't think they have a sense that they are different," this mother said, adding that the principal has been "entirely open to us."

Once a traditional school, where textbooks and workbooks were used extensively and teachers mostly offered lessons to the entire class, TAG has adopted the progressive teaching techniques that are the hallmark of the chancellor's new curriculum. Children are more likely to work independently or in small groups, and are encouraged to talk as well as to listen to the teacher. They choose their own books to read from classroom libraries and write papers on topics of particular interest to them.

On one of my visits, a 2nd grader was writing his own "book" entitled All About Arachnids, which, he explained, are "a group of bugs that have four pairs of legs: ticks, mites, spiders, scorpions, and harvestmen, better known as Daddy long legs." His research sources included *The World Book Encyclopedia*, a reference book typically used by much older children.

Fifth graders study topics in math that are often part of a 6th-grade math curriculum: pre-algebra, equivalent fractions, the areas of rectangles, measuring angles in triangles. "We try to accelerate it as much as we can," said 5th-grade teacher Rajendra Jaillal. "There are some kids here who could do high school math."

Reading is taught early. Many children enter the school already knowing how to read; nearly all can read by February of their kindergarten year. There is an emphasis on skills such as good handwriting and proper spelling, as well as plenty of test prep. At the same time, there are lots of class trips. One year, 1st and 2nd graders went apple picking upstate, then made applesauce. They wrote about the trip and used the applesauce recipe to learn math. Older children make frequent trips to the Harlem Meer, the nature center at the north end of Central Park. The trips are the basis for lessons on map-making, geography, or geology.

TAG shares a building with a performing arts program for middle school students and a District 75 school for severely disabled children. In 2004, TAG combined with the Talented and Gifted middle school in the same building to form a K–8 school.

Admission to kindergarten through 3rd grade is based on a multiple-choice test and an interview. (Admission for older students is based on test scores.) Tests are given between December and May. Children who pass the written test are invited for an interview. The interview tests the child's social maturity, ability to think, and ability to work collaboratively. In recent years, there have been three applicants for every seat. About 40% of the students come from outside District 4.

# PS 182: Bilingual Bicultural Mini-School
### 219 East 109th Street
### New York, NY 10029
### (212) 860-6031

**Admissions:** District 4 priority
**Grade levels:** K–6
**Enrollment:** 500
**Class size:** K: 21; 5/6: 34

**Reading scores:** \* \* \*
**Math scores:** \* \* \*
**Ethnicity:** 0%W 7%B 91%H 2%A
**Free lunch:** 97%

The Bilingual Bicultural Mini-School is a pioneer in bilingual education devoted to maintaining both the language and the cultural heritage of children whose home language is Spanish, while encouraging them to perfect their English. At the same time, BBMS has some English-dominant students whose families want them to learn a second language. One African-American father said his child enjoyed the multicultural environment of the school and the challenging homework in its gifted program.

Students study with the Ballet Hispanico; learn to play the traditional, specifically Puerto Rican guitar called the quatro; and work with the city's Museo Del Barrio. There are three programs: one for English language learners, one for children who are English dominant, and one for gifted students. Until they make the transition to English—and most do by 4th grade—students take math, science, and social studies in Spanish. BBMS is traditional in many ways—kids wear gray and white uniforms, for example—but the school operates in a highly creative way. Every month kids participate in school-wide projects based on a theme. One month the subject was kites, explored through artwork and writing, and culminating in the whole school's flying kites in the yard. Children zoned for PS 83 who want a bilingual, program are automatically admitted. Others may apply directly to the school.

In the same building, **PS 83**, (212) 860-5847, is a clean, safe, traditional school with a gifted and talented program that occasionally accepts children from outside the neighborhood. The school has a long-standing reputation for providing solid academics to its predominantly Latino student population. In recent years, parents have complained about the "rigid" atmosphere, the lack of music and art, and the "unhealthy" emphasis on test scores. Still, it's one of the higher-performing schools in the neighborhood and sought after by parents from as far away as the Bronx.

# Special Music School of America

## 127 West 67th Street
## New York, NY 10023
## (212) 501-3318
### *www.kaufman-center.org*

**Admissions:** citywide
**Grade levels:** K–8
**Enrollment:** 135
**Class size:** 15

**Reading scores:** * * * * *
**Math scores:** * * * * *
**Ethnicity:** 56%W 14%B 11%H 19%A
**Free lunch:** 13%

The Special Music School of America is an unusual public–private partnership designed to offer New York City children the kind of musical training previously found only in the "spetsshkola," or special schools of the former Soviet Union. Serving 135 students from all five boroughs, the Special Music School of America combines regular academic classes with unusually rigorous musical training, including individual lessons from Russian-conservatory trained musicians.

The Department of Education provides the academic director and the teachers for the school; the Elaine Kaufman Cultural Center, near Lincoln Center, provides the space; grants from the Annenberg Foundation, among others, pay for the music teachers and instruments. Children have two private lessons a week in piano, cello, violin, flute, or clarinet, as well as classes in music theory, chorus, and movement.

The academic classrooms are small, but the class size is small as well—only 15 children, so everyone gets plenty of attention. Teachers have been trained in the Reading and Writing Project at Teachers College. Fifth graders write "persuasive essays" on topics such as "Why Ruby Bridges Is a Hero" and "Why New York City is the Best City in the World."

The math program mixes traditional textbooks with the games and puzzles that are part of the TERC curriculum. For example, in one 4th-grade class, a boy and a girl played a game called "factor bingo" in which they had to find factors of various numbers and put chips on a chart on the corresponding number. The first child to put five chips in a row would win. Middle school students have an accelerated math program and may complete Math A, the high school or Regents-level course, before they finish 8th grade.

While the academics are solid, and children do very well on standardized tests, the passion and energy of the school are, not surprisingly, in the music program. Walk through the corridors and you'll peek into small music rooms where children receive individual instruction. In one room, you'll see a small child deep in concentration, seated on a bench at a grand piano, her feet too short to reach the pedals. In another, a child is practicing the violin; in a third, the cello.

In a music theory class, a group of children are taking musical "dictation." The teacher plays a tune on the piano, and the children write the tune in musical notation on paper lined with musical staffs. Children also study chorus and "eurhythmics," or movement.

First graders are expected to practice their instrument 1 hour a night, while 5th graders may need to practice 2 to 3 hours a night. Add that to academic homework of up to 1½ hours a day and a commute to school, and a child's day is completely full, with little time for other activities—Cub Scouts or ballet classes or just free time to play.

Like many schools with an arts focus, there is a tension between the academic and music programs. One mother claimed that a music teacher actually discouraged children from doing their academic homework because it takes time away from practice. "It's a balancing act, and sometimes [the music teachers] do get a little carried away," said another mother. But [the music program] is also a fabulous gift. And I think the academics are wonderful."

Parents say the new music director, Jenny Undercofler, a pianist who was director of the solfege (ear training program) at the Juilliard School, is better able to help students navigate the tensions between the two programs than her predecessor was. Academic director Jenny Ander says the school is "80% academics and 20% music." Still, it's clear this school is best for children who have a deep enthusiasm for music and who are willing to devote the time necessary to become proficient.

Open houses are offered four times a year. Testing for kindergarten admission begins in September. Children undergo two rounds of "assessment" to determine their musical talent. In the first round, a group of children plays "musical games." They may be asked to repeat a series of rhythms by clapping or beating on a drum. Those called back for a second round have an individual assessment. They may be asked to sing or play on a xylophone. There are typically 350 applicants for 15 kindergarten seats. "It absolutely does not matter whether the K/1 applicants have ever touched an instrument," said Ander.

The school occasionally has seats for children in upper grades. No prior musical experience is required for children applying to kindergarten, 1st, and 2nd grade. Applicants for 3rd grade must audition on an instrument. Fifth graders are not automatically admitted to the middle school. Applications are available on line at *www.kaufman-center.org* or by calling the school.

# PS 199

**270 West 70th Street
New York, NY 10023
(212) 678-2833**

**Admissions:** neighborhood school
**Grade levels:** K–5
**Enrollment:** 570
**Class size:** K: 25;5: 29

**Reading scores:** * * * * *
**Math scores:** * * * * *
**Ethnicity:** 64%W 10%B 17%H 9%A
**Free lunch:** 13%

Designed by Edward Durell Stone, the architect who designed the Museum of Modern Art and the General Motors building in midtown, PS 199 has grand white columns reminiscent of Lincoln Center; soaring ceilings with subtle, recessed lighting; and wide, gleaming white halls. It has a large auditorium, a beautiful gym, a well-equipped library and media/tech center, and several playgrounds that open out directly from ground-floor classrooms.

Strong, coherent leadership, a unified staff with a shared vision of education, and an active parent organization have made PS 199 one of the most popular and successful schools in the district.

"I love that there is one clear coherent curriculum, but each teacher puts her or his imprint on it. There's plenty of room for creativity and exploration, and yet regardless of the teacher, there's a clear consistent academic philosophy and curricula followed," a parent told the *West Side Spirit* newspaper, which awarded PS 199 the "Blackboard Award for Outstanding Elementary School" in 2004.

Don't be put off by the tours for prospective parents, in which the school is presented as a somewhat rigid, forbidding place were administrators are preoccupied with rules and regulations. Principal Carol Stock may have an imposing, formidable personality on first meeting, but she is unusually knowledgeable and thoughtful about education and has a talent for finding great teachers.

The school is one of the few in the district that's wheelchair accessible, and parents say the presence of handicapped children helps make the school a particularly gentle and tolerant place. All 4th graders take dance classes offered by the National Dance Institute. Children take part in "wheelchair ballet," with the able-bodied assisting those in wheelchairs.

Children who are physically handicapped but able to keep up with the regular curriculum without extra help are assigned to regular classrooms. Children with emotional handicaps or learning disabilities may be taught separately in two self-contained classes or included in general education classes with extra support from specially trained teachers.

The school strikes a balance between traditional and progressive teaching techniques. Children move through the hallways quietly and settle down to work quickly. Children sometimes sit at their desks and fill in old-fashioned worksheets with phonics drills and lists of spelling words.

The school has a long-standing collaboration with the Reading and Writing Project at Teachers College. Children learn to write by making up their own stories and inventing their own spelling—at least in the beginning. The administration believes children need to learn to communicate on paper before they learn "dictionary spelling" and that children write best when they feel there is a purpose to their work. "You're always writing for a real audience," said Stock.

The math curriculum is the progressive Everyday Math program developed by the University of Chicago, in which children experiment with different ways to solve problems rather than using one set formula given to them by the teacher. The curriculum is based on the notion that children learn math best by manipulating concrete objects they can touch and feel—plastic tokens or coins—rather than relying on the more abstract paper-and-pencil exercises.

Musicians from the New York Philharmonic Orchestra—some of whom send their own children to the school—work with teachers to develop music programs, and a musician from Julliard teaches chorus. Children sometimes get free tickets to performances at the Philharmonic.

The administration is philosophically opposed to gifted education, and children are not grouped by ability. The father of one high-achieving boy transferred his child from PS 199 to the high-powered Anderson gifted program because he felt the child wasn't challenged sufficiently. But Stock says children from Anderson also transfer to PS 199 because they are overburdened by unreasonable amounts of work. She said PS 199 allows children to work at their own pace and that some students read books such as *The Good Earth,* typically read by much older students. Other parents concur. "If your child can do a lot, he does a lot," said one mother of three. "If he can't, he can work at his own level."

Next to the school is a small garden with a gazebo. Children plant in the garden, watch birds, and bring their sketch pads to draw during art class. PS 199 has a wheelchair-accessible playground and an unusually large blacktop play area—an important plus for city children who live in small apartments.

Children outside the PS 199 zone are rarely accepted. Tours are offered only to those who live in the zone and show proof of address.

# PS 87

**160 West 78th Street**
**New York, NY 10024**
**(212) 678-2826**

**Admissions:** neighborhood school
**Grade levels:** K–5
**Enrollment:** 910
**Class size:** K: 25; 5: 28

**Reading scores:** ****
**Math scores:** ****
**Ethnicity:** 45%W 22%B 25%H 8%A
**Free lunch:** 19%

PS 87 is a big, noisy, exciting school with creative and enthusiastic teachers; a hyperactive parents' association that raises lots of money; a progressive curriculum; and a liberal philosophy that mirrors the West Side neighborhood it serves. It's aggressively democratic, earnestly multiethnic, and lots of fun.

Built in 1959, the school's long corridors, institutional green tiled walls, and flickering florescent lights are somewhat gloomy. But get over the off-putting first impressions, and the place begins to grow on you.

The corridors have bulletin boards covered with photos and kids' work from class trips that teach basic research techniques along with reading and writing: Children go to the local firehouse to interview firefighters, or to the post office to interview mail carriers, and then write up their findings.

The classrooms have an agreeable clutter of kid-friendly projects, and the children seem happy and relaxed as they paint, sing, write their own books, or work on computers. One day when I visited, a class was building a huge city with cardboard boxes colored with poster paints. In another class, the teacher was playing an old upright piano and teaching children to sing in harmony. In yet another, children were planting bulbs and seeds.

The parents' association raises $300,000 a year, which supports the library, music, art, science, technology, and kindergarten assistants. Kindergarten parents bring their children right to the classroom and may stay while the children get settled.

PS 87, heavily influenced by the philosophy of Bank Street College of Education, has an interdisciplinary curriculum based on social studies. For example, children might study bread: how to bake it, how to sell it, and what kinds of bread are made in different countries. They read books and write stories about bread. They visit a bakery. They learn arithmetic by measuring ingredients and by making change when they sell the bread.

The school is philosophically opposed to gifted classes. Children are not grouped by ability, and children receiving special education services are included in regular classes where they receive extra help. Teachers accommodate different abilities by offering children books of different difficulties on the same theme. In 4th grade, for example, a very strong reader might tackle *The Last of the Mohicans.* An average reader might try *Sign of the Beaver,* and a struggling child might read *Morning Girl.* Each child could then contribute to a class discussion about Native Americans.

Although the school's reading and math scores are more than respectable, teachers don't emphasize standardized tests. "I tell parents, if you're ultra-concerned about tests, this is not the place for you," said parent coordinator Anne Murney. "This isn't a school that goes nuts if we're scoring at this percentage or that on standardized tests. We're concerned about [teaching] humanity and ethics and getting along with one another—and that's something you can't measure on a test."

The school has a dual-language class, in which pupils study half the day in Spanish and half the day in English with a bilingual teacher. The children in the dual-language program stay together from kindergarten through 5th grade, and the goal is for all children in the program to be fluent in both languages by the time they graduate. The objective is to have equal numbers of children who have English and Spanish as their first language. In the past, however, more English-speaking children enrolled, and the English speakers tended to be less than fluent in Spanish when they graduate.

Some concerns: While most of the teachers are good, the quality of teaching is uneven. On one of my visits, transitions from one activity to another were slow, and some kids squirmed in a few classes. Richard Cogliandro, who became principal in 2003, brought some stability after a tumultuous period in which the school had lots of teacher turnover and three principals in 3 years. But parents say the school needs to give teachers more help to perfect their craft. "What we're lacking is staff development," said one mother who is active in the PTA. "When you have new teachers come in, they aren't getting the support they need."

Some teachers complain that the citywide emphasis on math and reading has squeezed out social studies and science, and at least one father complained that there was more test prep and less time spent on creative projects such as building model bridges. Still the school has a solid corps of faithful parents and energetic, thoughtful teachers.

PS 87 has long accepted applications from out-of-z[one], out-of-district children, and in recent years a substantial propor[tion of the] school's student body has come from outside the zone. Howev[er, De]partment of Education regulations on transfers are in flux, so ca[ll the] school for the latest admissions information. One change: Althoug[h] PS 87 has long admitted children from Districts 5 and 6 (serving Harlem, Washington Heights, and Inwood), in 2005 administrators were instructed to give preference to families living in District 3. The school has long welcomed children of different races as well as the children of gay and lesbian couples. Weekly tours for prospective parents are offered from November to March.

# ih Anderson School

West 84th Street
v York, NY 10024
(212) 678-2812

chool/G&T

**Grade levels:** PK–8
**Enrollment:** 870
**Class size:** K: 25; 5: 28

**Reading scores:** *****
**Math scores:** *****
**Ethnicity:** 53%W 12%B 23%H 12%A
**Free lunch:** 19%

PS 9 is divided into three programs: Anderson, one of most selective programs for elementary school children in the city; the gifted and talented (G&T) program, for children who score high at least in the 90th percentile on an IQ test; and the "Renaissance" program, which serves as a neighborhood school for children who live in the zone.

The Anderson program, with about 443 pupils, accepts children who score above the 95th percentile on an IQ test and who pass a demanding screening process. Open to children from all five boroughs, the program is accelerated, particularly in math, and very bright children have the opportunity to take part in advanced work such as national math competitions. The Anderson program has a new middle school, so those children may continue in the building through 8th grade. (Others, including children in the G&T program, also may apply to the middle school.)

On one of my visits, 2nd graders in the Anderson program were reading books generally read by much older children, such as the *Harry Potter* series or *Lemony Snickett's A Series of Unfortunate Events*. Third graders read myths from Central America, South Africa, and China, analyzed them, and then synthesized them to create myths of their own with titles such as "How the Sea Was Created" or "How Saturn Got Its Rings." Fourth graders read *The Witch of Blackbird Pond*, a story about the witch trials in Colonial New England more typically read by middle school students.

The G&T program, with about 197 pupils, is the most popular on the West Side. Although it is open to children who live within the district who score above the 90th percentile on an IQ test, children who live in the PS 9 zone get first preference and fill most of the seats. The children in the G&T program seem articulate and confident, and the teaching is solid. In a 4th-grade G&T class, children learned to add degrees of a circle by using a clock face—a very sophisticated way to tell time. In a 5th-grade class, children studying westward expansion worked on a project re-enacting the trials of settlers on the Oregon Trail. (Fifth graders also practiced square dances in the gym, a physical education class integrating their study of westward expansion.)

The Renaissance program, with about 230 pupils, includes neighborhood children who have not taken the test or who have scored below the 90th percentile. In a 3rd-grade Renaissance class, a teacher read aloud from *Teammates,* the story of Jackie Robinson's breaking of the color line in baseball. Samples of children's writing posted on the wall seemed quite sophisticated.

The school has limited special education services; a special education teacher is available to give children extra academic help, but there are no self-contained or collaborative team teaching classes.

An imaginative arts program serves children in the whole school. Museum educators on the staff of the Metropolitan Museum of Art and the Museum of Modern Art as well as the school's art teacher work with classroom teachers on ways to integrate the arts into their curriculum. Third graders studying Mexico, for example, might make papier-mâché masks in a Mexican style. Fourth graders studying Colonial America and the Revolution might see 17-century period rooms and the painting *George Washington Crossing the Delaware* at the Met.

The school places plenty of emphasis on basic skills, and the curriculum is more traditional than at some other West Side schools. Some parents complain there is too much emphasis on standardized tests and too much test preparation. At the same time, there are some progressive elements: Graded readers and textbooks have been replaced with works of children's literature, and the school has adopted the Everyday Math program. (the Anderson program uses Everyday Math as well, but at an accelerated pace, 1 year ahead of the other children.)

The curriculum is interdisciplinary. For example, children might take a trip on the Hudson River on the *Clearwater*, a replica of an 18th-century sailing ship, and learn about the environment today as well as the history of the 18th century.

For years, the Anderson program and the G&T program have had mostly white, middle-class children, while the Renaissance program has had mostly poor black and Hispanic children. Some parents said the school was divided into the "haves" and the "have-nots." That's beginning to change, if slowly: The Anderson program and the G&T program have had some success in recruiting nonwhite children. Almost all the children in the Renaissance program, however, are black and Hispanic. (One white parent who was zoned for PS 9 said she sent her children to PS 87 because she didn't like what she saw as racial segregation in the Renaissance program.) Standardized test scores for the Renaissance program are respectable, if not as high as in the other programs.

The administration is committed to ensuring that all programs have equal access to materials, supplies, and good teachers. "When trips are planned, it's not a G&T trip, everyone goes," said Principal Diane Brady. For example, all the kindergarten classes go on an apple-picking trip in the fall.

Each program has its own committee of the PTA. Some of the money the Anderson parents raise goes to school-wide projects, and some goes for special projects for children in the Anderson program. The PTA raises money to pay for assistant teachers in all the PS 9 classrooms.

The Anderson program has an open house in late September or early October. Applications are due in early December. Tours of the whole school are offered in December, January, and February. There are usually about 300 applicants for 50 kindergarten spots in the Anderson program. About half meet the cutoff of the 95th percentile on an IQ test. There are occasionally spots for children in other grades as well. If you have your heart set on PS 9, hang in there: Seats in the G&T and Anderson programs often open up in late spring or over the summer.

# PS 166

**132 West 89th Street**
**New York, NY 10024**
**(212) 678-2829**
*www.PS166.org*

**Admissions:** neighborhood school/G&T
**Grade levels:** PK–5
**Enrollment:** 580
**Class size:** K: 20; 4: 25

**Reading scores:** * * * *
**Math scores:** * * * *
**Ethnicity:** 39%W 23%B 34%H 4%A
**Free lunch:** 36%

PS 166 has one of the most popular gifted programs on the Upper West Side, a beautifully renovated building with plenty of computers, an active parent body that raises lots of money, and a good music and art program. The school has a pleasant outdoor "reading garden," designed by an architect–parent and built with a $50,000 grant for which a parent applied.

Once a school that served mostly poor black and Hispanic children, many of whom live in nearby housing projects, PS 166 has in recent years attracted a growing number of upper-middle-class white families—some of whom could afford private school. The upper-middle-class children are concentrated in the two "gifted and talented" classes in each grade.

A super-organized PTA has raised a substantial amount of money to pay for full-time classroom assistants in the lower grades, part-time assistants in the upper grades, and a one-day-a-week science teacher, as well as art and music supplies. The PTA raises about $300,000 a year, in part by asking each family to contribute $1,500 a year. The PTA is "dedicated to providing the children with as many amenities as the ones existent in private schools," one mother said. Partly as a result of this fundraising, the gifted and talented program has become second only to PS 9 in the number of applicants in the district. The school is wheelchair accessible and a substantial number of children receive special education services. Teachers are "young with a lot of energy, and very enthusiastic" and are "good with socialization" as well as academics, a mother said. Children learn to play the piano in class. The afterschool program includes lessons in guitar, piano, Irish-step dancing, chess, yoga, art, origami, and ballet. The chess team has gone to the national finals. There is a fee for the afterschool program.

One downside: the building seems racially segregated. The G&T program is mostly white and middle-class, while the rest of the school is mostly poor and Hispanic. A parent who is active in the PTA said the middle-class children tend to attend private nursery schools, and so do better on the IQ test that determines admission to the G&T program. The poor children, on the other hand, may start kindergarten without having attended any preschool at all. This mother said the G&T program is more racially integrated in the upper grades.

One father, who lives in the zone, complained that the principal was brusque and unresponsive, and refused to meet with him to discuss the possibility of enrolling his disabled son. (The principal said she referred him to the guidance counselor.) By contrast, another father described the school as "very open and friendly." Tours are offered from October through February.

# PS 163

## 163 West 97th Street
## New York, NY 10025
## (212) 678-2854

**Admissions:** neighborhood school/G&T
**Grade levels:** PK–5
**Enrollment:** 634
**Class size:** K: 25; 5: 32

**Reading scores:** \* \* \*
**Math scores:** \* \* \* \*
**Ethnicity:** 18%W 31%B 46%H 5%A
**Free lunch:** 62%

PS 163 suffered a downturn when it lost its popular principal a few years back. Now, under the effective leadership of Principal Virginia Pepe (who has a doctorate in educational administration), PS 163 is making a comeback. PS 163 is one of the few schools whose gifted and talented program is well-integrated racially and economically. Children of black professionals make friends with middle-class whites, and English speakers mix with Spanish speakers in the unusual "dual-language gifted program." There is one English-only gifted class in each grade, and one "dual-language" gifted class, in which children study in both Spanish and English, in each grade.

Pepe has revamped and improved the dual language programs, which once offered English speakers only a smattering of Spanish. Now children spend one day (or half a day) in a class with an English-speaking teacher, then the next day (or the rest of the day) across the hall with a Spanish-speaking teacher. All the books, bulletin boards, and lessons are offered in the language of the classroom, and children now learn much more of the second language, Pepe said.

The school is particularly welcoming to children with special education needs. On one of my visits, I saw two autistic children successfully integrated into one class, and a child with Downs Syndrome integrated into another. The school has collaborative team-teaching classes that combine special needs children and those in general education. These classes have two teachers, one of whom is certified in special education.

Many teachers have been trained in the Teachers College method called the Writing Process, in which children learn to write even before they can read, stringing together letters as they sound out words to approximate spelling. The school also has a collaboration with Fordham University, which offers tutoring to children with reading difficulties as part of a program sponsored by the Ennis William Cosby Foundation

Some concerns: the desks and chairs are worn, and some of the rugs could use vacuuming. Not every teacher is a star. The school serves more working-class families than rich ones, and, as a result, the PTA has not been able to raise the huge sums that other PTAs in District 3 have raised. But Pepe is assembling a talented, dedicated staff, and the school's future is promising. Call to arrange a tour. Tours are offered betwwen October and January.

# PS 333: Manhattan School for Children
## 154 West 93rd Street
## New York, NY 10025
## (212) 678-5867
### *www.manhattanschool.org*

**Admissions:** District 3
**Grade levels:** K–8
**Enrollment:** 540
**Class size:** K: 29; 8: 32

**Reading scores:** ****
**Math scores:** ****
**Ethnicity:** 45%W 24%B 22%H 9%A
**Free lunch:** 13%

Manhattan School for Children is an earnestly egalitarian school with a super-involved parent body and a group of teachers who take kids seriously. Serving 540 children in grades K to 8, MSC is a relaxed, laid-back place where kids wear caps backwards and call teachers by their first names. Parents are welcome, even in the middle school.

"Don't look at it as a place you'll be sending your children," parent coordinator Tatiana Hoover tells prospective parents. "Look at it as a community you'll be joining."

Housed in the former Joan of Arc Junior High School, Manhattan School for Children attracts involved, activist parents: an eclectic mixture of artists, journalists, bankers, Columbia University professors, and women who work as nannies.

It was founded in 1993 by parents who were dissatisfied with their neighborhood public school but who didn't want their children to go to private school—either because they couldn't afford it, or because they believed in public education and wanted their children exposed to kids from different races and social classes. The result is a small, welcoming, racially diverse school where parents come right to the classroom to drop off their children.

Fathers often stop by to eat lunch with their kids—served not in a noisy cafeteria but in the relative coziness and calm of the kids' own classroom. A wide corridor serves as a meeting place for parents, kids, and teachers during the day. By the coffee pot, you'll hear two mothers chatting in Spanish, and several fathers planning a winter fund-raising event. Parents of different races seem to feel comfortable together. The school welcomes interracial families and children of gay and lesbian couples.

Children call grown-ups by their first names. The school has an unusually dedicated staff that works far longer than required by contract and an extremely active group of parents who are involved not just in fund-raising but in decisions such what teachers to hire. Student teachers and parent volunteers in the classroom ensure that kids get plenty of attention.

Classrooms are sunny and cheerful, and there are plenty of books and supplies. The school has a dance studio, an art studio, a science lab, and a nice handicapped-accessible playground surrounded by red oak trees and shrubs.

There's a lot of singing and dancing. In one class, 1st graders were doing a "chicken dance," flapping their arms like chickens and singing as their teachers played on the piano. Third graders in a creative music class performed a Native American dance. Dance, drama, and art are each offered twice a week.

There is a lot of room for creativity. Children make remarkable block towers, cook pasta and bread, or take a trip to the natural history museum or to an environmental center upstate.

Parents describe the school as warm and nurturing. One mother said her shy son, who was overwhelmed in a large elementary school, immediately felt at home at Manhattan School for Children, where he has made friends and developed self-confidence. Parents say Principal Susan Rappaport is unusually accessible, going so far as to give out her home telephone number. The school is increasingly attracting middle-class and upper-middle-class parents, and the Parents' Association raises a substantial amount of money.

The school, which is wheelchair accessible, is in the forefront of "inclusion," integrating severely disabled children in general education classes. *New York Times* reporter Lisa Belkin chronicled the triumphs and struggles of Thomas Ellenson, a motor-impaired, nonverbal child who has cerebral palsy, in a September 2004 magazine piece. The school goes to great lengths to help disabled children take part in regular classes. For example, a keyboard with pictures allows a child who cannot speak to express himself.

Admission is open to children living in District 3. For details, see the school's website: *www.manhattanschool.org*. Tours are offered in the fall. Parents must fill out an application that describes their interest in the school. "We're trying to find a good match between who we are philosophically and parents' expectations of what they want," said Rappaport. A mother added: "What they are really looking for is diversity and interesting parents who will be involved."

# PS 75: Emily Dickinson School

### 735 West End Avenue
### New York, NY 10025
### (212) 866-5400

**Admissions:** neighborhood school
**Grade levels:** K–5
**Enrollment:** 856
**Class size:** K: 22; 5: 29

**Reading scores:** * * *
**Math scores:** * * * *
**Ethnicity:** 19%W 27%B 46%H 8%A
**Free lunch:** 50%

Like the neighborhood it serves, PS 75, is a gritty, idealistic place, committed to teaching the children of Columbia University professors alongside the children of new immigrants from Mexico. Although the corridors are a bit gloomy and the furniture is old and scratched, the school has a spirit that's indomitable.

"There are moments when I really weep, because I have this little utopia," said Atina Grossman, a history professor whose son graduated the school. "My small, blond, spaced-out little intellectual has developed an ability to deal with others, to really negotiate in the world."

The walls are a dreary buff color, the florescent lights flicker, and the black floors make the corridors dark. But the classrooms are bright and cheery and the sweat equity on the part of parents has brought the school a well-equipped and cheerful new library, which also serves as a meeting room. Many of the staffers are parents who couldn't bear to leave PS 75 when their children graduated, including the business manager, the art teacher, the music teacher, and the librarian.

Parents used their collective muscle to build an unusually pleasant playground, with a gazebo surrounded by horse chestnut trees. The gazebo serves as an informal meeting place for parents waiting to pick their children up at the end of the day.

The school's teaching methods have evolved in recent years. The school has introduced the Teachers College Readers and Writers Workshop, which encourages children to write from their own experiences, constantly revising and editing their drafts. Each classroom has its own library, and children have plenty of access to fun-to-read picture books and children's literature.

"It's really revolutionized the way reading and writing are taught," said Principal Bob O'Brien. "It teaches children to write in a variety of genres." Kids still practice how to form letters on lined paper in workbooks here—not the free-form writing on unlined pa-

115

per popular at some progressive schools—and there's plenty of emphasis on phonics, spelling, and grammar. Kids learn cursive in 3rd grade.

Math, too, has undergone a transformation, with the introduction of the progressive Everyday Math curriculum. In one 5th-grade math class, children made up dream projects on how they would spend $1 million. One child researched how much it would cost to build a restaurant—down to the details of the price of coffee.

The school has long been known for its dual-language program, in which Spanish-speaking and English-speaking children are taught together and English is spoken one day, Spanish the next.

Other dual-language programs in the district struggle to attract enough Spanish speakers to make the programs really work. In this one, because the teachers are unusually capable and the balance between English-dominant and Spanish-dominant speakers is more even, children really seem to learn both languages. Both languages are spoken on the playground—and that helps as well. "I love the fact that they're playing with native speakers," said an English-speaking mother. "They just pick it up by osmosis," another mother said.

The dual-language program has the added advantage of small class size—about 20 in kindergarten and about 26 in 5th grade. In 1st grade, children might have a grammar lesson on identifying verbs. "*Qué es un verbo?*" a teacher asks. "*Montar? Montar un bicicletta es un verbo—muy bien.*"

By 4th grade, children are proficient enough to write their science reports in Spanish. "In 4th grade, doing a report on butterflies is a challenge," said an English-speaking mother. "To do it in Spanish is a real challenge."

Kindergartners have chess instruction from a teacher who taught social studies at Bronx High School of Science—before he decided he liked PS 75 better.

The school is philosophically opposed to gifted programs, and children of different abilities are grouped together. Parents say the teachers are skilled enough to reach every child, and many graduates go on to selective middle schools such as the Delta honors program. O'Brien tries to accommodate every child. One very bright child, bored in a regular class, was moved to a dual-language class: The extra work of learning a second language provided her with the challenge she needed, O'Brien said. The school's math coach takes a group of 5th graders who are particularly strong in math and helps them work on a special project, such as graphing attendance for the whole school. Finding challenges for high-achieving kids is "something we need to do more of," O'Brien said.

The school is also committed to giving children who are struggling the extra help they may need. Nearly 50 volunteers from the Jewish Community Center give children individual tutoring. Special education services are mostly integrated into regular classes. There are several collaborative team teaching classes with two teachers, one of whom is certified in special education. Some severely handicapped children from District 75, including a few with autism and mental retardation, are integrated into regular classrooms, with extra assistance offered right in the class. "I believe it's a civil rights issue to have kids served in the mainstream," rather than segregated in self-contained special education classes, O'Brien said.

A few downsides: The cafeteria is loud, crowded, and unappealing. On rainy days, kids watch videos in the auditorium because there isn't a good place to play inside. Because of the layout of the bathrooms, kindergartners and 1st graders must go to the toilet as a group, with their teacher, at specified times. (Older children may sign out of class to use the bathroom.) Although the quality of teaching is good overall, a few teachers are uninspired. And, although the teachers spoke to children in gentle voices during my recent visit, I heard a few school aides shout at kids.

Pluses: The school is unusually accommodating to working parents. Children may be dropped off at 8:00 a.m., and the after-school program is strong. Parents drop children right in their classrooms—a nice start to the day.

Tours run from October to January. In recent years, there have been as many as 250 applicants for about 10 seats for kindergartners from outside the zone. "Let us know you want to be here," said O'Brien. "Keep telling us you really want to be here."

# PS 187: Hudson Cliffs School

## 349 Cabrini Boulevard
## New York, NY 10040
## (212) 927-8218

**Admissions:** neighborhood school   **Reading scores:** ****
**Grade levels:** K–8                 **Math scores:** ****
**Enrollment:** 874                   **Ethnicity:** 21%W 3%B 69%H 7%A
**Class size:** K: 25; 8: 35          **Free lunch:** 56%

PS 187 has a wholesome, Norman Rockwell feel to it. Perched on cliffs overlooking the Hudson, the school's 75-year-old building was recently renovated, so it boasts the best of quaint fixtures and high ceilings with none of the associated wear and tear.

A traditional school serving children in kindergarten through 8th grade, PS 187 takes pride in the number of students it sends to the city's elite, specialized science high schools. In recent years, 10 to 20% of its graduates have been admitted to Stuyvesant, Bronx Science, and Brooklyn Tech. "All the children feel the push to achieve academically here," said a teacher.

On a quiet residential street near Fort Tyron Park and the Cloisters, PS 187 prizes discipline, safety, and order. Teachers sometimes snap their fingers to keep order. Kids shush each other at first sign of noise. The school has a "silent lunch"—children may not talk in the cafeteria, but listen to music instead. (They may talk and play on the playground after lunch.)

The school's detractors may call it rigid. But PS 187 also has enthusiastic fans who say the emphasis on structure and routine makes them and their children safe.

Classrooms and hallways, especially in the younger grades, are bright, cheerful, and decorated with children's work. Many teachers favor tried-and-true techniques: Children work on worksheets or copy poems from the chalkboard. Some teachers rely on textbooks to teach reading; others use children's literature extensively. Some teachers encourage children to move around in class a bit as they work, for example, on a science experiment; others prefer they remain seated at their desks. But despite the differences in styles, teachers are unified in their philosophy: Expect high standards and accept no nonsense.

"We all have the same vision. We have school-wide expectations, and then teachers develop their own style," said Principal Janet Aravena, who was a teacher at PS 187 for 25 years before becoming principal in 1998.

PS 187 is a community institution. At least eight of its teachers and administrators attended themselves as children, and many of them were classmates of parents who now send their children there. A handful of teachers have worked at the school since the 1970s.

Some school traditions go back years. Each departing 8th-grade class hangs a gift of artwork in the gym, for example. The school has had a science fair each year for half a century, and the yearly field day—called "Country Fair Day"—started in the 1970s.

The school has many arts programs and extracurricular offerings. The music teacher puts on four musical productions a year, two for 5th–8th graders, one for 1st and 2nd graders, and another for the 3rd and 4th graders. The Parents' Association also pays a professional dance company to teach the children movement, and after-school programs include sports, art, homework help, and high school prep.

Like many other schools in the city, PS 187 suffers from overcrowding. One of the music teachers has classes on the stage. There's no storage space, and supplementary academic services are administered in rooms that used to be closets, Aravena said. The guidance counselor for the entire school also serves as the high school advisor. The parents we talked to want to enhance the technology the school makes available to students, such as computers, so that's one of their fund-raising goals.

# Amistad Dual Language Academy
## 4862 Broadway
## New York, NY 10034
## (212) 554-8021

**Admissions:** District 6
**Grade levels:** K–8
**Enrollment:** 403
**Class size:** 25

**Reading scores:** N/A
**Math scores:** N/A
**Ethnicity:** 7%W 6%B 83%H 4%A
**Free lunch:** 72%

The Amistad Dual Language School offers instruction in both English and Spanish as a way of teaching Spanish to English speakers and English to Spanish speakers. The bright and sunny classrooms are filled with students' work—not displays of work from past lessons, but evidence of works in progress: poster board covered with Post-it notes that students can move as they participate in a lesson, for example, and lined sheets of paper on which the teacher has recorded the results of a recent experiment. None of this material hangs around for long, says Principal Miriam Moreno-Pedraja, because that would mean a class isn't moving ahead as it should.

Half of the children are native speakers of English, and half speak Spanish at home. Instructional time is divided between Spanish and English. In kindergarten and 1st grade, language alternates by day; in grades 2–5, the language alternates by week. The teacher speaks only in the language stipulated by the schedule.

All of the teachers are certified to teach in both languages, and their competence is reflected in the general tone of the school, which is very relaxed. When we visited, there was no need for any of the teachers to snap at students or raise their voices, because they all seemed to enjoy the task at hand—even the middle school students, who in other schools tend to get a little rowdy. Most teachers are recruited from Bank Street College's teacher education program, and most work as student interns before being hired on the staff.

The school participates in the Black Rock Forest, a program run by a consortium of educational institutions that gives students from both private and public schools the chance to explore and learn from a nature preserve on the west bank of the Hudson River.

Until recently, Amistad was not designated as a separate school, but rather a program within a larger school, and its test scores were reported as part of the larger school. Now that Amistad has been designated as a school in its own right, its test scores, which have been disappointing, will come under more scrutiny. The challenge is how to raise them without sacrificing the features of the curriculum that make Amistad special. So far, the faculty is relying on a combination of very mild test preparation and various strategies designed for those who need help. Students receive some instruction in test-taking strategies. There's also a three-person intervention team, and some of the paraprofessionals have been trained in reading remediation techniques. Teachers provide individual preparation for students who are interested in applying to the city's specialized high schools.

Children from District 6 are eligible to apply. Call the school to arrange for a tour and enter your child's name in a lottery that takes place in March. Thirty percent of the seats in the school are reserved for children living in the immediate neighborhood. The lottery is designed to achieve an equal number of boys and girls as well as an equal number of Spanish and English speakers.

In the same building, the **Muscota New School**, (212) 544-0614, serves 320 children in kindergarten through 5th grade. A small, progressive school open to children living in District 6, Muscota offers a warm, nurturing atmosphere; lots of parent involvement; and a multicultural curriculum. The school doesn't celebrate "religious or commercial holidays," lest someone feel excluded. Instead, they substitute their own homegrown festivities, such as "Mad Hatter's Day." Parents say they like the lengthy reports Muscota teachers write to supplement official report cards. In addition, teachers and parents meet twice a year for "family conferences," and otherwise as needed.

On a recent visit, most of the teachers were saw were solid, and some were outstanding, such as the one whose 4-year-old students seem fluent in American Sign Language. But a few others seemed to be struggling with classroom management.

Some parents say they would like more focused, structured classrooms; a faster pace of instruction; and more homework. Others are passionate defenders of the school. "It is a safe place for children to play, learn, and grow without feeling all the pressures and constraints that are often needlessly put upon them by this current 'test-taking' administration," said a teacher whose two children attended Muscota.

# WORTH WATCHING: MANHATTAN

Here are some new schools (or established schools that have taken a new direction) that are promising and worth a visit. Some accept children from all five boroughs; others consider children from outside their immediate attendance zone, if not from the whole city.

## Lower East Side

Several small progressive schools on the Lower East Side welcome parent involvement and accept children from outside the immediate neighborhood.

**The Children's Workshop School**, 610 East 12th Street, 10009, (212) 614-9531, is an intimate, welcoming school founded in 1993 by teachers who had worked at Central Park East II, the alternative elementary school in East Harlem. "This school belongs to the children," says Principal Maria Velez-Clarke, co-founder of the school. Kids are encouraged to speak their minds, and grown-ups care deeply about the well-being of students. "Kids are taught that expressing yourself through art and writing are equally important," says Dorothy Cantwell, a parent and the school's parent coordinator. Colorful quilting projects are displayed in the hallway outside the main office. As part of their study about water, 1st and 2nd graders took a trip to the little red lighthouse, which sits beneath the George Washington Bridge, and then wrote and illustrated their own books about the landmark. Students go to the Union Square Market to learn how food is produced, and 4th graders go on a week-long trip to a farm in upstate New York.

Classrooms are stuffed with books and blocks, and hallways display student art projects. All classes have mixed-grade groupings. Students are taught to work together in groups and are given classroom responsibilities. In a 1/2nd-grade classroom, a job board displayed a photo of each child, with a description of his or her duty beneath it: One child was the class table scrubber, and another was in charge of snack bowls. The school is fairly relaxed, and students can be chatty during independent reading time or in the hallways. Transitions between classes can be noisy. The school has a fabulous, brand-new library, with warm lighting, wood furniture, and a laptop computer lab. Students may lounge on the deep maroon carpet in the storytelling area. There is a free after-school program run through the Virtual Y. There is one self-contained class for students with special education needs. Other students with special needs are integrated into regular classrooms. Tours are offered twice a month. Priority is given to children living in District 1.

Housed in the same building is the **East Village Community School**, (212) 982-0682. Formerly called Lower East Side School, the school has unimpressive test scores, but parents say it offers something that standardize tests can't measure. "I picked this school because I want [my children] to love learning, I want them to grow into strong, caring people, I want them to take a responsible role in a democratic society, and I want them to understand and respect people who are different from themselves," parent Linda Levy wrote.

Also on the Lower East Side is **PS 188: The Island School**, 442 East Houston Street, 10002, (212) 677-5710, a small, spacious school serving mostly Spanish-speaking, low-income students, many of whom who live in an adjacent housing project. The building is open until 6 p.m. on weekdays, and almost all students stay after school, getting help with homework and participating in a wide range of activities. PS 188 sprawls over four floors of a massive, attractively renovated building, which it shares with a special education program. Classrooms are large, bright, and imaginatively decorated; the gym is commodious and the new library is striking. Computers and multimedia digital equipment abound. There's a music room for the school's violin program, a vast multipurpose room with a play theater for young children, and a room, decorated with posters of trailblazing women, for an after-school girls' program. "Our mission is to give the kids in this neighborhood all the offerings you'd get at Dalton [a private school]," Principal Barbara Slatin said.

## Chinatown

**PS 42**, 71 Hester Street, 10002, (212) 226-8410, a neighborhood school that straddles the boundary between Chinatown and the Lower East Side, has won a spot on the state's list of most improved schools. Test scores place PS 42 among the top 15% of city schools—a remarkable achievement considering that more than 90% of the students are poor enough to qualify for free lunch and many start kindergarten speaking only Chinese. Principal Rosa O'Day insists that staffers "take teaching and learning very seriously, but not at the expense of humanity." During our visit, teachers proudly showed off children's fluffy renderings of baby chicks and commented knowledgeably about students' home lives and work. The warmth starts at the top. When O'Day entered a 1st-grade classroom, children eagerly swarmed around her to show off a project they were working on—creating tiny folded slips that opened to reveal drawings of the people they wanted to be when they grow up. (One boy wanted to be mayor.) Fifth graders published a class newspaper and researched story topics of their choosing. A class of students of English-as-a-Second-Language wrote letters to Mayor Bloomberg protesting the closing of a neighborhood firehouse that the kids had visited earlier in the year. The school provides bilingual classes for its immigrant students. There are two guidance counselors, one of whom speaks Chinese. One downside: The school's corridors are narrow and feel cramped.

## Midtown

**PS 51: Elias Howe School**, 520 West 45th Street, 10036, (212) 757-3067, is a charming, cohesive, highly successful school. Even though 80% of the children are poor enough to qualify for free lunch, PS 51's test scores were high enough to be placed on the chancellor's list of 209 schools exempted from the mandated curriculum. A 2nd grader summed up his feelings about the school in a phrase posted on the wall of his classroom: "We are a community. We stick together like peanut butter and jelly." All the grown-ups seem to know every child, so no one goes unnoticed, and everyone pitches in to solve problems and to lend a hand. For both reading and math, classes break up into small groups. Teachers, teaching assistants, student teachers, and volunteers each work with a group, so the classrooms are richly staffed for instruction. Children make up their own books: In one class, inspired by a popular writer, Kevin Henkes, they wrote books called "Stephen the Worrier," "Help, I'm Lost in Macy's," and "Stuck in Space." There are lots of math games, which parents also have been using at home. The art teacher features projects that complement classroom studies, like Chinese pen and ink drawings done by kids learning about China in social studies. She also has kids study Calder, Warhol, and Grandma Moses, and produce work inspired by them or produce a "message to the world," inspired by Peter Shuman's block prints.

## East Harlem

A number of schools in **East Harlem** have a tradition of accepting children from outside their regular attendance zone. **PS 108**, 1615 Madison Avenue, 10029, (212) 860-5803, is a pleasant, calm place that values strong teaching. Students are expected to adhere to the dress code—a uniform of white tops and dark slacks—and the assistant principal regularly sends letters home or calls parents to make sure the policy is enforced. "This is a strict, but very, very nurturing environment," says Principal Lourdes Arroyo, who joined the school in 2001, after many years as the head of the Bilingual Bicultural Mini-School. Teachers we met seemed particularly caring, among them one who was quietly comforting a student who was in tears on the day of our visit. (The principal told us that the child had just been placed in a new foster home.) Arroyo knows the students by name and was familiar with the projects that were going on in many classrooms. Students know her and, in each classroom we visited, greeted her with a collective, "Good morning, Mrs. Arroyo!" A neighborhood school, PS 108 sometimes accepts children from outside the zone.

Sharing a building with PS 108 is the **EH Block School**, 1615 Madison Avenue, 10029, (212) 860-7967, a tiny school with just seven teachers and 110 students. The Block School offers strong teaching in an intimate setting, and its reputation has spread through word of mouth since its inception in the 1970s. "It's like a little family," explained a teacher. "We have a lot of children whose parents went here." Students wear uniforms—khaki pants and white tops—and teachers we spoke to seemed energetic. The hallways and classrooms are well decorated, cheery and bright, and filled with displays reflecting creative projects.

East Harlem is also home to a number of charter schools—tuition-free schools that operate independently of the Department of Education. **Harbor Science and Arts Charter School**, 1 East 104th Street, Suite 603, 10029, (212) 427-2244, is a small, welcoming school with only one class on each grade. Staffers know every child by name, and teachers often work with kids in small groups or individually. This 1–8 charter school has a comfortable balance between pushing kids to solid academic performance and allowing them to cultivate strength in the arts. Through collaboration with the Harbor Conservatory, a privately run theater and arts program also located in the building, students are exposed to drama, art, African dance, and percussive music once a week. In early grades, teachers use games such as "red light, green light" to reinforce vocabulary. In teaching children to read, the school emphasizes phonics through 2nd grade, and then switches to a balanced literacy approach, which combines phonics and whole-language. The math curriculum relies on practice, review, and testing at regular intervals. In a science class, students worked on essays about water conservation.

**Harlem Children's Zone Promise Academy Charter School**, 175 West 134th Street, New York, NY 10030, (212) 368-3470, is part of an ambitious plan to revitalize Central Harlem and save the lives of children in a community that has long been gripped by poverty, poor health, and failed schools. "We have a whole community of kids shackled by a history of failure who have sort of given up and thrown in the towel—and we expect those kids to compete with other people's kids," said Geoffrey Canada, President and CEO of Harlem's Children's Zone, a community organization that sponsored the school. "We make a promise to our parents: If you give us your kids, we're going to guarantee that those kids are going to be successful." The school day goes from 8 a.m. to 4 p.m., and the school year runs through August. The after-school program for the elementary grades operates from 4 p.m. to 6 p.m., while middle and high school after-school activities run until 7:30 p.m. Both programs provide breakfast, lunch, snack, and dinner. Both children and staffers adhere to a strict dress code. The school has a maximum class size of 25, and a minimum of two adults in each classroom. Admission is by lottery. Call in the fall.

# Harlem

**PS 180**, 370 West 120 Street, New York, NY, 10027, (212) 678-2849, has been reborn under Peter McFarlane, whose doctoral thesis at Columbia University's Teachers College explored strategies for school change. Students wear uniforms and are generally well behaved and engaged in their work. Classes are small. Kids work in groups and individually, while the teacher and sometimes an assistant work one-on-one with kids. PS 180 starts at prekindergarten and, in a sense, ends at college. Every year, 5th graders tour colleges on the East Coast. At the end of the term they visit one out of town for several days. Representatives from Marymount and Ithaca Colleges familiarize them with financial aid and the admissions process. The object is for all students to "view college as a viable and realistic goal," says McFarlane. Principal since 1998, he has hired excellent teachers and built a community through the school leadership team and other parent activities. Now, McFarlane is concentrating on professional development. Although the school has made marked improvement in achievement and is rich in equipment, programs, and community partnerships, McFarlane calls PS 180 a struggling school. Most-recent scores show gains in reading and math scores, but McFarlane continues to push for improvement.

**Future Leaders Institute,** 134 West 122nd Street, New York, NY, 10027, (212) 678-2798 (website: *www.futureleadersinstitute.org*), is a small, ambitious school in a community that is home to many schools with very low achievement levels. It was founded in 1999 by a husband–wife team, Marc Waxman, who had taught at the respected

KIPP Academy in the Bronx, and Gianna Cassetta, a former teacher at PS 198 in Manhattan's successful District 2. They wanted to combine the progressive academics that are a hallmark of District 2, with features that made KIPP successful—an extended day and extra financial support from a nonprofit organization. The result is a pleasant, well-financed school where students attend classes from 8:30 a.m. to 5 p.m. and participate in a 3-week summer session as well.

The extended school day allows more time for academics, and each child gets a full hour of science instruction each day—a rarity for younger students. In the later part of the day, professionals from the community teach enrichment activities such as violin and track. Unfortunately, the school has had to take on more students than it originally envisioned, leading to larger class size in some grades: While some classes are as small as 20 students, others are as large as 35. Students entering the school with weak skills in the older grades have made it difficult to create the continuity of instruction that the school aims for, and the larger number of students threatens to undermine the small school culture.

Despite the stresses, the school does a good job of creating a safe and purposeful environment. With its strong leadership and talented teachers, Future Leaders Institute is working hard to give all children—including those who transfer in from other schools with very low levels of skills—the tools they need to succeed. In 2005, it became a charter school, open to children in all five boroughs by lottery.

## Washington Heights

**Hamilton Heights Academy**, 475 West 155th Street, New York, NY 10032, (917) 507-4460, was founded by parents looking for alternatives to the overcrowded and undistinguished neighborhood schools in District 6. The school, housed within PS 28, opened in September 2002, with 18 students in one kindergarten class and plans to add a grade each year until 5th grade. Initially, the academy encountered resistance from longtime, mostly African-American residents who feared their children would be excluded from a school proposed by the newcomers, mostly white parents. After some fence mending, the founders made clear that the school was open to all. Now, all parents are working together to shape a school based on a shared vision of progressive education.

A typical day begins with the kids taking off street shoes and putting on their school shoes. This helps keep street germs outside and create a home slipper feel inside. Teachers start the day with an activity time, when the children can do things like engage in creative play or dress up in capes, chef hats, and dresses. When activity time ends, the teacher simply says, "Hands up!" Students stop what they are doing and raise their hands above their heads quietly, so they can hear the next instruction. This continues on through shared reading, word study, writer's workshop, math investigations, and story time. Parents are not only welcomed, but trained by the teachers so they can be more useful in the classrooms, which each has a paraprofessional too. This may be the only school where there are, on occasion, too many adults; sometimes the large number of parents can be distracting to the teacher. Admission is by lottery. Priority is given to District 6 students.

A sweet school in Washington Heights is **PS 178**, at 12-18 Ellwood Street, 10040, (212) 569-0327, serving 460 children in prekindergarten through 2nd grade. The school, housed in a clean, spacious building that used to be a nursing home, has an art room, a science room, a gym, a library, an occupational therapy suite, and even an outdoor play area on the second floor. The PS 178 faculty is studded with stars. Teachers attend workshops at Columbia University's Teachers College, and experts from TC visit the school on a regular basis.

One mother praised what she called the "well-crafted balance between nurture and discipline" and the "welcoming, generous spirit" of Principal Deirdre Budd, who "is always available to parents." This mother said, "The children all know what is expected of them and are very respectful of one another, just as the teachers, staff, and administration are respectful of the children." Another parent praised "the sincerity and hard work" of teachers, staff, and administrators.

A neighborhood school, PS 178 accepts children outside its attendance zone in its gifted and talented dual-language program.

PS 178 also houses the **Washington Heights Academy**, a small program initiated by a group of neighborhood parents in cooperation with Region 10. The Academy opened with its first kindergarten class in September 2004, and plans to add one grade per year to become a K–8 program. Parents who organized support for the new program said they loved PS 178, but wanted a school that would continue beyond 2nd grade. While most of the program's seats are reserved for families from the PS 178 zone, some seats are available for children from other parts of District 6. Contact Lynne Herndon at (212) 781-0223 or blherndon@verizon.net.

# Bronx
# Schools

**District 10**
1   PS 24
2   PS 81
3   PS 51: Bronx New
4   PS 23: New Children's

**District 11**
5   PS 108
6   PS 175: City Island

**District 8**
7   PS 304: Early Childhood Lab
8   PS 69: The New Vision School

**District 12**
9   Bronx Little School

**District 7**
10  PS 179

# THE BRONX

Good public elementary schools in the Bronx are few and far between. A few middle-class neighborhoods such as Riverdale and City Island have good schools, and a few principals in very poor neighborhoods have managed to build schools that offer a first-class education. But the overall picture is bleak, and many concerned Bronx parents send their children to school in Manhattan or to private schools near home.

Are things getting better or worse? Mayor Michael Bloomberg's reorganization of schools in 2003 brought a more consistent approach to teaching, as well as better-quality books and supplies. The mayor's decision to consolidate District 7, serving the South Bronx, with District 2, serving the Upper East Side, has brought the schools of the South Bronx the same high-quality teacher training that the schools of the Upper East Side have long enjoyed. Two teacher recruitment programs, Teach for America and the New York City Teaching Fellows, have brought new blood to beleaguered schools.

But the gains are uneven across the borough. High teacher turnover remains a problem, and there is still a critical shortage of qualified teachers and principals in the borough. The Bronx public schools have long been seen as a training ground for the Westchester public schools just a few miles to the north. Talented teachers and principals often leave the Bronx for schools in Westchester, where class size is smaller, working conditions are easier, and salaries are higher.

The mayor's reorganization of the school system consolidated six old districts into three regions. However, for the purposes of school choice, students still apply to schools within their old districts (with a few exceptions). Region 1 comprises the northern and western parts of the borough, including the old Districts 9 and 10. The regional office is at 1 Fordham Plaza, (718) 741-7090. Region 2, including the eastern and central Bronx, comprises Districts 8, 11, and 12. Its offices are at 1230 Zerega Avenue, (718) 828-2440. Region 9, which also includes a large swath of Manhattan, has absorbed District 7 in the South Bronx. Its offices are downtown, at 333 7th Avenue, New York, NY 10016, (212) 356-7500.

# PS 24: Spuyten Duyvil School
### 660 West 236th Street
### Bronx, NY 10463
### (718) 796-8845

**Admissions:** neighborhood school
**Grade levels:** K–5
**Enrollment:** 726
**Class size:** K: 22; 5: 30

**Reading scores:** ****
**Math scores:** ****
**Ethnicity:** 44%W 14%B 30%H 12%A
**Free lunch:** 19%

PS 24 has the highest test scores in the Bronx and ranks in the top 15% citywide—a remarkable achievement considering it has a large number of children receiving special education services. The school serves as an anchor in this multiracial community, and parents say one of its greatest strengths is its ability to teach children of different groups to get along with one another.

"We don't just have whites and African-Americans and Hispanics and Asians," said a mother who is active in the Parents' Association. "We have Jews and Muslims, every religion, the children of firefighters and policemen, lawyers and doctors. That's the real magic—and why I didn't want to live in the suburbs."

The administration welcomes parents in the day-to-day life of the school, not only as fund-raisers. Parents are trained as tutors to help kids who are struggling to read. Parents are invited on field trips and to "writing celebrations" in their children's classrooms.

PS 24 is housed in a pleasant, two-story, red-brick building on a street lined with maple trees. Built in the 1950s, the building is spotless, with shiny floors and polished brass stair rails. It has an art studio, a well-equipped library, and a science room that even has a working planetarium. Instrumental music is offered in all grades once or twice a week. Classrooms are large and sunny.

The class size is somewhat smaller than typical for public schools, with 20–24 children in kindergarten through 3rd grade and 24–30 in grades 4 and 5. The classes mix children of different abilities in grades K–3. There are "accelerated" classes in 4th and 5th grades for children who need more challenge.

PS 24 has been in the forefront of the move to integrate children receiving special education services into general education classrooms. Increasing numbers of children are receiving special services within regular classrooms, although the school still has several self-contained, or segregated, classrooms, said Principal Mark Levine, a former special education supervisor. Some of the self-contained classes are in tiny rooms that once were offices for teachers, but they are well equipped with books and supplies.

The administration has been working with Teachers College to train staff in the Writing Process, which encourages children to write with a passion about topics that interest them. Children, with their teacher's guidance, may choose books from bins labeled with topics such as "folktales," "friends," and "insects." The school still has phonics workbooks, in which, for example, children draw lines to match rhyming words "tail" and "nail"—which the principal says is a way to ensure that children get basic skills in addition to the more creative aspects of reading and writing.

Similarly, in math, the school strikes a balance between traditional arithmetic drills and methods that emphasize an understanding of math concepts.

The school has long struggled with the concern of some parents that the brightest children are sometimes bored and that overburdened teachers cannot challenge all students sufficiently. That concern has been eased, particularly in the lower grades, by the approach to reading that allows each child to choose a book that matches his or her ability and by the open-ended writing assignments in which children may write quite simple or quite sophisticated essays. Another response has been to offer accelerated classes for high-achieving 4th and 5th graders.

Teacher turnover is a problem, as it is in many New York City public schools. Many experienced staffers leave for higher-paying jobs in the suburbs. Still, most parents are more than satisfied with the education their children receive. "It's safe, warm and nurturing, and it offers a solid, comprehensive, nonfaddish education that's well rounded," one mother said.

Admission is limited to children living in the zone.

# PS 81

## 5550 Riverdale Avenue
## Bronx, NY 10471
## (718) 796-8965

**Admissions:** neighborhood school
**Grade levels:** K–5
**Enrollment:** 625
**Class size:** K: 25; 5: 30

**Reading scores:** ****
**Math scores:** ****
**Ethnicity:** 36%W 16%B 38%H 10%A
**Free lunch:** 29%

PS 81 is housed in well-kept, red-brick building designed in the Georgian architectural style and accented with tall Palladian windows. It has a large blacktop playground shaded by mature maple trees. In the northernmost corner of the Riverdale section, the school is just a few blocks from the Yonkers border. It serves a mix of children, both well-off and poor, from 60 different ethnic groups and speaking 22 different languages, including Arabic, Russian, Hebrew, Korean, the African language Twi, and the languages of Uzbekistan and Pakistan. Teachers believe that building citizenship is particularly important in a school that serves many new immigrants, and the theme of citizenship permeates the school. For example, children "caught" being good get special awards, and 5th graders serve as big brothers/sisters to younger students. Every morning, children and staff stand, hand over heart, facing the American flag, to recite *The Pledge of Allegiance.* "It sets the tone for the school," said Principal Melodie Mashel, whose own children attended the school years earlier.

The teaching is solid, test scores are high, and the children are engaged in their work. The day of our visit, 4th graders were busy crafting "edge-of-your-seat" descriptions to help make their writing more exciting and tension-filled. A 5th-grade class was wrapping up a study of fantasy writing inspired by their reading of *The Wizard of Oz.* The school has two self-contained special education classes and one 5th-grade accelerated learning class for high achievers. Admission is limited to children living in the zone.

# PS 51: Bronx New School

**3200 Jerome Avenue**
**Bronx, NY 10468**
**(718) 584-8772**

**Admissions:** District 10
**Grade levels:** K–5
**Enrollment:** 253
**Class size:** K: 25; 5: 25

**Reading scores:** * * *
**Math scores:** * * *
**Ethnicity:** 15%W 31%B 51%H 3%A
**Free lunch:** 43%

Bronx New School was founded by a group of parents who wanted a safe, informal, welcoming school where children felt they could share their worries with their teachers as if they were at home. Modeled after the Central Park East schools in East Harlem, the Bronx New School takes pride in its nontraditional approach to learning.

Children call teachers by their first names. Classrooms have rugs, sofas, and pillows. The school is so small that all 11 classroom teachers can sit around a table in the teachers' lounge and talk about anything from curriculum development to the problems a particular child may be having.

On one visit, the smell of homemade biscuits wafted through the halls. Baking teaches children how to read a recipe, how to measure ingredients, and how the ingredients change when heat is applied—lessons in reading, math, and science. Children study drama once a week with a non-profit group of performing artists called Dreamyards.

Housed in a converted warehouse on a street lined with auto repair shops near the Bronx High School of Science, the school has no playground, gym, or auditorium. Windows face the elevated subway tracks of the number 4 train, and the whole school rumbles every few minutes when a train goes by. But, despite the unglamorous surroundings, kids and teachers alike seem happy and engaged.

The school offers regular tours to prospective parents in October through January. Admission is by a lottery conducted in March. Children in District 10 may apply.

# PS 23: The New Children's School
## 2151 Washington Avenue
## Bronx, NY 10457
## (718) 584-3992

**Admissions:** neighborhood school
**Grade levels:** K–2
**Enrollment:** 660
**Class size:** K: 17; 2: 21

**Reading scores:** tests not given
**Math scores:** tests not given
**Ethnicity:** 2%W 35%B 61%H 2%A
**Free lunch:** 89%

PS 23 is an oasis of calm and order in a rough and run-down neighborhood in the Belmont section of the Bronx, halfway between the Bronx Zoo and Bronx Community College. The sunny and cheerful building, opened in 1991, has a library that's superior to most public library branches, a well-equipped computer lab, and an award-winning "sight and sound" playground equipped with drums, bells, and a periscope for children to explore during recess.

But even more impressive than the physical plant is the quality of teaching and the leadership of Principal Carolyn Jones, who has been with the school since its inception. "I don't think of this as a job," said Jones about her tenure at PS 23. "It's what I love to do." She's been able to recruit teachers from the top schools of education in the city, including Teachers College, Columbia University, and Bank Street College of Education. A lot of the teachers don't stay long. Like a number of good schools in the Bronx, PS 23 is seen as a training ground for teachers who want to go to the Westchester suburbs. Still, the quality of instruction is stellar enough for the Department of Education to have designated PS 23 a mentor school in math, literacy, and special education—sharing its innovations in instruction and curriculum development with principals from all over the city.

Jones rules the school with an obsession for detail. Not a paper clip is out of place. Every book and every crayon is set out for a purpose. Each classroom is the same. Each has tables instead of desks, a rug to sit on, a toy kitchen, wooden blocks, crayons sorted by color within little plastic cups, an art area, a terrarium, and lots of attractive, fun-to-read books in a special reading area.

The orderliness permeates the entire school, including the hallways, the playground, and the lunchroom. "The kids are purposeful here," said Jones. "They are too busy to misbehave." Every moment of the day is treated as instructional time. Children sing songs in the hall as they move from one class to another—a way to keep them together and focused. Specialty classes like art and computer often start with the reading of a book, and each lunch period starts with a poem read in Spanish and English.

The school is very structured yet quite free and intimate. It is not uncommon to see teachers sitting on the floor alongside the children during a group lesson or activity. The layout of the classrooms encourages children to explore, make choices for themselves, and work independently—all in tune with the uniform curriculum rolled out in most city schools in 2003. PS 23 is light years ahead of the many city schools still struggling to stock their classroom libraries and cope with the transition from traditional graded readers. The school is dripping with books ranging from professional development literature and guided-reading series (multiple sets of books for teachers to use with small groups of children at the same reading level) to unique selections of books for each grade in well-stocked classroom libraries. At Jones's insistence, students don't repeat books from one grade to the next in order to keep them moving forward with their reading.

The school is barrier free and has a substantial special education population, including both physically disabled and mentally retarded students. Its small, well-maintained gym is used exclusively to offer children physical and occupational therapy and is stocked with an impressive selection of therapeutic equipment normally found in professional physical therapy facilities. Teachers in special education classes use the same techniques and equipment as others in the building.

The school also has a large number of children who speak only Spanish.

Test scores are unavailable for the school because it goes through 2nd grade only, and children are first tested in 3rd grade. Most pupils are zoned for the school. Parents from outside the neighborhood also may apply for admission.

# PS 108: Philip J. Abinanti School
## 1166 Neill Avenue
## Bronx, NY 10461
## (718) 863-9829

**Admissions:** neighborhood school
**Grade levels:** K–5
**Enrollment:** 570
**Class size:** K: 25; 5: 29

**Reading scores:** ****
**Math scores:** ****
**Ethnicity:** 33%W 12%B 41%H 14%A
**Free lunch:** 58%

There's a sense of excitement about learning at PS 108, where children are happy, relaxed, and engaged in their work. Teachers take pride in the warm and nurturing atmosphere they have created, and children have a good rapport with the principal and the rest of the staff.

This neighborhood school serves new immigrants from India, Pakistan, China, and the Dominican Republic as well as native-born Irish-Americans, African-Americans, and Latinos. Two major teaching hospitals, Albert Einstein and Jacobi, are in the school zone, and the children of doctors and other staffers (many of whom are newcomers to this country) attend.

The school has an unusually successful program in English as a Second Language and a well-regarded inclusion program to integrate disabled children in regular classes with extra help. The art program integrates reading and writing with arts skills.

Students wear uniforms of light blue shirts and dark blue slacks, with dark blue sweat suits on gym days. Students stand with straight posture as they move quietly through the halls. The building is clean and orderly. Samples of children's artwork and writing are displayed throughout.

Kindergartners "publish" stories that are three or four sentences long, then invite parents to a "writing celebration" where the children read and autograph their work. There are rich classroom libraries in each room. Some textbooks are used, but there are also good selections of biographies, memoirs, books of fantasy, and children's classics.

Math lessons have plenty of manipulatives—small blocks children use to add, subtract, multiply, and divide. The school adopted the Chicago Math program (also called Everyday Math), in which children are encouraged to find their own solutions to problems, several years before the curriculum was adopted citywide.

Although administrators post an "honor roll" of high-achieving students, they also post a "merit roll" of well-behaved children who work particularly hard—even if their grades aren't the highest. Also posted are charts entitled "Citizens of the Month," honoring children's good deeds and "random acts of kindness."

"We create a culture in the building in which children value one another," said Principal Corinne Rello-Anselmi. "Kids clap and cheer each other on."

PS 108 was recognized in 2003 as one of the most improved schools in New York State. In 1999, 40% of students met state standards for reading. By 2004, that number increased to 63%. Admission is limited to children living in the zone.

# PS 175: The City Island School
## 200 City Island Avenue
## Bronx, NY 10464
## (718) 885-1093

**Admissions:** neighborhood school
**Grade levels:** K–8
**Enrollment:** 430
**Class size:** K: 20; 8: 29

**Reading scores:** ****
**Math scores:** ****
**Ethnicity:** 65%W 9%B 22%H 4%A
**Free lunch:** 25%

City Island, surrounded by Long Island Sound and connected to the mainland by a bridge, looks more like a New England village than most people's idea of the Bronx. It has inlets filled with sailing boasts, Victorian houses with big porches, summer beach bungalows that have been converted for year-round use, and one commercial street with seafood restaurants, sail makers, and antique shops. It's the kind of place where lots of mothers stay at home with their kids, where parents keep an eye on one another's children, and where kids can walk or ride their bikes to school.

"There is a feeling of safety and security," one PS 175 parent said. "There are people around who know your children, and you know other people's."

PS 175 is housed in an untraditional, even bizarre, building. Constructed in 1975, it was apparently an attempt to turn the educational philosophy of the "open classroom" into an architectural style. Rather than having classrooms with walls, the 2nd floor of the building is one large, open space, divided only by brick pillars holding up the roof. Movable blackboards and bookshelves divide the space. Giant picture windows on the 2nd floor give splendid views of the Long Island Sound. In contrast, the 1st floor has no windows, except for the classrooms lining the periphery of the common area, a cavernous open space that encompasses the main entrance, cafeteria, and "the pit," a sunken stage that serves as a quasi-auditorium without walls.

In 2003, in response to a problem with overcrowding that had forced some classes to be held in the cafeteria, the school opened "learning cottages"—red-colored annexes that house 2nd and 3rd grades. The cottages have classrooms that are smaller than average in size, but are clean and well-maintained, and can accommodate classes of 25. Initially, parents were uneasy about the annexes, but have since welcomed the results: No more classes in the cafeteria.

For years the school embraced old-fashioned methods of instruction: teachers standing and lecturing to the entire class, children reading from readers, and lots of worksheets and quizzes. These days, well-stocked classroom libraries have replaced the readers, children gather for group lessons on rugs, and child-centered activities are as much a part of learning as teacher-driven lessons. Principal Milagros Efre-Lopez says the citywide curriculum reforms rolled out in 2003 helped make the changes possible. "It gave me the opportunity for professional development and to implement a research-based curriculum," said Efre-Lopez. "We were able to get rid of the basal readers."

There has been some grumbling about the changes. Some parents say they preferred the school under the previous administration, and a few even threatened to take their children out. But others defend Efre-Lopez and the changes she has implemented. "The entire staff from the principal to the custodian, from the teachers to the security staff, show nothing but care and concern for the education and well-being of all the children," one mother said.

The school continues its long-standing tradition of welcoming parents into the building every morning to recite *The Pledge of Allegiance* with their children. Parents say that it eases children's transition from home to school and allows parents to get to know teachers. Lopez enjoys it for the sense of community it engenders.

The school won a grant from the Lincoln Center Institute to teach performing arts. Groups such as the Metropolitan String Quartet perform at the school. As part of a Region 2 initiative, consultants from Princeton Review, the test prep company, work with the school, supplementing the curriculum with academic exercises and assessments to help parents and teachers monitor a child's progress.

Parents say the only complaint they have about their children's education is the fact there's no high school on the island. Many parents opt for private schools on the mainland, and some move to the suburbs when their children graduate from 8th grade.

Approximately 70% of the students attending PS 175 live on the island. Space permitting, variances are given to off-island students. However, the location of the school does not lend itself to an easy commute. While many off-island students handle the daily trek by car or bus without a hitch, there are some who struggle with chronic lateness and poor performance because of the distance they must travel everyday. Efre-Lopez cautions off-island families to consider carefully the burden that the commute will entail, when deciding whether the school is right for their child.

# PS 304:
# The Early Childhood Lab School at PS 101

2750 Lafayette Avenue
Bronx, NY 10465
(718) 822-5307

**Admissions:** District 8
**Grade levels:** K–5
**Enrollment:** 419
**Class size:** K: 22; 5: 28

**Reading scores:** * * *
**Math scores:** * * *
**Ethnicity:** 33%W 19%B 44%H 4%A
**Free lunch:** 69%

A tiny kindergartner strolled into the principal's office—unannounced and without an appointment—during our visit and asked, "Can I read you my story?" She read her work confidently and was rewarded with words of encouragement.

This relaxed rapport between children and adults is typical of PS 304, a school where classes are organized so that every child receives individual attention. Kids create their own books, write their own memoirs, and make "author studies" comparing several books by the same author.

The PS 101 building houses two schools with first-rate programs: an elementary school, PS 304, and a middle school, MS 101 (also known as the Maritime Academy). Founded in 1998 as a "professional development site," the two schools are designed as places for teachers from around the district to visit regularly to hone their skills. (The building also houses PS 10.)

At the elementary school, teachers are unusually adept at helping children get along socially as well as academically. While many schools seem to cater to girls' habits and personalities, this school is a place that seems to understand boys particularly well, perhaps because teachers are forgiving of quirks.

A boy who preferred to sit in a chair, for example, wasn't forced to sit on the rug with his classmates at meeting time. The teacher explained that the boy had a hard time focusing when he was on the rug and preferred the chair. This small accommodation allowed him to be more comfortable and attentive.

Children (and boys in particular) seem to be unusually cooperative: Two boys sat together in a big rocking chair, each reading a different book. Boys in art class shared their materials without a squabble.

The spirit of collaboration was evident even in the cafeteria. Most cafeterias are either chaotic or super-disciplined, with rigid rules of behavior. At this school, children may play with dolls, share their comic books, or roam from table to table in an atmosphere that's relaxed but not out-of-control.

All the children have lunch at the same time. This gives the whole staff time for a lunch meeting each Monday, as well as staff development for each grade during the rest of the week.

Music by Mozart and Beethoven is played throughout the day. Large colorful rugs and rocking chairs adorn the bright rooms, where children's artwork is on display. Each classroom has a rich library of fiction, poetry, nonfiction, biographies, and historical novels, color coded so that students can choose books of an appropriate level of difficulty.

In most elementary schools, the classroom teacher gives lessons in most academic subjects. At PS 304, children travel to a special room to learn math and science from a spirited and energetic teacher who gives Ms. Frizzle (the star of the PBS *Magic Schoolbus* series) a run for her money.

There is a strong emphasis on test preparation, with Saturday workshops, lunchtime activities, and parent workshops beginning 2 months before the city exams.

Parents help out, not only in typical PTA fund-raising, but also as school volunteers. They write grants and lobby the district and state for extra funds.

Admission is open to children living in District 8. Contact the school or the Region 2 office for more information.

# PS 69: The New Vision School

### 560 Thieriot Avenue
### Bronx, NY 10473
### (718) 378-4736
### *http://ps69bronx.org*

**Admissions:** neighborhood school
**Grade levels:** PK–4
**Enrollment:** 467
**Class size:** K: 25; 4: 25

**Reading scores:** **
**Math scores:** ****
**Ethnicity:** 2%W 24%B 71%H 3%A
**Free lunch:** 80%

"Who got a phone call from me last night?" asks Principal Alan Cohen as he bounces into a 3rd-grade classroom at PS 69 in the Clason Point section of the Bronx. Two students raise their hands. "What did I say to you?" Cohen asks. "You asked me if I was feeling better," answers a boy who had been feeling sick the day before. "And what else?" asks Cohen. "To remember to read for 30 minutes," the boy answers. "And did you?" Cohen asks. The boy nods his head and cracks a smile.

During his hour drive home each day, Cohen uses his cell phone to call students to remind them to do their homework. A former district official who became the school's principal in Fall 2003, he exudes contagious enthusiasm. "He gets on the loudspeaker each morning and tells the kids: 'You go to the best school in the city, you have the best teachers, and you are the best kids!'" the assistant principal told us. "And the kids believe it. And we believe it too."

While Cohen concedes that the school still has a way to go before it is, indeed, "the best," PS 69 has a palpable spirit of improvement. Take its scores on standardized tests in math, for example. While only 28% of 4th graders met or exceeded standards in 2000, fully 74% met or exceeded them in 2004. In reading, the 4th-grade numbers jumped from 24% in 2000 to 49% in 2004. (Third-grade reading scores did not improve in 2004, and in fact dipped to 31% from 43% in 2003. Cohen attributes this to new teachers and a lack of emphasis on test prep stamina, two things that he says the school is working on.)

Lessons we observed were focused and students were well behaved. Class sizes at PS 69 are relatively small by city standards—most registers are in the mid-20s. We visited several classrooms where students were engaged in silent, independent reading, or gathered on a rug in front of the teacher to discuss a book with the whole class. In math, students were using manipulatives—such as blocks and rods—to practice adding or dividing numbers.

Located in a working-class neighborhood, PS 69 is housed in two buildings—a traditional red-brick structure erected in 1923 and a low-ceilinged annex that was constructed in the 1970s and today contains the kindergarten and 1st grade. Both buildings are nicely decorated with student work on the walls, but facilities are limited: The library, art room, and music room could all use work, and the cafeteria is cramped. The gym is makeshift. Still, the overall tone of the school, with its neat, book-filled classrooms, is pleasant, and the buildings are clean and orderly. The principal told us that he personally checks the bathrooms each morning to make sure they are stocked with soap and paper towels.

There are lots of other signs suggesting that the school's staff really cares about the kids: Aides play games with the students at recess, and children at risk of being held over are each "adopted" by an adult in the building, so that they get special one-on-one attention. The school also benefits from an enthusiastic parent coordinator, involved parents, and an effective conflict resolution program. An English language learner teacher works with students who are just learning English. There are five self-contained special education classes for children with special needs.

The school is not perfect, and Cohen admits there is plenty of work to be done. Reading and math scores need to be still higher, he says. Some teachers are young and don't stay long before moving on to graduate school. While the school does have a teacher center, where teachers get some professional development, there is no reading coach. Nevertheless, these gaps seem far overshadowed by the school's sense of purpose, energy, and optimism. "We have a vision here," Cohen said to us on our tour, as the half-dozen parents and staffers who were accompanying us nodded in agreement. At PS 69, everyone seems to be aiming high.

# Bronx Little School
## 1300 Boynton Avenue
## Room 135
## Bronx, NY 10472
## (718) 860-8181

**Admissions:** citywide
**Grade levels:** PK–5
**Enrollment:** 130
**Class size:** 15–22

**Reading scores:** ***
**Math scores:** ****
**Ethnicity:** 1%W 31%B 64%H 4%A
**Free lunch:** 90%

If you're feeling down, a visit to Bronx Little School will cheer you up. The happy children, the teachers who work day and night on behalf of the kids, and the principal who knows how to balance academic rigor with a nurturing environment will give you hope for the future of public education in the Bronx.

Housed in the former Monroe High School, Bronx Little School is modeled after Central Park East in East Harlem. The school opened in 1999 under the jurisdiction, curiously enough, of the Alternative High School Division. (Monroe High was divided into several mini-schools, one of which serves elementary school children.) For its first few years, Bronx Little School had the freedom to develop its own curriculum and hire its own teachers, completely independent of the beleaguered district in which it was located, District 12.

Now it's part of Region 2 and subject to the same rules and regulations as other schools in the city. Principal Margaret Harriman, luckily, knows how to satisfy the demands of the region for solid test scores and implementation of the new curriculum, while maintaining her vision of what a school should look like.

The classrooms are spacious and bright, with plenty of books, blocks, water tables, Legos, and costume boxes. Each room has an attractive wooden loft with soft cushions. Children may grab a cushion in the loft and find a quiet corner to read. Or they may dress up as Romeo and Juliet and use the loft as a balcony from which to stage their act.

There are plenty of trips and activities. Some children took an overnight trip to Vermont to learn about farm life. One child won a spelling bee among a network of 30 schools in Region 2.

Children warm to the loving atmosphere in the school. One child spoke so little in class when he first came that teachers feared he might be autistic. It turned out he was quiet just because he had never trusted grown-ups enough to speak. Little by little, he came out of his shell, and when we saw him, he seemed to be a happy and secure boy.

The principal and teachers communicate well with one another and with the children. Kids wave happily to the principal, whom they call "Meg," and eagerly show off their work when she visits their classes. The school emphasizes social and emotional development as well as academic success. There is only one class per grade. Class size is small, and teachers give individual attention.

Parents are welcome to visit anytime. Classroom labels are written in both Spanish and English—helpful to the Spanish-speaking parents who make up the bulk of the parent body. There is a range of income levels among the families, including poor Mexico immigrants and middle-class employees of Verizon and Time Warner.

Some concerns: The school doesn't have a special education teacher. Although the children don't have much contact with the high school students, sharing a building can be difficult.

Bronx Little School is open to children from anywhere in the city. Apply in May.

# PS 179

### 468 East 140th Street
### Bronx, NY 10454
### (718) 292-2237

**Admissions:** neighborhood school
**Grade levels:** PK–5 (projected)
**Enrollment:** 260
**Class size:** K: 20; 4: 28

**Reading scores:** * * *
**Math scores:** * * *
**Ethnicity:** 1%W 30%B 67%H 2%A
**Free lunch:** 100%

A gentle, welcoming school in a poor neighborhood, PS 179 is striving to give the children of the South Bronx the same high-quality education that children in middle-class neighborhoods receive. With class trips to the aquarium, the zoo, the ballet, and the natural history museum, teachers bring children to a world outside their neighborhood. Teachers read aloud to their classes every day, exposing students to classics of children's literature. And they draw parents into the life of the school, encouraging them to help with homework to an extent that is uncommon in high-poverty schools.

"I want to make sure the children get the same things that children get downtown," said Principal Sherry Williams, whose own history makes her well suited to begin to close the gap between rich and poor schools. Williams grew up in the neighborhood, attended PS 5, PS 161, PS 131, and MS 149, all nearby, then won a scholarship to attend a private boarding school in New England. She graduated from Simmons College in Boston and returned to teach in the Bronx.

PS 179 was founded in 2002, replacing PS 40, a school that was closed because of low academic performance. The new school shares the old PS 40 building with Mott Haven Village School, which was founded as an alternative school in the mid-1990s. The two now are zoned, neighborhood schools. Students who live at addresses with even numbers are assigned to PS 179; students with addresses that are odd are assigned to Mott Haven Village.

Like other children in poor neighborhoods, most kids at PS 179 begin school lagging behind their middle-class peers. Many have limited vocabularies (one child didn't know the word for "tiger," for example) and they may not know the alphabet, colors, or numbers. Teachers at PS 179 try to fill in these gaps by urging parents to read to their children for 20 minutes a day, and, if the parents are unavailable, by arranging for older siblings or other relatives to fill in. Class trips expand children's vocabularies—the child who didn't know the word *tiger* learned it on a trip to the zoo.

Although PS 179 has embraced the chancellor's new curriculum, which replaces textbooks with fun-to-read picture books, Williams has placed more emphasis on phonics, teaching children to sound out words letter by letter, than is typical in schools following the new balanced literacy approach to reading. In one class, children were practicing spelling—now called "word study"—with markers on lap-sized, wipe-off white boards. In another class, children were playing "letter bingo"—learning to identify sounds and letters—and tracing letters on laminated boards. Starting in kindergarten, the school identifies kids who seem to be having difficulty and gets them extra help after school—rather than pulling children out of their regular classes as often is done elsewhere. "It costs more, but I think it's more beneficial," said Williams.

The school has a large Spanish-speaking population, as well as Chinese newcomers and African immigrants speaking languages such as Twi and Mandingo. They receive instruction in English as a Second Language.

Like a lot of schools in high-poverty areas, PS 179 struggles to recruit experienced teachers. Most of the staff is young and could benefit from more time in the classroom. But Williams appears to have created a school with a collegial atmosphere where kids are focused on their work and teachers feel they get the support they need. PS 179 is a school to watch.

# WORTH WATCHING: THE BRONX

## Fordham

**PS 33**, 2424 Jerome Avenue, Bronx, NY 10468, (718) 584-3926, is an academic haven located in one of the poorest Congressional districts in New York State. Principal Elba Lopez says the well-run, clean building she oversees today is not what she encountered when she first came to the school in the early 1990s. "Discipline was horrendous, the morale of the staff was low, and our math and reading scores were to the ground," she says. The first line of attack was discipline and classroom management. Lopez also made it a point to hire teachers who were from, and who understood, the community. Then she worked to make parent involvement a central piece of daily school operations. Today, PS 33 parents trained in the "reading recovery" method help students before classes begin or after school. The PTA, which takes students who have shown significant improvement to the local McDonalds for a monthly celebration party, is welcome to use the principal's office. The school developed popular Saturday supplemental-learning classes for parents as well as children. And it launched a 6-week summer program for children about to enter kindergarten, so they could begin to learn their ABCs and 123s before starting school. PS 33 has a large Spanish-speaking population.

## Morris Heights

**PS 315: Lab School for Children**, 2246 Jerome Avenue, Bronx, NY 10453, (718) 584-7441, is a small K–8 school open to all children in District 10. There's one class in each grade, a comfy feel, and the determination to boost student learning. Located in what used to be a bowling alley, the school has colorful classrooms with plenty of "word walls" (vocabulary lists), rugs, and other touches to make kids feel that this is their space. Roomy kindergarten classes contain lofts for creative play. In this environment students work well in teams and seem focused on their studies. We spoke with students who were articulate and willing to explain what they were studying and how. One thing bothered them: the absence of windows in the building. The cafeteria doubles as an auditorium, with a portable stage and sound equipment, and the school compensates for the lack of a gym with a daily "literacy and movement" class. The day of our visit the teacher was working with a special education class, reading from the book *Aida* by Leontyne Price. Each student played a different character, acting out the story as the teacher read—and all were intensely interested, hanging on every word. A dance and drama word wall hangs in this class too.

## Co-op City

At **PS 153: Helen Keller School**, 650 Baychester Avenue, Bronx, NY 10475, (718) 904-5550, children in wheelchairs mingle with the able-bodied, and every child, from the super-high achieving to most mentally disabled, is seen as a useful member of the school community. Most of the school's children are general education pupils who live in Co-op City, but PS 153 also houses the district's gifted program and several citywide programs for children who have special education needs, including hearing impairment, emotional disturbance, physical disabilities, and autism. One mother was thrilled that her son, who is hearing-impaired, was able to attend a gifted class and still get speech therapy and training in lip reading. His teacher wore a microphone while he wore a special radio-operated hearing aid. The school has a special ed gym teacher who is in a wheelchair, and a teacher for the deaf who is hearing-impaired. Children are chosen for the gifted program according to a test given in all District 11 schools in kindergarten. Free busing is provided. The district gifted coordinator may be reached at (718) 904-5563.

## Soundview

**PS 100**, 800 Taylor Avenue, Bronx, NY 10473, (718) 842-1461, in Soundview–Clason Point, has long had a reputation for success in the community, with a good attendance rate and stable reading and math scores. A gifted and talented program, starting in 1st grade, is open to children zoned for the school. Teachers have breakfasts and lunches together to discuss students' performance in each subject and keep kids from falling through the cracks. The school has a dance program, as well as Studio in a School, and student artwork covers the ceiling and every corridor. While other schools in the Bronx often suffer from lack of supplies, PS 100 is full of blocks, reading books sorted in bins, and computers. Lessons can be fun. When we walked into the room of one upper-grade math teacher, she commented, "Oh no! You've caught us gambling," as she engaged the students in tossing coins and spinning wheels to help them learn probability. Children are grouped by ability starting in kindergarten. Special education classes are well equipped, cheerful, and indistinguishable from the general education rooms. Children sit for an informal evaluation in the fall to determine where they should be placed. They are asked a range of questions—from ABCs to their home addresses.

At **PS 119**, 1075 Pugsley Avenue, Bronx, NY 10472, (718) 822-5198, involved parents, a solid teaching staff, and an energetic principal work together to inspire the children. PS 119 is a clean and cheerful school in a working-class neighborhood of two-family homes and low-rise apartment buildings near the Parkchester train station in the Soundview section. While many other schools in the Bronx have suffered from rapid teacher turnover, poor building maintenance, and weak leadership, "this is a school that never really went down," said Principal Lydia Bassett Tyner, who has a bachelor's degree from Harvard and a master's degree from Bank Street College of Education. "It's a hard-working, vigilant community that really works with the school in a positive way." Built in 1939, the red-brick building still has original details such as shiny wood floors, oak coat closets, and large wood-framed windows. An addition built in the 1990s houses a large gym, a sunny cafeteria, and an auditorium. The school is overcrowded, with portable classrooms on the playground and 1st-grade classes housed in a middle school next door. PS 119, which once served mostly Puerto Rican and African-American children, now includes a number of immigrants from Bangladesh, China, Korea, Yemen, India, and Guyana. Some girls wear "hijab," or head scarves worn by some observant Muslims.

## South Bronx

**PS 154**, 333 East 135th Street, Bronx, NY 10454, (718) 292-4742, is a sweet and welcoming school serving children from one of the poorest and most dangerous areas of the city. Some of the students live in homeless shelters or in foster care, and many of their parents are high school dropouts. Housing projects nearby are known for drug-dealing and gang fights. But the classrooms in the 1960s-era brick PS 154 look like what you might expect in a middle-class neighborhood, equipped with blond-wood tables, pretty molded wooden chairs, and rich classroom libraries with fun-to-read books by authors like Dr. Seuss and Ezra Jack Keats. Classrooms for the youngest children have cloth hand puppets, sand tables, wood blocks and housekeeping corners with dress-up boxes and child-sized wooden kitchens. Grown-ups never seem to raise their voices, and the atmosphere is calm and orderly. Principal Cynthia Ballard introduced the Reading and Writing Workshop method devised by reading guru Lucy Calkins. Similar to the progressive curriculum since imposed citywide, the workshop model encourages each child to choose a different picture book to read, rather than having everyone in the same class read the same textbook. Test scores have crept up gradually, and while only about 40% of the children meet state standards, PS 154 has been removed from the state's list of low-performing schools.

# Hunts Point

Surrounded by old warehouses and auto mechanic garages, **Bronx Charter School for the Arts**, 950 Longfellow Avenue, Bronx, NY 10474, (718) 893-1042, which opened in 2003, is a pleasant oasis in a poor neighborhood. The exterior is covered with colorful ceramic tiles and the main office is right in the lobby, without any walls to divide the office from the entrance. The doors are covered with Crayola crayon colors, and student projects are displayed proudly throughout the spacious halls. Students have 6 hours a week of instruction in music, theater, dance, and art, and art specialists work alongside classroom teachers to integrate the arts into the curriculum. Kids learn percussion, *melodica* (a wooden Spanish recorder), and keyboard. By 4th grade they are able to read music and take up band instruments. There is a small violin program sponsored by Midori & Friends. The school also works in partnership with Lincoln Center and the Guggenheim Museum. Students wear Bronx Arts T-shirts that come in a variety of colors (and may wear a different color each day of the week if they choose). All classes in the school have collaborative team teaching (CTT). CTT classes have two teachers, one of whom is certified in special education, and a mix of general education pupils and children with special needs. Parents are welcome. Executive Director Xanthe Jory has a firm, businesslike manner but is also gentle with children. Applications are available in January and due by March. Children are chosen by lottery.

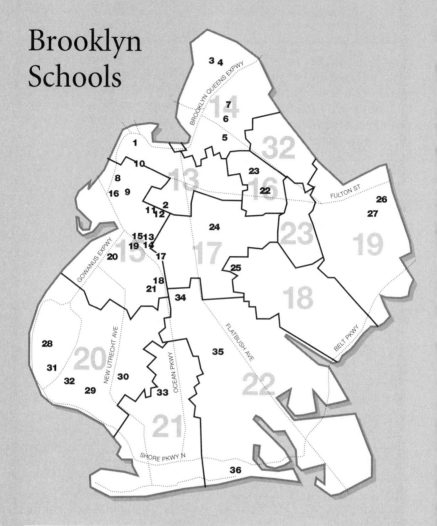

# Brooklyn Schools

**District 13**
1   PS 8: Robert Fulton
2   PS 282: Park Slope

**District 14**
3   PS 31: Magnet School for the Arts and Humanities
4   PS 34: Oliver H. Perry
5   Beginning with Children Charter
6   PS 250
7   PS 132: Conselyea

**District 15**
8   PS 29
9   PS 58: Carroll
10  PS 261
11  PS 372: Children's
12  PS 321
13  PS 107
14  PS 39
15  PS 10
16  PS 146: Brooklyn New
17  PS 154
18  PS 130: Parkside
19  PS 295: Studio School of Art and Culture
20  PS 172
21  PS 230

**District 16**
22  PS 21
23  PS 308

**District 17**
24  PS 161

**District 18**
25  PS 235

**District 19**
26  PS 7
27  PS 89: Cypress Hills Community

**District 20**
28  PS 185
29  PS 229
30  PS 247
31  PS 104: Fort Hamilton
32  PS 204: Vince Lombardi

**District 21**
33  PS 177

**District 22**
34  PS 139
35  PS 193
36  PS 195

# BROOKLYN

From the elegant 19th-century brownstones of Brooklyn Heights to the dilapidated public housing towers of Coney Island, the city's most populous borough has an extraordinary variety of places, people—and schools. Brooklyn has orderly, traditional schools where children wear uniforms and read Shakespeare, and progressive schools where children call teachers by their first names and flop on rugs and pillows on the floor. It has schools that are well run and helpful to parents, offering clear information and regular school tours, and schools with an appalling history of weak leadership and low performance.

For many years, each of the borough's 12 districts operated as an independent fiefdom. Each tried to lure the best students from other districts—while making it next to impossible for its own students to find out anything about schools outsides its borders. Each district—and sometimes each school—had its own admissions criteria.

Under Mayor Bloomberg's 2003 reorganization of schools, the 12 districts were consolidated into five regions. The districts still exist, at least on paper, but their staffs have been reduced dramatically and you may not get a live human on the telephone. You may have better luck reaching someone at the regional offices. (But don't count on it—there's voice-mail Purgatory in the regional offices as well.) On the positive side, there has been some attempt to make consistent rules about admission to schools.

The leadership in Region 8, which includes a large swath of the borough from Willliamsburg to Sunset Park, has been particularly strong, and there have been steady improvements in many of the neighborhood schools in recent years. Teachers increasingly are drawn to the region, known for its staff development and lively approach to education. Particularly good are the schools in District 15, which includes Park Slope.

The other consistently strong district is District 20 in Bay Ridge, which is part of Region 7. Strong principals, effective leadership from the regional office, and parents who make their children's education a priority have made the schools good across the district.

Most children in Brooklyn attend their neighborhood schools, but if your child's zoned school is unsatisfactory, there are a number of opportunities for school choice. Some schools have federal magnet grants designed to encourage racial integration by attracting children from outside the immediate neighborhood. A number of schools offer gifted and talented programs that admit children from across a district. And there are a few charter schools that admit children by lottery. For profiles of schools not listed here, see *www.insideschools.org*.

While some transfers between districts are possible, it isn't always easy. Only your own district is obligated to accommodate your child. Some schools are overcrowded and won't accept anyone from outside their zone, while others recruit children from outside the neighborhood. Children who are enrolled in certain low-performing schools may be able to transfer under the provisions of the federal No Child Left Behind Act. Rules about transfers, or "variances," change from year to year, so you'll have to call your regional office for updated information.

## Region 8: Williamsburg to Sunset Park

Region 8 covers the old Districts 13, 14, 15, and 16 and encompasses the neighborhoods of Williamsburg, Brooklyn Heights, Fort Greene, Carroll Gardens, Park Slope, and parts of Sunset Park and Bedford-Stuyvesant. The region encourages parents to shop around, and some of the options are quite attractive. Children living in a school's zone are admitted automatically. Then children living outside the zone, but inside the district in which a school is located, are considered. Children living in the region but outside the district get second preference. Students living outside the region may apply to these schools as well. Applications are available from the office of student placement, 131 Livingston Street, Room 309, Brooklyn, NY 11201, (718) 935-3900. The application deadline varies from year to year, but it's usually in the winter. For information about gifted and talented programs, call the regional G&T coordinator, Donna Baker, at (718) 330-9305.

Seven schools (two of which are profiled here) received federal magnet grants in 2004 to encourage racial integration by introducing innovative programs designed to attract children who otherwise might not attend. Children zoned for each neighborhood school are still guaranteed admission, but children from outside the zone and the district also may apply through the magnet programs. Tours are offered in the fall or winter. Applications are available at the regional office or at individual schools. Call the regional magnet coordinator, Joe Gallagher, at (718) 935-3675 or e-mail *jgallag@nycboe.net* for details.

Deputy Chancellor Carmen Farina, who was superintendent for District 15 and later superintendent for the region, offered strong and effective leadership to the district during her tenure and still offers guidance to the schools from her post in the central administration. Many schools that were not-ready-for-prime-time several years ago offer promise today.

**District 13** includes the stately homes of Brooklyn Heights, the pleasant brownstones of Bedford-Stuyvesant, and the housing projects of Fort Greene. Unfortunately, the schools have not been successful as a whole, although there are a few bright spots. Under the direction of the new regional office, there have been some improvements, which are reflected in the following profiles. Some parents send their children to gifted and talented programs, called LEAD. Call the regional G&T coordinator at (718) 330-9305.

**District 14** includes Williamsburg and Greenpoint, the Brooklyn neighborhoods just over the Williamsburg Bridge from Manhattan. Polish-American Greenpoint has a small-town, Old World feel to it, with butchers and pastry shops, a church with a steeple, row houses, and neighbors who know one another. Williamsburg, with large Hispanic and Orthodox Jewish populations, has long had the feel of a village from another time and place. Now, Greenpoint and Williamsburg are rapidly gentrifying, with trendy boutiques and restaurants catering to hip artsy types who were priced out of Manhattan. Both neighborhoods have large manufacturing zones, and artists have built lofts in old industrial buildings.

The schools have long been traditional, and some have been quite successful. Now, as part of Region 8, they have begun to adopt some more-progressive teaching methods while maintaining their attention to basic skills. (Some District 14 parents seeking a still more progressive approach to education send their children to the alternative schools in Manhattan's District 1.)

Parents in **District 15**—which runs from Carroll Gardens to Sunset Park—have long shopped for elementary schools the way parents elsewhere shop for colleges. Starting in the winter and continuing through the spring, parents visit schools, fill out applications, have their children tested, and bite their fingernails waiting to see where they've been accepted. It's harder to get into schools outside the zone than it once was, because popular schools are filling up with children from the immediate neighborhood. Moreover, the shopping around isn't as necessary as it once was because many of the ordinary, zoned neighborhood schools have improved. So check out your neighborhood school before you drive yourself crazy with a long search. The district, which includes the beautifully restored turn-of-the-twentieth-century brownstones of Park Slope and the run-down housing projects of Red Hook, has some of the best and most creative schools in Brooklyn. (Not every school is a gem, however, so visit before you enroll your child.)

The region has organized schools in "clusters," grouping the schools around common themes and pairing the best schools with those that are struggling. Teachers and principals are encouraged to visit other schools within their cluster to share successful ideas and techniques.

There is occasionally room for children from outside the district in some of the schools, although those parents may have to wait until June or even later to find out whether the school they want has space for their child.

**District 16**, in the Bedford-Stuyvesant section of Brooklyn, has mostly low-performing schools. Two notable exceptions are profiled here.

## Region 6: from Crown Heights to Bergen Beach

Region 6, including the old Districts 17, 18, and 22, encompasses a large swath of Brooklyn from Crown Heights (home of the annual Caribbean Day parade on Labor Day when 1 million people revel in North America's version of *Carnival*) to the sleepy seaside community of Bergen Beach. The region is as varied as any in the city: There are large Victorian houses on tree-lined streets in Crown Heights and Ditmas Park and suburban neighborhoods like Mill Basin, where 10-year-olds may walk safely by themselves to a bowling alley. Neighborhood schools are still the norm in this region, but there are a handful of noteworthy programs that accept children from across the district or even the borough. The regional offices are at 5619 Flatlands Avenue, Brooklyn, NY 11234, (718) 968-6100. The office of gifted and talented programs coordinator is Christopher Roma-Agvanian, (718) 968-6104.

**District 17** encompasses East Flatbush and Crown Heights. The district has a mix of large houses on tree-lined streets and more modest apartment buildings. Much of the neighborhood is divided between blacks (including many Caribbean immigrants) and Orthodox Jews, who generally send their children to private yeshivas. For information about gifted programs, call the regional coordinator, Christopher Roma-Agvanian at (718) 968-6104.

**District 18**, serving Flatbush and Canarsie, is home to many immigrants from the Caribbean. The district's gifted programs, ASTRAL, Javits, and Soar, have a history of accepting children from outside the district. Applications are usually available in October. Tests are administered in January. For information, contact the regional coordinator, Christopher Roma-Agvanian at (718) 968-6104.

**District 22** is a huge district that stretches from Ditmas Park, with its grand Victorian houses, in central Brooklyn, to the sleepy seaside community of Bergen Beach on Jamaica Bay. Most of the schools have had a traditional philosophy, although progressive methods are now being introduced. Every school in the district has a gifted program called Eagle. (Six schools have the Eagle program for prekindergartners.) Applications are available in January. Testing is available in Chinese, Haitian Creole, Russian, Spanish, and Urdu. Parents are notified in May and June. PS 193 in the Midwood section is the site of the Center for the Intellectually Gifted, or CIG, program, a small program for children who score exceptionally high on the test. For information about gifted programs, call Christopher Roma-Agvanian at (718) 968-6104.

## Region 7: Bay Ridge to Coney Island

Region 7 (including the old Districts 20 and 21) encompasses a stretch of southern Brooklyn from Bay Ridge to Coney Island. Children tend to go to their neighborhood schools. However, both districts have a number of gifted programs that admit children from across the district. Call the gifted coordinator, Joseph Giamportone, at (718) 759-3927. The region's main offices are in Staten Island, but there is a satellite office at 415 89th Street, Brooklyn, NY 11209, (718) 759-4900.

**District 20**, in the southwest corner of Brooklyn near the Verrazano Bridge, includes the pleasant residential neighborhoods of Bensonhurst, Borough Park, Bay Ridge, and parts of Sunset Park. Single-family houses with small yards are popular and there are two- and three-family houses and apartment buildings as well. The area once had large Italian and Norwegian populations, and now includes many immigrants from the Middle East, Asia, the former Soviet Union, China, and Central America. Because of overcrowding, there isn't a lot of school choice. High-achieving children may apply for gifted or Delta programs outside their neighborhood. Call the regional office at (718) 759-3927. The district is well run and most of the neighborhood schools are quite good. So don't overlook your neighborhood school, even if it isn't profiled here. See *www.insideschools.org* for schools not included here.

**District 21** encompasses a stretch of southern Brooklyn from Bensonhurst and Midwood to Coney Island and Sheepshead Bay. A long sandy beach, the New York Aquarium, a boardwalk stretching from Coney Island to Brighton Beach, and, of course, the amusement park at Coney Island make these Brooklyn neighborhoods popular tourist destinations.

Bensonhurst, once largely Italian-American, now has a sizable Asian population. Midwood is increasingly an Orthodox Jewish community. Coney Island is predominantly African-American, and

Sheepshead Bay has many new immigrant communities, particularly families from Russia. A number of schools serve children in kindergarten through 8th grade—an attraction to parents who want their children to avoid the city's sometimes-chaotic middle schools. The district elementary schools are generally well run.

The district has a gifted program called Sigma in a number of schools. Parents may complete an application in the early fall. The district office evaluates children for placement the following year. Call the gifted coordinator, Joseph Giamportone, at (718) 759-3927.

## Regions 4 and 5:
## Bushwick and Ocean Hill-Brownsville

Region 4, serving schools in Bushwick, includes several districts in Queens as well as the old **District 32**. Its offices are at 28-11 Queens Plaza North, Queens, NY 11101, (718) 391-8300. Call Cheryl Quatrano, the gifted and talented coordinator, at (718) 397-5472 for information about gifted programs.

Region 5, serving Ocean Hill-Brownsville and East New York, includes the old **District 23** and **District 19** as well as parts of Queens. Its offices are at 8201 Rockaway Blvd., Ozone Park, NY 11416, (718) 642-5800. The gifted and talented programs coordinator is Sherry Copeland, who may be reached at (718) 642-5871.

Districts 23 and 19 have long been among the most beleaguered in the city. But, under the administration of regional superintendent Kathleen Cashin, there are some glimmers of hope. A number of schools we visited seemed to be making headway against enormous odds.

# PS 8: Robert Fulton School

## 37 Hicks Street
## Brooklyn, NY 11201
## (718) 834-6740
### *www.ps8pta.org*

**Admissions:** neighborhood school/magnet program
**Grade levels:** PK–5          **Reading scores:** \*\*
**Enrollment:** 300             **Math scores:** \*\*\*
**Class size:** K: 15; 5: 28    **Ethnicity:** 13%W 65%B 19%H 3%A
                                **Free lunch:** 90%

The zone for PS 8 includes the million-dollar brownstones of Brooklyn Heights, but until recently most well-off parents in the area sent their children to private schools or to better-regarded public schools. PS 8 served mostly poor children from nearby housing projects.

Now, both middle-class and well-off families are coming back, attracted by an energetic new principal, Seth Phillips from PS 94 in Sunset Park; an able staff developer, Olivia Ellis, from Park Slope's sought-after PS 321; and an activist, multiracial group of neighborhood parents eager to help. Enrollment is growing, and test scores, while still low, are on the rise. Parents, once excluded from the school, are encouraged to bring their children right to the classrooms.

Built in 1906, PS 8 has stained glass in some of its windows and a bas-relief sculpture on one wall. Sun streams in through large windows, and the floors are painted a cheerful yellow. The school is strongest in the lower grades. The prekindergarten classroom is a model of what a preschool should look like: tadpoles in the tank; children bustling around to different centers, some playing at a water table, others writing; the walls plastered with student artwork. Both kindergarten rooms are welcoming and well equipped, with young, energetic teachers.

Children may receive special education services in collaborative team-teaching classes, which mix special education students and those in general education, and are led by two teachers, one of whom is trained in special education.

In 2004, PS 8 received a magnet grant, making it a Magnet School for Exploration, Research, and Design. The school has collaborations with the Guggenheim Museum, Brooklyn Center for the Urban Environment, Marquis Studios in DUMBO, Studio in a School, and the Rotunda gallery, which will help the school build an art gallery. Children from outside the zone are encouraged to apply.

# PS 282: Park Slope School
### 180 Sixth Avenue
### Brooklyn, NY 11217
### (718) 834-6965

**Admissions:** neighborhood school/gifted program
**Grade levels:** K–6
**Enrollment:** 652
**Class size:** K: 20; 6: 28

**Reading scores:** ****
**Math scores:** ****
**Ethnicity:** 4%W 59%B 34%H 3%A
**Free lunch:** 57%

Long the highest performing school in District 13, PS 282 has a gifted program that attracts children from across Brooklyn and even from other boroughs. It has a strong music and art program, a science room with animals, a room just for chess, a fabulous gym and physical education teacher, and a spacious, attractive building with room for children from outside the zone.

For years, the school had a reputation as a rigid, highly structured place, with mountains of homework, lots of worksheets, and punitive attitudes toward discipline. Now, a new principal, Magalie Alexis, has made the school a more human place, adding rugs and classroom libraries, decreasing the homework load, and introducing teachers to new ideas by encouraging them to tour other successful schools.

In a prekindergarten class, children build Legos, play in a sandbox, and pile up blocks. In the 2nd-grade wing, classrooms had comfy couches lined with teddy bears. Worksheets are gone, and the principal encourages children to write their own "books" which are presented at "publishing parties."

The school, steeped in tradition, is still more formal than others in the neighborhood. Children walk quietly through the halls in straight lines. Teachers tend to stay for years and many parents attended PS 282 themselves. Alexis, herself a PS 282 alumna, pointed out to us teachers who were there when she was a child, including the beloved physical education teacher. Some teachers stay on even after they retire, helping out a few days a week.

Call the school's parent coordinator for tour dates and details about admissions. For information about the gifted program, call the region's gifted coordinator at (718) 330-9305.

# PS 31:
# Magnet School for the Arts and Humanities
## 75 Meserole Avenue
## Brooklyn, NY 11222
## (718) 383-8998

**Admissions:** neighborhood school/magnet program
**Grade levels:** PK–5          **Reading scores:** \* \* \* \*
**Enrollment:** 643          **Math scores:** \* \* \* \* \*
**Class size:** K: 26; 6: 32          **Ethnicity:** 31%W 2%B 56%H 11%A
                                    **Free lunch:** 74%

At PS 31, students walk quietly down the hallways, and prekindergartners politely push in their chairs when they are asked to gather on the classroom rug. But students also kick up their heels enthusiastically in dance class, where they "shake their buttons" to the merengue, or stomp in line as the music urges, "Everybody dance now!"

A very high-performing school with a reputation for being traditional, PS 31 recently has started incorporating some more-progressive approaches to teaching reading and math. Many teachers still give lessons from in front of the classroom, but students also are encouraged to work in groups or to learn math concepts by using manipulatives like blocks and rods.

"We're structured, but we work in groups, very cooperatively," said one staff member who has been at the school for 30 years. "It's very different than it was 10 years ago. There's a lot more freedom." The school has a strong cadre of teachers, its hallways and classrooms display interesting student projects, and it is exceptionally neat and clean—the light-blue hallways literally glisten.

The school boasts a host of arts programs—including keyboards, flutophone, ballroom dance, and Spanish language classes—thanks to a magnet grant that it received in 2004. The school also offers after-school activities, as well as a Saturday academy.

The school accepts all students within its zone boundaries. Because the school's building originally was intended as a temporary space, PS 31's zone is actually about a mile away from the school itself. Zoned students are provided with transportation. In addition, because the school receives federal magnet funding, it must admit a certain number of students through a lottery. Students throughout the city may apply, although transportation is not provided for students admitted through the lottery. Call the school for tour dates.

# PS 34: Oliver H. Perry School
## 131 Norman Avenue
## Brooklyn, NY 11222
## (718) 389-5842

**Admissions:** neighborhood school  **Reading scores:** \*\*\*\*
**Grade levels:** PK–5                 **Math scores:** \*\*\*\*\*
**Enrollment:** 477                    **Ethnicity:** 72%W 1%B 22%H 5%A
**Class size:** K: 22; 5: 28           **Free lunch:** 69%

Built as a hospital during the Civil War, PS 34 has a pretty brick fa-çade with a gambrel roof described in a plaque as "early Romanesque revival." The former wards have been divided into classrooms. There are no hallways: Teachers and pupils must pass through one another's classrooms to get to their seats.

But the staff has made a virtue out of necessity in the school's unusual physical plant. Teachers rarely raise their voices—too many people would hear them if they did. There seems to be a mutual respect for everyone's work. There's a gentle hum of children and adults talking: The school is neither silent nor chaotic. PS 34 is small enough that everyone knows everyone else.

Children wear uniforms of white shirts, blue pants, and navy blue sweaters. The school emphasizes phonics and continues to use graded readers to supplement children's literature. But PS 34 also has adopted Teachers College's methods of teaching reading and writing, and an administrator said, "The children have really bloomed with the new programs."

Children are not grouped by ability, but some high-achieving children in grades 3–5 are taken out of their classes one period a day for "enrichment." They learn about photography and make "sun-prints" with light-sensitive paper, watch a Charlie Chaplin film at the Museum of the Moving Image, or draw self-portraits. The school has wireless Internet access and an impressive technology program. Children in grades 3–5 study violin. There is no gym or auditorium. There are monthly open houses for prospective parents.

# Beginning with Children Charter School
## 11 Bartlett Street
## Brooklyn, NY 11206
## (718) 388-8847
### *www.bwccschool.org*

**Admissions:** citywide
**Grade levels:** PK–8
**Enrollment:** 450
**Class size:** K: 25; 8: 25

**Reading scores:** * * *
**Math scores:** * * * *
**Ethnicity:** 9%W 35%B 55%H 1%A
**Free lunch:** 70%

Beginning with Children Charter School is a small, welcoming school with bright and spacious classrooms, skylights that light the hallways, and a beautiful, well-equipped library with padded armchairs, wall-to-wall carpet, and a computer research center.

A charter school, Beginning with Children is not bound by certain rules and regulations of the Department of Education. The school has considerable private financial support from the Beginning with Children Foundation, a nonprofit organization set up to raise extra funds for the school, and, as a result, it is not as battered by the vagaries of budget cuts as most public schools and its facilities are pleasanter than most.

A prosperous couple, Carol Reich, a psychologist, and Joseph Reich, a financial advisor, founded Beginning with Children in 1992 as a public–private partnership. They wanted to offer financial support for an autonomous public school in exchange for a say in how to run it. At the time, before the state passed a law creating charter schools, Beginning with Children reported directly to the city schools chancellor. It converted to charter status in 2000 and now is governed by the state education department.

The school is affiliated with Pfizer Inc., a pharmaceutical company. Pfizer donated the building the school now occupies and provides ongoing support ranging from use of their photocopier when the school's is out-of-order to offering its employees as mentors to middle school students.

Beginning with Children actively encourages parents to help out in their children's classrooms. A father who owns a carpentry shop made cubbies and coat racks for the school. An artist-father worked on art projects in a prekindergarten class. A number of parents have been trained as classroom volunteers by the nonprofit group Learning Leaders.

Parents appreciate the warm relationships between children and staff. "The teaching staff is absolutely wonderful," said one mother.

Teachers combine progressive and traditional teaching methods. "We take an eclectic approach," says the school's principal, Cynthia Baily, who taught at the school for 6 years prior to becoming principal, and before that taught in Manhattan's District 2. Children use textbooks as well as the small blocks called manipulatives to study arithmetic. They learn to read with picture books and literature—not graded readers—but teachers offer explicit instruction in phonics as well. Science and social studies are integrated into reading as much as possible. Second-grade students studying deserts in science, for instance, may read books on desert plants and animals in reading groups.

The school has two science labs—one for students in prekindergarten through 2nd grade, and the other for 3rd through 5th graders. Prekindergartners might make healthy pizzas to learn about nutrition or learn about the snails or mealworms in the science room. Fourth graders do experiments to learn about why objects sink and float, and 5th graders build terrariums to learn about ecosystems and the water cycle. "It's all about students discovering as they do it," said the upper-grade science teacher.

The school does not have a gymnasium (students use the cafeteria as a gym space), but there is a gorgeous, brand-new outdoor playground, replete with a track, jungle gym, and some little gazebos.

Beginning with Children School serves grades pre-K through 8 (with the middle school two blocks away from the elementary school). It is open to children citywide. Kindergarten spots are filled by lottery, with preference given to siblings of children already enrolled in the school. There are far more applicants than seats available. Applications are accepted throughout the year. Tours are conducted in January. Call the school for tour information. The lottery is held in February.

# PS 250

**108 Montrose Avenue**
**Brooklyn, NY 11206**
**(718) 384-0889**

**Admissions:** neighborhood school
**Grade levels:** PK–5
**Enrollment:** 953
**Class size:** K: 20; 5: 34

**Reading scores:** ****
**Math scores:** ****
**Ethnicity:** 1%W 12%B 73%H 14%A
**Free lunch:** 80%

PS 250 has solid teachers, well-behaved kids, and a stellar attendance record. Most students go on to IS 318 for middle school, which in turn sends a good number of children to the city's specialized high schools. "Our students leave here with a strong work ethic and good attendance habits," says Nora Barnes, who became principal in 2003, after more than a decade as the school's assistant principal.

Fifth graders typically spend an hour to an hour-and-a-half completing their homework each night, and they leave the building well prepared for middle school. The teachers we saw were excellent, and classrooms we visited were well focused, hands-on, and productive.

But PS 250 isn't only about hard work. Teachers and administrators also care about teaching children to be kind. Barnes, a former library teacher with an easy smile and patient manner, speaks gently to children. Teachers we saw uniformly treated students with kindness, and children—who often work together in groups or pairs in their classrooms—seem to act with respect toward one another as well. "Because nice matters," reads a sign posted on the door of one of the school's pre-K classrooms.

The school's test scores are well above average for schools with similar demographics.

The school is in a working-class Hispanic neighborhood that has had an influx of artists and recent college graduates. Rents are rising, which has forced some families to move out and led to a dip in the school's enrollment. The school building is well kept and pleasant, featuring a nice auditorium, a gym, a good-sized cafeteria, an early childhood playground, and a larger schoolyard for older kids.

# PS 132: Conselyea School
### 320 Manhattan Avenue
### Brooklyn, NY 11211
### (718) 599-7301

**Admissions:** neighborhood school
**Grade levels:** PK–5
**Enrollment:** 588
**Class size:** K: 25; 5: 28

**Reading scores:** ***
**Math scores:** ****
**Ethnicity:** 27%W 11%B 56%H 6%A
**Free lunch:** 72%

Located in an area where old-time bagel shops are making way for artsy, young brunch spots, PS 132 seems poised to change with its neighborhood. Principal Beth Lubeck-Ceffalia, who took the helm in 2003 after 2 years as assistant principal, has rearranged and redecorated much of the school; she invited local artists in to paint colorful murals.

Despite the school's awkward physical layout and lack of space (the middle school is housed in a "module" connected to the main structure), the building's overall tone is inviting and pleasant. Teachers we observed were warm and competent, and students were well behaved.

The school benefits from strong leadership and is catching the interest of many community parents who once might have traveled over the Williamsburg Bridge to send their children to well-regarded elementary schools in lower Manhattan. A new "Mommy and Me" program is bringing parents of preschoolers, and even some parents-to-be, into the building, thereby helping to strengthen support for the school in the community.

Once a traditional school, PS 132 has adopted progressive teaching techniques, such as encouraging children to work in groups. A 4th-grade teacher read part of a story about snowflakes aloud to her class and then asked students to turn to one another and make predictions about what would happen next in the tale. The lesson encouraged students to work together and learn from student-to-student conversations.

PS 132 has a small group of children receiving special education services, and all special needs students are mainstreamed into regular classrooms.

# PS 29

**425 Henry Street
Brooklyn, NY 11201
(718) 330-9277
*www.ps29.com***

**Admissions:** neighborhood school
**Grade levels:** PK–5
**Enrollment:** 770
**Class size:** K: 20; 5: 31

**Reading scores:** ****
**Math scores:** ****
**Ethnicity:** 49%W 19%B 24%H 8%A
**Free lunch:** 32%

A strong neighborhood school with an unusual level of parent involvement, PS 29 increasingly is attracting neighborhood families who once might have sent their children to private school. The school has solid academics as well as good programs in music and art.

Principal Melanie Raneri Woods says her "passion is literacy," and her focus on teaching children to write well is evident throughout the school. Starting in the earliest grades, children's essays are posted on bulletin boards for all to see. Each month, a new one is added, so children and adults can observe the progress throughout the year.

The assistant principal specializes in math, and the classes we saw seemed lively. Third graders made broad jumps, then measured how far they had jumped. Science classes have lots of projects and experiments. Kids enjoy the animals in the science lab: gerbils, frogs, turtles, fish, and a 9-year-old rabbit with glaucoma.

Intermingled with the academics are seven "specialities" or enrichment classes that meet weekly, such as drama or playwriting. These bring kids together from different classes and different ages, and include children from the school's four special education classes.

Parents are active in the life of the school: They don't merely raise money, but also help out during the day, particularly at lunchtime. A stockbroker-father led a class in a stockmarket game; a lawyer helped kindergartners decorate cakes; a former Rockette gave tap-dancing lessons; and a parent who described herself as "untalented" taught kids to play Scrabble.

Parent volunteers lead "lunch clubs" in poetry, gardening, Spanish, knitting, and French, and help pay for instructors from the Brooklyn Conservatory of Music who teach a lunchtime band and string ensemble. One father, who works nights, comes to coach a 4th- and 5th-grade basketball team. (The custodian coaches an opposing team.)

Children seem to get more exercise than is typical at public schools. The physical education teacher is talented and makes the best of a smaller-than-average gym. (She also gives writing assignments to kids—a sign of how seriously the school takes writing.) The administration puts a premium on getting children outside to play at recess. On the day of our visit, it rained in the morning but stopped by lunchtime, so the principal sent the children out to play. Children go out even when there is snow in the corners of the playground. (The snowy areas are taped off, so kids can play in the rest of the yard.) The playground is unusually well supervised, and kids play with hula hoops or kick a ball between soccer goals.

The building is old, and, with old wiring, there isn't a lot of technology. The bathrooms (with toilets with hard-to-flush discs) could use a renovation. The school is large, with five to seven classes in each grade. The kindergarten classes have lots of emphasis on reading and writing, and one mother said she transferred her daughter out because the child felt she needed less academic pressure and more time to play. But most parents are enthusiastic about the school, and some like it so much they even move into the neighborhood just so their children can attend.

The school is well integrated both racially and economically. It has upper-middle-class and wealthy families as well as working-class families and those who live in housing projects. The school has a nice mix of whites, blacks, Hispanics, and Asians. New immigrants include many Arabic-speaking children from the Middle East.

The school offers self-contained special education classes, including one for children with Asperger's syndrome, a form of autism that's associated with poor social skills but high levels of intellectual ability. Children with special needs are integrated in general education wherever possible, particularly during "enrichment" periods. There are three full-day prekindergarten classes, and an after-school program one parent described as "fabulous." Tours are offered in November and January. Admission is mostly limited to children living in the zone.

# PS 58: The Carroll School
### 330 Smith Street
### Brooklyn, NY 11231
### (718) 330-9322

**Admissions:** neighborhood school
**Grade levels:** PK–5
**Enrollment:** 452
**Class size:** K: 15; 5: 26

**Reading scores:** ****
**Math scores:** ****
**Ethnicity:** 36%W 17%B 41%H 6%A
**Free lunch:** 62%

The kindergarten classrooms at PS 58 have doors that open on a small playground equipped with a red, yellow, and blue climbing gym. Parents bring their children directly from the playground into the classrooms in the morning and stay for a while to read aloud or play games with the children. The kindergarten rooms have inviting dress-up corners and toy kitchens, beds for dolls, block areas, colorful curtains, and mountains of books, just the things to make a small child feel at home.

"I'm trying to create the feeling of a large living room, where everyone is learning together," said Joyce Plush Saly, who has been principal of PS 58 since 2002. "Soft voices, lots of conversations between students, and between students and teachers. I'm a little worried when I go into a classroom and they are not talking."

With Brooklyn New School Principal Anna Allanbrook as her mentor and the Reading and Writing Project at Teachers College as a continuing source of support, Saly has created a charming neighborhood school, where neither adults nor children raise their voices, where children are happy and focused on their work and teachers have plenty of opportunities to learn from one another. Academic standards are high, and the quality of children's work is impressive. But there's also attention to developing children's social skills and carving out plenty of time for play.

The nondescript orange-brick exterior of the school is typical of 1950s school construction, but the staff has made creative use of the space inside. Round wooden tables and chairs have been placed in the widest corridors, so children or teachers can meet in twos and threes to read or work on projects together. Former locker rooms and closets have been put to use as places for teachers to work with small groups of children. One large room is set aside for art projects organized by Studio in a School, and two rooms are used as science rooms. (One is filled with terrariums the children have made.) There are three self-contained special education classrooms.

Children learn to work independently from the earliest grades. Even 1st graders can read quietly to themselves, allowing their teacher to have individual conferences. By 5th grade, children are capable of quite sophisticated research. In one 5th-grade class, children were writing research papers on topics such as Sojourner Truth's role in the women's movement and Andrew Jackson's skill as a general. Saly said the children are not expected to write a simple biography, but rather to write about how an historical figure was affected by the Civil War or had an impact on the war. "We're not looking for a regurgitation of facts, but using facts to support a larger idea," she said.

Recess comes before lunch, both to encourage children to get plenty of exercise and to give them unstructured time to make friends. An energetic physical education teacher organizes games on the large playground for older children in nice weather and continues indoor recess in the large gymnasium when it rains. The staff has managed to find ways for children to get indoor exercise on two out of three rainy days: Children take turns dancing in the cafeteria, playing games in the gym, and reading in the auditorium—a refreshing change from schools in which cartoons are shown on rainy days.

Saly's relentless, even obsessive, drive to shape the school in her vision may have alienated some long-time staff at this once traditional school, but the principal makes no apologies for easing out teachers who don't share her philosophy of education. She hired 17 teachers just 1 year, and most of the staff has been hired since her arrival.

When she sees something wrong, she won't let up until it's been fixed to her satisfaction. Disgusted by mouse droppings in a prekindergarten class soon after her arrival, Saly got after the custodian not just to keep rooms clean, but also to plug every crack and hole in the building with steel wool. It took five weekends of hard work—but it was successful.

On my visit, she interrupted a teacher reading aloud to her class, and encouraged her to pull her rocking chair closer to the children, seated on the rug, so they could see the pictures in the book better. She told another teacher she wanted to see drafts posted on the bulletin board—not just children's final work—so they could see the process that led to the final product.

Class size was unusually small at the time of our visit—and unlikely to stay that small. PS 58 once accepted many children from outside the school zone (and may again in the future), but Saly was reluctant to take variances until she knew the plans for Upper Carroll, the middle school housed in the same building. With plans in the works to move Upper Carroll to another building, PS 58 is being forced to expand both in class size and in the overall number of classrooms. Call the parent coordinator for tour dates.

# PS 261

## 314 Pacific Street
## Brooklyn, NY 11201
## (718) 330-9275

**Admissions:** neighborhood school
**Grade levels:** PK–5
**Enrollment:** 780
**Class size:** K: 20; 5: 27

**Reading scores:** ****
**Math scores:** ***
**Ethnicity:** 29%W 42%B 25%H 4%A
**Free lunch:** 52%

PS 261 Principal Judi Aronson says success in adult life depends not just on academic achievement, but also on learning to get along with different kinds of people—and her school is the perfect place to learn that.

Every possible ethnic group is represented here: Pakistanis, African-Americans, Mexicans, and even a white Rastafarian from Paris. Many children are from interracial families, so you may meet an African-American-Filipino, or a Hawaiian-Argentine, or the adopted Chinese child of a white mother. Gay and lesbian parents are welcome. PS 261's PTA is racially integrated—a rarity in New York City schools.

The school is also economically integrated. It has American-born children of architects, lawyers, artists, and new immigrants from the Middle East; prosperous families from brownstone Brooklyn; and poorer families who live in housing projects. Children come from across Brooklyn—Sheepshead Bay and Clinton Hill, Bedford-Stuyvesant and Park Slope—attracted by the small class size and the relaxed, laid-back atmosphere.

Kids call their teachers by their first names, and even the principal is called "Judi." The yellow-brick exterior with green trim may look institutional, but inside the classrooms look as homey as living rooms, with couches, chairs, and rugs on the floor. Teachers have a chance to meet regularly with one another to plan lessons. One teacher who came from a more traditional school in Manhattan said she was thrilled by the level of collaboration among the staff at PS 261.

The school has discovered many ways for children to connect with one another and even to fight the mass consumerism so prevalent in our society. One teacher encouraged children to make—not buy—holiday presents for one another, and children came up with enchanting ideas, like a purse made from old blue jeans, or a diary, or a necklace.

In most of the classes I visited, kids seemed happy and engaged. The quality of writing was good, and teachers seemed to know how to work individually with children to revise and improve their work. One 1st grader wrote:

"I went to my country house. It was great because . . ."

"Oh! You're using ellipses!" the teacher exclaimed admiringly. "What do you think you need to add to make it more interesting?"

In the upper grades, a few classes were unfocused, with slow transitions between activities. In one case, a teacher was so frustrated by her inability to get the children to be quiet that she slammed the door so loudly it could be heard down the hall.

Other concerns: Some classroom rugs could use a good vacuuming. The children complain of dirty bathrooms, and the teachers complain of mice—both common issues in New York City schools. Test scores are only average for the city.

But most of the teachers keep their children on task, and the school is a warm, cozy place with many parents who love it. "We have not had one disappointing teacher in all our years [at PS 261]," said the parent of a 6th and a 2nd grader who said she could have afforded private school. "The teaching staff is remarkable, talented, energetic, and committed to incorporating the latest thinking in education. The diversity of the families and students brings tears to your eyes, and while cooperation is never perfect between all those diverse groups, I've never seen it work as well in any other arena."

PS 261 has a strong after-school program, and a "Grandparents Day" attended not only by students' families but also by residents of a nearby nursing home. Children go to performances at the Metropolitan Opera or take part in "an intergenerational band" along with parents and teachers.

About half the students come from outside the immediate neighborhood. Open houses are held in November and March. A lottery is held in February. Kids who apply from outside the zone are requested to spend a day in the school before enrolling.

# PS 372: The Children's School

**512 Carroll Street**
**Brooklyn, NY 11215**
**(718) 624-5271**
*http://ps372.csd15.org*

**Admissions:** lottery
**Grade levels:** PK–5
**Enrollment:** 586
**Class size:** 25

**Reading scores:** * * * * *
**Math scores:** * * * * *
**Ethnicity:** 58%W 13%B 17%H 12%A
**Free lunch:** 58%

The Children's School is the city's most radical—and successful—experiment integrating disabled children with general education pupils, side-by-side, all day long, in the same classrooms. Surprisingly, it seems to work—for high achievers as well as children with multiple disabilities. The secret? Strong leadership, small ratios of grown-ups to children, and an extremely competent staff that allows children to progress at their own pace, whatever their talents and abilities.

The school has become one of the most popular in Brooklyn, not only for children with special needs but also for those with strong academic and social skills. "We've had refugees from gifted programs," one teacher said. That's because children who are extra bright are often bored even in the highest track of a traditional school. At the Children's School, children's quirks and eccentricities are not only tolerated but valued, and teachers manage to accommodate a wide range of abilities and personalities.

Every class has two teachers, at least one of whom is trained in special education. The teachers work as a team, and, like partners in a good marriage, they encourage each other, pick up the slack when one is flagging, and complement each other's strengths and weaknesses. "It's much more intense than my marriage," one teacher said of her relationship with her teaching partner. "I feel worse when I argue with her than when I argue with my husband."

If one teacher runs out of ideas—or patience—for dealing with a child, the other can step in with a fresh perspective. Having another super-qualified grown-up in the classroom not only eases the enormous physical strain of teaching in elementary school; it also eases the isolation and loneliness many teachers feel.

In some inclusion programs, the special education teacher is treated like a junior partner whose job it is to control the "bad" kids. At the

Children's School, both teachers are equal, and each works with both the disabled children and those in general education.

Each class has 25 children, 40% of whom receive special education services. Each class has at least one "paraprofessional," or teacher's aide; some have two. Some children have mild learning problems and may need only a little extra help—say, speech therapy for a lisp. Others have severe emotional or academic difficulties. Some have a mix of high intelligence and unconventional behavior. One 1st-grade girl, for example, could read college-level texts but was unable to sit on the rug at circle time. When she wandered off from the group during morning meeting, the teacher said, "Location"—a gentle reminder that brought her back to the rug. "We don't expect kids to have a cookie-cutter behavior in order to have access to an enriched program," the teacher said.

Children seem to be able to concentrate even if one of their classmates is acting oddly. The teachers are skilled at dealing with social issues and behavior problems. If, for example, one child has a temper tantrum, staffers teach other children to just walk away and wait it out. And kids seem tolerant of the occasional outburst. "They learn to ignore things, or ask another child, 'are you okay?' with a pat on the shoulder," a teacher said. Of course, the fact that there are many grown-ups in the class to deal with a child who is having a bad day means that the other children can continue their lessons without interruption. "You have so many staff people and so much attention, it's unbelievable," said a mother.

The school, housed in two buildings separated by a play yard, is clean and orderly. Classrooms are well stocked with a range of books attractively displayed. There are plenty of blocks—even in 2nd grade, an age at which most schools expect children to sit at desks and not "play." Exceptional artwork decorates the walls—created by the kids with the help of parents. Some projects integrate art, science, and social studies, such as a 10-foot cardboard model of the Brooklyn Bridge, which helped children learn about design, balance, and their neighborhood.

Many progressive schools have strong programs in reading and writing, and the Children's School is no exception. The Children's School also seems adept at teaching math and science—two areas that too often are neglected in otherwise good elementary schools. The school uses Everyday Math, a "new math" or "constructivist" curriculum developed by the University of Chicago. An unusually able 5th-grade teacher, Vicky Holland, who has a master's degree in math education, has found a way to let each child move at his or her own pace, rather than insisting on the whole-group instruction that's typical of most math classes. In the classroom, each child may be working on a different math problem. Several children may work individually on math websites on computers in the classroom—either as enrichment for advanced students or as drill for those who need extra practice. The class uses the problem-solving approaches that are typical of the new math, but also uses arithmetic drills that are common to traditional lessons.

A welcoming science room is filled with guinea pigs, turtles, lizards, snails, and plants. A terrarium mimics the ecosystem of a forest floor, and children can watch changes over time, such as the decomposition of a log. The day I visited, 3rd graders stood in small groups around tables examining owl pellets—the regurgitated, undigested parts of animals the owls had eaten—and identifying whether the animals were shrews, moles, or birds according to their bones.

"Oh, Miss Rita, we have whiskers," a child said.

"It's not really whiskers, it's teeth," said another.

"Ugh, don't remind me. Look, another set of teeth," said a third.

Teacher turnover is low, and many staffers are happy to have their own children in the school. "They were encouraged to be creative," said a teacher whose children graduated from the Children's School. "And there is no sense of competition in the sense of 'I'm smarter than you.' Even in kindergarten, they help each other out. They really build good citizens."

Arthur Mattia, formerly assistant principal of the school, took over from the founding principal, Lorraine Boyhan, in 2004, and the transition to the new administration seems to have been smooth. The school is open to children from across the district (and children who are zoned for three schools in District 13: PS 9, PS 133, and PS 282), although most kids come from surrounding neighborhoods. Open houses are January through March. Applications are accepted in January. Admission is by lottery held by the regional office, and there are far more applicants than spaces available.

# PS 321

## 180 Seventh Avenue
## Brooklyn, NY 11215
## (718) 330-9395
### *www.ps321.org*

**Admissions:** neighborhood school    **Reading scores:** * * * * *
**Grade levels:** PK–5    **Math scores:** * * * * *
**Enrollment:** 1,275    **Ethnicity:** 61%W 18%B 16%H 5%A
**Class size:** K: 20; 5: 30    **Free lunch:** 21%

PS 321 has achieved almost mythic status in Brooklyn. Many families move to the neighborhood just to get their children into PS 321, and real estate agents tout the school when they are selling houses and apartments.

It's a cheerful and academically strong school with a progressive philosophy and a politically liberal parent body. A strong principal, a fine teaching staff (many of whom have master's degrees), and an active Parent–Teacher Association (which raises more than $100,000 a year) are the keys to PS 321's success.

Many teachers, as well as the principal, Liz Phillips, live nearby and some send their own children to the school. The principal is unusually hard-working and knowledgeable about education, and is both accessible to parents and well liked and respected by the staff. "There's a sense that we're all in this together, that we all have the best interests of the kids at heart," a teacher said.

The school is large—too large, many parents say—with eight to ten classes in each grade. Built for 1,000 pupils, the school is badly overcrowded with 1,200. Some children are housed in portable classrooms on the playground. Nonetheless, the school has managed to reduce class size to 20 in kindergarten through 2nd grade. A new playground has improved the atmosphere at recess. Kindergartners have lunch in their classrooms, and 4th and 5th graders may leave school for lunch, easing some cafeteria congestion.

The school has pioneered an inclusion program that integrates students receiving special education services with those in general education. These classes, one in each grade, have two teachers, one of whom is certified to teach special education, and a part-time assistant. The school also has a few segregated, or self-contained, special education classes.

While writing and the humanities have long been the school's strength, math and science instruction have improved substantially in recent years. Phillips has appointed an assistant principal to concentrate on math and science. All students get at least one full period of math daily—more than is typical for elementary schools—and math work is displayed as prominently at writing and art projects. Children are sometimes grouped by ability for math, so able students may work on challenging projects while students who are struggling can get the help they need. The teachers appear to be competent in math, and their supervisors are clear about what they are trying to achieve.

While the school uses progressive teaching techniques for math in the classroom, homework is more likely to be traditional worksheets with which parents are more familiar. As a result, Phillips said, "parents are happier than they've ever been" and test scores have soared, particularly among children from less affluent families.

There are two science labs and three science teachers. A 1st-grade class made a life-size paper mache tree with squirrels, birds, bats, and other creatures to replicate the ecosystem of Prospect Park. Fifth graders with a strong interest in science bred fruit flies. Other 5th graders created their own robots powered by mini-computers.

Writing remains a great strength of the school. Phillips is a former faculty member of the Teachers College Reading and Writing Summer Institute at Columbia University, and PS 321 has had a 25-year history of using the Writing Process to teach children to write. Children write several drafts of each paper and continually revise their work. They "publish" their work at "celebrations" to which parents are invited.

On the first Friday of each month, parents are invited to read with their children in their classrooms. Hundreds typically come, and some stay for coffee and parent workshops in the auditorium. Parents are enthusiastic about "curriculum" workshops at which the principal explains clearly what teachers' goals are for each grade and what's going on in the classrooms.

In a 2nd-grade "writers' workshop," most children worked independently as the teacher spoke with a girl about a piece she was writing about her trip to the beach. "I see a trtl on the shore sleping," the girl wrote. Rather than correcting spelling on a first draft—that would come in later drafts—the teacher encouraged the girl to write more about the turtle she saw sleeping.

"Write what you remember. Write why your memories were so special," the teacher said gently, in a voice hardly above a whisper. "What did the turtle look like? What did the shore look like? What were the smells? Did you hear the wind blow? You heard frogs jumping! Try writing about the sounds you heard, and if you heard absolutely nothing, write about that." The girl listened intently and then went back to work while the teacher helped another child.

In early grades, academics are presented in a playful way. One 1st-grade class, for example, visited Prospect Park, then built wooden block replicas of the landmarks they had seen and labeled them: picnic house, skating rink, Grand Army Plaza. Their work combined lessons in writing (the labels), math (measuring the blocks and learning how triangles and curved arches fit together), and social studies (learning about their neighborhood).

By 5th grade, the subject matter is more complex, but the approach is similar. Children visited Gettysburg, then used toy soldiers to create a diorama re-enacting the Battle of Bull Run. Children read original documents and historical fiction about the Civil War: Abraham Lincoln's speeches, diaries of young soldiers, biographies, and a picture book about the Underground Railroad called *Follow the Drinking Gourd*.

Two tours are held, one in January and one in February.

# PS 107

## 1301 Eighth Avenue
## Brooklyn, NY 11215
## (718) 330-9340

**Admissions:** neighborhood school
**Grade levels:** PK–5
**Enrollment:** 467
**Class size:** K: 18; 5: 30

**Reading scores:** ****
**Math scores:** ****
**Ethnicity:** 38%W 12% B 44%H 6%A
**Free lunch:** 58%

Parents whose children were zoned for PS 107 once clamored for admission to the most sought-after school in the neighborhood, PS 321. But Principal Cynthia Holton has energized PS 107, test scores have increased substantially, and parents who once might have considered private school are now enrolling their children here.

"I used to beg people to come on the tour but no longer," said PTA co-president Nica Lalli. "We've gone from 10 people on a tour to 50 or 60."

Holton has made the school more open to parents, promoted collegiality and communication among the staff, and encouraged teachers to develop new teaching techniques. Taking the lead from PS 321, PS 107 offers "First Friday," inviting parents into classrooms to read to the children. Some parents are trained to work regularly in the classroom. One big advantage to PS 107: It's small so everyone knows everyone else.

The school integrates the arts and social studies. As part of the Arts Alliance program, members of Studio in the School, Lincoln Center, and Arts Connection work with faculty and students. "It used to be that old crumbly art projects were displayed in locked cases in the hallway," said one mother. "Now there is a rejuvenated curriculum for kids with arts integrated."

Hallways are bright, cheerful, and decorated with exciting artwork. The principal, trained in the Writing Process by Lucy Calkins at Teachers College, has concentrated on improving the teaching of writing, and examples of children's work show she has succeeded.

As the sense of community has grown, parents have begun to work to help the whole school, and not just their own child's class. A 1st-grade parent runs a book club for 5th graders called the "Remarkable Readers Club." Children read such sophisticated books as *Twelve Angry Men* in the morning before school.

Tours are held December through March.

# PS 39

**417 Sixth Avenue**
**Brooklyn, NY 11215**
**(718) 330-9310**
*www.ps39.org*

**Admissions:** neighborhood school
**Grade levels:** PK–5
**Enrollment:** 379
**Class size:** K: 19; 5: 31

**Reading scores:** ***
**Math scores:** ****
**Ethnicity:** 25%W 31%B 36%H 8%A
**Free lunch:** 69%

With 20 or fewer children in kindergarten through 3rd grade and fewer than 400 children in the building, PS 39 is a cozy school where children and teachers get to know one another well. It's a school with a lot of hugs: kids hug one other, their teachers, and visiting parents. It has a nice racial balance, with roughly equal numbers of whites, blacks and Latinos as well as a sprinkling of Asians, and an economic mix of middle-class and poor children.

The school has two full-day prekindergarten classes with their own entrances and doors leading onto a nice playground. Parents may bring children right into the classrooms. On one of our visits, prekindergartners made their own peanut butter, cracking open peanuts and putting them in a blender with oil.

A 19th-century building with a brick exterior and an elegant mansard roof, PS 39 has a peculiar interior that resembles a railroad flat. Tiny classrooms are connected to one another without any hallways. It's a bit awkward, but parents say the unusual layout just adds to the sense of intimacy in the school. PS 39 offers "a high quality education in a small, secure, loving environment," one parent said. Some nice extras: a strong chess team (that competed in a national chess championship in Nashville one year) and a dance curriculum. In recent years, PS 39 has had room for children from outside the zone. There are monthly tours from November to March.

# PS 10

## 411 Seventh Avenue
## Brooklyn, NY 11215
## (718) 965-1190
## *http://ps10.csd15.org*

**Admissions:** neighborhood school
**Grade levels:** PK–5
**Enrollment:** 600
**Class size:** PK: 18; 5: 28

**Reading scores:** * * *
**Math scores:** * * *
**Ethnicity:** 17%W 7%B 70%H 6%A
**Free lunch:** 84%

PS 10 is located in a rapidly changing area of Brooklyn, on a block where the neighborhoods of Windsor Terrace, Greenwood Heights, and South Park Slope converge. As the affluent neighborhood of Park Slope creeps farther and farther south, boutiques and cafes are springing up on the blocks around the school. The school is changing as well, thanks to an energetic administration led by Principal Concetta Ritorto, who took the helm in September 2003 and who formerly taught at nearby PS 321 in Park Slope, one of Brooklyn's most sought-after schools.

PS 10 is bright and cheerful, student work adorns the walls, and the school's test scores are on the rise. Teachers are excited about a new "kindergarten academy for the talented," for zoned students who have been screened for talent in art, music, or writing.

"In this school, the only word I can use is 'Renaissance,'" said the school's parent coordinator, Madeline Seide. Samantha, a 5th grader who was acting as one of our student guides, agreed. "There's a lot more creativity on the walls now," she said. Mitra, our other 5th-grade student guide, said he particularly liked the technology program at the school. His class wrote poems about the Civil War, and then incorporated them into a slide show.

The school has a particularly strong special education program—something students, teachers, and administrators stress with pride. There are several self-contained special education classes, as well as a growing inclusion program, in which students with special education needs share their classroom with general education students. PS 10 is housed in a barrier-free building. "Typical kids are friends with kids in wheelchairs," said the parent coordinator, who is herself the parent of a child with a disability. "Tolerance levels are high." PS 10 is a zoned, neighborhood school, though some students are admitted from outside the zone.

# PS 146: Brooklyn New School
## 610 Henry Street
## Brooklyn, NY 11231
## (718) 923-4750

**Admissions:** Region 8 preference
**Grade levels:** PK–5
**Enrollment:** 500
**Class size:** K: 25; 5: 28

**Reading scores:** ****
**Math scores:** ****
**Ethnicity:** 35%W 36%B 21%H 8%A
**Free lunch:** 36%

Brooklyn New School, an alternative school founded by parents and teachers in 1987, has become one of the most successful and sought-after in Brooklyn. The quality of teaching is consistently good, the leadership is strong, and the curriculum is creative and fun.

There are no chalkboards, desks, or textbooks. Instead, there are comfortable couches, tables and chairs, and fun-to-read picture books. Students call teachers by first names. On any given day, you may find half the school away on trips: to museums, Jamaica Bay National Wildlife Refuge, Prospect Park Wildlife Center, or even an overnight camping excursion.

The writing program is particularly strong. Children write in different genres: poetry, short stories, news features about sports events, and persuasive essays. They are expected to write several drafts, revising and improving their work repeatedly before they "publish" it—prepare a final copy to share with others. The teachers inspire children to write for pleasure, and some children write far more—and with greater depth and understanding—than is typical for children their age. A 3rd grader wrote several "novels" of three single-spaced typed pages. In one class, students wrote essays about such profound topics as "Why do you die?" and "Why are there bad people?"

The staff manages to challenge children of different abilities while finding a common ground within a class. Children choose their own books for independent reading, so, for example, one 3rd grader may be reading a sophisticated text such as *The Lord of the Rings* while a classmate reads an easier book from the *Magic Tree House* series. In addition, the teacher chooses a text for the whole class to read together—a prize-winning work of children's literature with lots of pictures. The shared book is easy enough for the weak readers to understand, but has literary qualities that the more advanced students can appreciate when, for example, children analyze the way an author develops a book's plot and characters.

Science and social studies are taught with fun projects—not textbooks. A 3rd-grade class studying Native Americans made wigwams from sticks and Indian dolls from cornhusks. They wrote essays on "A Day in the Life of a Lenape Indian," made artwork in the style of Native Americans, and presented a computer project on their study of an Indian tribe. Children built a wigwam next to an historical house in Prospect Park.

Children dissect animals such as mice or tarantulas in science class and take frequent nature and hiking trips. One class used the nearby Gowanus Canal as a laboratory to study water quality. They even built an impressive historical model of the canal in their classroom. The school organizes regular overnight trips to an environmental center in the Poconos, where students study Native Americans and take ecological hikes. The administration has been successful in applying for grants from private foundations to pay for extras, and the PTA is aggressive about fund-raising as well.

There is a well-regarded, after-school program, with classes in music, dance, theater, and sports.

The school uses the TERC math curriculum, which teaches children to create their own solutions to problems rather than simply plugging in a formula given to them by the teacher. Some parents have complained that the math curriculum doesn't challenge bright kids, particularly in the upper grades, and that all children need more emphasis on basic skills. In response to these concerns, teachers have begun incorporating other math programs into their lessons. Many teachers use Math in the City to supplement. "Where we find a gap [in TERC] we figure out what we can bring in," he said.

There is one special education class and one collaborative team teaching class. The special education teacher came from District 15's Children's School, which has been lauded as a model for the successful integration of children with special needs into a general education environment. One of the innovations she brought with her is the use of FM units—mini microphones which help the teacher get the attention of a class without raising her voice. It has been so successful that the principal has given the units to teachers in other classes where students seem to have trouble focusing or making the transition from one task to another.

The school has flourished under the leadership of Anna Allanbrook, a long-time teacher as the school who was named principal in 2000. The Brooklyn School for Collaborative Studies (BCS), a middle school that is an extension of Brooklyn New School, opened in 2001 with Alyce Barr, a long-time Brooklyn New School teacher, as director. In 2005, BCS added a 9th grade as well, in the first step towards becoming a 6–12 school. Brooklyn New School admits according to a lottery held in March. Open houses begin in December.

# PS 154

**1625 11th Avenue**
**Brooklyn, NY 11215**
**(718) 330-9333**
*www.ps154.org*

**Admissions:** neighborhood school/magnet
**Grade levels:** PK–5
**Enrollment:** 400
**Class size:** PK: 18; 4: 25

**Reading scores:** ****
**Math scores:** ****
**Ethnicity:** 55%W 8%B 29%H 8%A
**Free lunch:** 40%

A welcoming mosaic, made by parents and children, hangs in the entryway to PS 154. On the first Friday of every month, parents come into the classrooms and read aloud to the children. Then the grown-ups go downstairs to drink coffee, eat donuts, and catch up on news with one another. At lunchtime, the cafeteria staff makes homemade meals such as stew and noodles—not the microwaved lunches sent from a central kitchen typical at most city schools. Parents and children may join in evening events such as a "family dance" on a Friday night.

These are things that give PS 154, housed in a three-story, red-brick building constructed in 1907, a homey feel in a neighborhood that's mostly Irish-American, Italian-American, and Hispanic, with many working-class families and lots of stay-at-home moms. As the neighborhood has become more gentrified, PS 154 has begun to attract professional families as well.

Just two blocks from Prospect Park, PS 154 takes advantage of its location: First graders interviewed the maintenance manager of Prospect Park ("Why do you chop down trees?") and the zookeeper ("How do you keep the animals clean?") A magnet grant has allowed the school to have a formal collaboration with the Brooklyn Museum as well as the zoo and the Botanic Garden.

Principal Richard Goldstein was assistant principal at PS 321 for many years and has recruited some PS 321 teachers as his senior staff. Small class size means everyone gets attention; the small size of the school overall gives children a sense of community and belonging. The classes in the lower grades are enchanting, and the upper grades are getting stronger.

There is room for children from outside the zone. The school has open houses from December to March. Anyone in the region may apply through the magnet grant. Applications are due in March.

# PS 130: Parkside School
## 70 Ocean Parkway
## Brooklyn, NY 11218
## (718) 686-1940

**Admissions:** neighborhood school
**Grade levels:** PK–5
**Enrollment:** 542
**Class size:** K–2: 20; 5: 31

**Reading scores:** ****
**Math scores:** ****
**Ethnicity:** 17%W 23%B 35%H 25%A
**Free lunch:** 95%

PS 130 exudes warmth. "From the principal to the office staff, they go out of their way to help and guide, and seem to always wear a smile," a parent said. Parents are welcome, and on the morning of our visit one parent was reading to a small group of boys in a hallway.

More than two thirds of the students at PS 130 speak a second language at home, including Spanish, Cantonese, Haitian Creole, Urdu, and Bengali. The administration works hard to teach children how to resolve conflicts peacefully. We saw a tile mosaic that children from India and Pakistan had created together. Afterwards, they were able to discuss the tension they had felt working with kids from the other country.

Instruction seemed uniformly strong for both high-achieving students and those who need extra help. In a 3rd-grade class, the subject was China, and research topics included the Great Wall, communism, and the Chinese school system. Fifth graders read aloud essays on a variety of challenging topics—libraries, subway- and bus-fare hikes, smoking, and the death penalty.

The school is committed to integrating the arts with academic instruction. Hallways display handsome quilts made of squares created by each class. Photographs in the hall feature "Character Day," when children and staff dressed up as literary characters. Students put on a puppet show, with scenes created from real life.

The 105-year-old building shows its age in some ways, but it also is nicely maintained. There is no gym. After-school programs include theater, chess, photography, knitting, softball, and basketball.

# PS 295: The Studio School of Arts & Culture

### 330 18th Street
### Brooklyn, NY 11215
### (718) 330-2230

**Admissions:** neighborhood school    **Reading scores:** ∗∗∗
**Grade levels:** PK–5    **Math scores:** ∗∗∗
**Enrollment:** 367    **Ethnicity:** 25%W 8%B 61%H 6%A
**Class size:** K: 24; 5: 15    **Free lunch:** 74%

PS 295 was founded in 1995 at the urging of a group of parents who wanted a small, informal school where parents are always welcome and the arts are integrated into the curriculum. The school attracts an eclectic mix of families, including recent immigrants from Central America and the Middle East who live in Sunset Park and artists, dancers, and actors from Fort Greene and Park Slope.

The nonprofit organization Arts Connection brings music, visual arts, and dance to the school. Every class has dance at least once a week, taught by a full-time teacher. Children learn dance notation—a dance alphabet—and learn to "read" dance—just as children who learn musical notation learn to read music.

Children play "bingo" with symbols of dance notation instead of letters or numbers. (Winners then dance the dance represented by the symbols.) Children follow the method developed by Hungarian-born Rudolf Laban, one of the founders of modern dance and the inventor of the most widely used system of dance notation.

Principal Nora Polansky heads up a great staff. Frequent field trips—to the American Museum of Natural History, the post office, and the food co-op—help bridge the gap between the children of new immigrants and more prosperous families, by giving them shared experiences. Parents and children attend Family Nights at the the Brooklyn Museum of Art.

Parents frequently help in the classroom. For example, in one class a parent who is a lawyer discussed law once a week and arranged a trip to a courtroom. An actor-father taught theater.

PS 295 has inclusion classes to integrate students receiving special education services with general education pupils. These classes, also called collaborative team teaching, or CTT, have two teachers, one of whom is certified in special education.

There is generally room for as many as 30 children from outside the small zone. Tours are held October through April.

# PS 172: The Magnet School
# for Leadership in the 21st Century

### 825 Fourth Avenue
### Brooklyn, NY 11232
### (718) 965-4200

**Admissions:** neighborhood school, magnet
**Grade levels:** PK–5          **Reading scores:** ****
**Enrollment:** 563          **Math scores:** *****
**Class size:** K: 23; 5: 30          **Ethnicity:** 15%W 2%B 80%H 3%A
                                      **Free lunch:** 98%

PS 172 is one of the top-scoring schools in the district—a great achievement considering that 98% of the pupils are poor enough to qualify for free lunch and about 80% of the parents are non-English-speaking immigrants from Mexico, Ecuador, and Poland, many of whom work long hours in restaurants and factories. Teachers from across the country visit PS 172, seeking to emulate it.

What's the key to success? A coherent reading and writing program in which children learn to work independently while their teacher works individually with a classmate. Teachers, using techniques from the Teachers College Reading and Writing Project, hold conferences with each child two to three times a week, helping them find appropriate books to read and showing them how to edit and revise their written work.

Principal G. J. Spatola does not believe in gifted programs and there is no "top" class in any grade. But all students are challenged because the work is adapted to each child's interests and ability, he says. In a 4th-grade class, for example, some children read books from the Babysitters Club series and the Harry Potter series, while a girl who was a recent immigrant from Mexico read the picture book *A Pocket for Corduroy* in Spanish. Using yellow Post-it notes, she wrote down elements of the plot in Spanish.

The school integrates art into the curriculum. Fourth graders studying the Iroquois tribe made Native American weavings in art classes. Fifth graders studying Asia made Japanese-inspired fans, and Chinese calligraphies. Mayan artifacts, made by the students out of clay, were displayed alongside essays about the "Mayan Mystery," exploring why the Mayan people disappeared.

The school has an eclectic approach to math. Even within a classroom, some children might be doing sums using "ball-park estimates" and rounding up to the nearest 10 with pencil and paper, while other children may be using plastic cubes and rods (manipulatives) to find the same answer. There are as many math projects and graphs posted on the hall bulletin boards as there are reading and writing projects. One project was to find the range, mode, and average number and color of M&M chocolates in a bag.

There is an attractive, well-equipped science lab in the school, with a "question box" in which children place their queries on topics that interest them. Each week, the science teacher selects one and the children research the answer. A sample question: "Why do birds have beaks instead of mouths?"

There is an extensive after-school program, offering both remedial help in academics and recreation. The school received a magnet grant designed to encourage racial integration by attracting more white students. As part of the magnet theme of "leadership," 4th and 5th graders have internships with local politicians.

The building is quiet and orderly. Classrooms are a bit cramped, and the cafeteria does double duty as a gym. Parents trained as "Learning Leaders" help out in the classroom.

One mother praised the "very caring and compassionate" teachers who care for the children "just as if they were at home." Another complained that the principal is "too strict." For example, children may go outside to play at lunchtime, but are not allowed to run on the playground because of the principal's fears that they may get hurt.

Tours are held from February through May. Parents are welcome to arrange visits at others times as well. There are some openings for children from outside the neighborhood. Apply in March.

# PS 230

## 1 Albemarle Road
## Brooklyn, NY 11218
## (718) 437-6135

**Admissions:** neighborhood school/gifted program
**Grade levels:** PK–5      **Reading scores:** ****
**Enrollment:** 1,070      **Math scores:** ****
**Class size:** K: 20; 5: 28      **Ethnicity:** 23%W 3%B 32%H 42%A
     **Free lunch:** 66%

PS 230 is a huge, orderly school that serves a largely immigrant population, including many Bengali students and children from Yemen, China, and Eastern Europe. A gifted program, with two classes of 25 or fewer children in each grade, attracts students from across District 15.

The school has two buildings: a new, cheerful, and brightly lit annex for children in prekindergarten through 1st grade and a clean but older main building for children in 2nd through 5th grades. Unfortunately, there is no outdoor playspace for the lower-school students.

Classrooms and hallways display a lot of student writing. Many lessons revolve around research and nonfiction reading: Students might prepare a PowerPoint presentation on famous explorers as part of a social studies lesson, or learn about Aztec masks in art class.

On one visit, 3rd graders in the gifted class worked on double-digit multiplication, while 5th graders read and watched a stage production of Shakespeare's *Othello*. One class made a 19th-century "time line" marked with "The War for No Good Reason" (the War of 1812), "Ellis Island," and "Yellow Journalism," as well as the dates of inventions such as toilet paper and potato chips.

Parents are encouraged to participate in the school. On one visit, a parent volunteer was meeting with her "book club" in a hallway. The students were sitting Indian style, or lounging on their bellies, fully engaged in the discussion. "This is my second book club!" one student announced. "It's my third!" another offered.

The school has partnerships with the Mark Morris Dance Company and Art Works. There is a full-time dance teacher and a music teacher.

Students apply for the gifted program through the Region 8 office. Open houses are held in January.

# PS 21

### 180 Chauncey Street
### Brooklyn, NY 11233
### (718) 493-9681

**Admissions:** neighborhood school    **Reading scores:** \*\*\*\*
**Grade levels:** PK–5                 **Math scores:** \*\*\*
**Enrollment:** 750                    **Ethnicity:** 0%W 93%B 6%H 1%A
**Class size:** K: 20; 5: 28           **Free lunch:** 78%

Children like PS 21 so much they come back after they've graduated to work with younger children at the school's Saturday and after-school programs. The school is a community institution, an orderly, cheerful, and relaxed place with a clear sense of common purpose. The principal's high expectations translate into a consistently high level of achievement for the school's pupils, despite the fact that most of their families are poor enough to qualify for free lunch.

"This school has a long-standing culture of excellence and rigor," says Principal Harold Anderson, who grew up across the street from the school and is himself a graduate. "Our main goal is to create productive members of society. Well-respected individuals."

Indeed, many of the lessons we observed encouraged students to think about the world around them. In one class, for example, 1st graders Tiasia and Yasmine were writing poems about Martin Luther King, Jr. Tiasia wrote:

*Peace is like a smile.*
*Peace is like sunshine.*

When asked what they have learned about Dr. King, Yasmine offers: "That he was an outstanding citizen. And he died in 1968." Then, she adds, "When my baby brother gets to be 4, I'm going to teach him about Dr. Martin Luther King."

Much of the school's philosophy aims to foster this kind of tight relationship between home and school, and to teach students that learning doesn't end at the end of the school day. The school operates on the idea that parent involvement and empowerment are key to student performance and to the school's success. "We have a culture of excellence and rigor, and much of that is based on the parents," says Anderson, who has a warm, competent manner and who himself seems a fatherly figure to many of the school's students. "Our parents

192

are the number one educators of the children. We're just helping them. We inform and educate parents and, in turn, parents buy into our rules and our culture." That means accepting the school's dress code and homework policy and recognizing the necessity to participate in the school's Saturday, after-school, and early morning programs when children need extra help.

The school's tone and philosophy are traditional. Girls wear burgundy plaid jumpers. Boys wear gray trousers, white shirts, and burgundy plaid ties. Children concentrate on basic skills and test preparation. They learn to read from basal readers and textbooks, and have frequent drills in phonics. Still, while the school was deemed successful enough to receive a waiver from the new, progressive math and reading methods that were introduced citywide in 2003, PS 21 nevertheless is incorporating some of the more progressive teaching methods, particularly the "workshop model" method, in which lessons combine whole-class lessons, groupwork, and independent work. "We still do a lot of direct instruction," says Anderson. "But now we're doing group mini-lessons." Teachers increasingly are incorporating children's literature into lessons, in addition to basal readers.

Teachers accompany children to the lunchroom and eat with them. Children are taught to be polite and respectful. ("Our students are so well behaved we get compliments all the time," said one teacher, who takes her students on frequent field trips.) The school has no gifted program. The principal believes that children learn best in classes with mixed abilities. PS 21 is a neighborhood school, and children from outside the zone are not eligible for admission.

# PS 308

### 616 Quincy Street
### Brooklyn, NY 11221
### (718) 574-2372

**Admissions:** neighborhood school/selective program
**Grade levels:** PK–8
**Enrollment:** 1,013
**Class size:** K: 25; 8: 30

**Reading scores:** ***
**Math scores:** ***
**Ethnicity:** 0%W 92%B 5%H 3%A
**Free lunch:** 96%

PS 308 has a solid reputation for preparing students in this African-American community for Brooklyn Technical High School and other selective high schools. Many times each day, children hear that they are the "best of the brightest" who will create a "village of gifted people." The school attracts children from as far away the Bronx, and one child even came from Queens—in a special van adapted for his wheelchair.

The principal, Dr. Gail Bell-Baptiste, is an imposing woman who's not afraid to ease out staffers—or out-of-district children—who don't meet her high standards. "If she can make you strong, she will. If not, she'll get rid of you," said a mother who was so impressed with the school that she drove her son from Floral Park, Queens, each day—an hour away.

Parents say the principal is affectionate and playful as well as tough. Many children greet her with a hug, and she has been known to jump "double dutch" in the interior playground just outside her office. Her office, filled with knickknacks, dolls, and statuettes, is a magnet for small children. Parents praise the "structure" and solid education and say the school is welcoming. Good behavior is expected—and demanded. Hallways are orderly. Children seem happy.

For years, PS 308 was a school reserved for gifted children. Any child in the neighborhood could attend in kindergarten and 1st grade, but those whose test scores weren't high enough were asked to leave at the end of 1st grade. Children from outside the zone are still tested for admission to the gifted classes. All classes are grouped by ability.

"All children in the school are gifted—some academically, others in chorus or band," said the principal. "If you put kids in this atmosphere, 9 times out of 10 they'll do well."

Every student in the upper grades is required to read the *New York Times* each day, and students have thoughtful discussions about the front-page news. Eighth graders typically complete 9th-grade math and accelerated courses in Spanish, English, and social studies—and receive Regents or high school credit. The school has a very skilled chess team. One year, seven students qualified for the national championships in Missouri. The school has a steel band that performs for community events. The school offers "talent periods" on Friday afternoon in which children can learn to sew, knit, cook, or "put together computers and take them apart again," the principal said. Most students wear uniforms.

The building is overcrowded and has an awkward layout around a central courtyard. Classrooms, many with old-fashioned cloakrooms, have odd nooks and crannies in which students may work independently. Kindergartens and many 1st grades share huge rooms with makeshift room dividers as partitions. Prekindergarten classes are housed in nearby day care centers.

A neighborhood school, PS 308 also admits children from outside the zone in grades 1–6 who pass an entrance exam given in the spring. A tour is offered in January, when applications are available.

# PS 161

### 330 Crown Street
### Brooklyn, NY 11225
### (718) 756-3100

**Admissions:** neighborhood school     **Reading scores:** ★★★★
**Grade levels:** K–8                                 **Math scores:** ★★★★
**Enrollment:** 1,220                               **Ethnicity:** 1%W 90%B 7%H 2%A
**Class size:** K: 29; 5: 34                        **Free lunch:** 83%

PS 161 is a traditional school that combines old-fashioned values and a sense of decorum with a well-regarded reading program that encourages children to love literature.

This overcrowded school consistently has the highest test scores in the district and is highly sought-after by parents in the know. Although the school doesn't officially accept anyone from outside the neighborhood, it's an open secret that some parents fudge their addresses to enroll their children.

Students wear blue plaid uniforms with yellow blouses or shirts. Principal Deborah Barrett, wearing a blue and white uniform and smart school blazer herself, greets students and parents as they come in every morning, admonishing students who aren't properly attired. Children are quiet, but not silent, as they move through the halls.

"It's orderly, but the children don't feel as though they are in prison," said a mother active in the PTA. "It's not just sitting and listening all day." Small children might act out the story of Winnie-the-Pooh stuck in Rabbit's hole, while older children might debate a topic in the news.

Teachers say the secret to the school's success is successful test preparation combined with a coherent reading program that is consistent from grade to grade. Children have plenty of drill in phonics and also read classics of children's literature such as *Charlotte's Web* and *The Lion, the Witch, and the Wardrobe*. The school gives children practice tests. Those who score just below the state standard on the practice tests get extra one-on-one tutoring from teachers or parent volunteers. It's a form of triage, to be sure, because it gives extra help to children on the low side of average rather than those who are really struggling, but it has the effect of bringing the school's overall scores up.

Three reading teachers opened a bookstore in the school with the intent of "flooding the neighborhood with books." Paperbacks are sold at cost—$1 apiece. Children who staff the bookstore and write book reviews in a school newsletter are "paid" in bookstore script that can be used to buy books. "We wanted to get books into the hands of children," said teacher Diane Yules. "We can help them learn to read but if they don't get books of their own they won't become readers."

The school has a bright, pleasant library. The principal invites kindergartners and 1st graders to come to her office to read to her. Older children submit book reports to the principal. Student teachers from a nearby yeshiva visit to learn techniques for teaching reading.

PS 161 is a school that emphasizes the basics, and there aren't many "extras." One parent complained that the atmosphere is "all work and no play," that the children are "overloaded" with homework, and that the school would benefit from more art programs. But even given these criticisms, this parent called PS 161 a "jewel in the community."

PS 161 has a tiny, selective middle school. For details, see *New York City's Best Public Middle Schools* or *www.insideschools.org*.

There is a long waiting list of children wishing to attend PS 161. Large classes mean there isn't a lot of individual attention. Still, parents are satisfied. "Parents and teachers work together," a mother said. "There's a lot of teaching of morals and values. And there's a lot of love in that school."

# PS 235: Lenox School
### 525 Lenox Road
### Brooklyn, NY 11203
### (718) 773-4869

**Admissions:** neighborhood school/gifted program
**Grade levels:** PK–8          **Reading scores:** ★★★★
**Enrollment:** 1,543          **Math scores:** ★★★★
**Class size:** K: 23; 5: 30    **Ethnicity:** 1%W 95%B 3%H 1%A
                                 **Free lunch:** 70%

PS 235 is a gigantic neighborhood school with a large gifted program that attracts children from all over Brooklyn and even from other boroughs. Parents who work at nearby Kings County Hospital commute with their children; others pay for a private bus. Despite its unwieldy size, PS 235 has a long history of excellence and its reading scores place it among the top 15% of city elementary schools. It is one of the 209 schools that the chancellor exempted from the standard curriculum in 2003.

The tone of the school is traditional, reflecting, in part, the values of parents who attended formal schools in the British tradition in the West Indies. Children wear uniforms: blue plaid jumpers for girls, plaid neckties for boys. They are expected to be silent during morning line-up as they wait for their teachers.

Classics such as *The Wind in the Willows* and Shakespeare's *Julius Caesar* are on the reading lists. Many teachers have been trained in the Writing Process. Science is taught with hands-on experiments, and the math curriculum teaches children to think logically—not merely to add and subtract.

The school places an emphasis on dance and visual arts, and has an after-school program that offers homework help as well as lessons in violin and African dance. Dancers and artists from Jacques D'Amboise's National Dance Institute are at the school 5 days a week and a group of children from PS 235 win scholarships to study with NDI in Manhattan every Saturday for a year.

PS 235 occupies three buildings, each more than a mile from the others. The main building—large and old but adequately maintained—houses general education children in prekindergarten through 5th grade, as well as gifted classes for prekindergarten and grades 3–5. (The outside yard space also is filled with portable classrooms.) The annex, several miles away, is a bright and cheerful "Early Childhood

Center" shared with PS 135. Children in PS 235's gifted program attend this annex from kindergarten through 2nd grade.

The third building houses the Lenox Academy, a selective middle school for grades 6, 7, and 8, also administered by the principal of PS 235, Janice Knight. There is no apparent logic to putting one principal in charge of these three far-flung buildings, and traveling among the sites is an obvious strain.

PS 235 has suffered somewhat from the flight of the black middle-class from East Flatbush to the suburbs in recent years. Increasingly, the school is made up of children of the working poor—parents who value education but who may work several jobs and not have much time to help with homework or to volunteer at the school.

Even so, the school has an active PTA. Many parents accompany their children to the library on weekends and manage to find time to volunteer as tutors and to chaperone class trips. One father who worked nights even volunteered during the day as a school security guard.

A few concerns: Some parents say the homework load is "overwhelming." The cafeteria and playground could be better supervised. A few parents complain of discipline issues and say they notice a difference in the behavior of students in the gifted program, called SOAR, and those in general education classes. There are sometimes fights in the hallways and in the cafeteria. But parents also praise the principal and parent coordinator for being "accessible" and say the teaching is "excellent." One mother said: "The focus is on working hard. Good work is kind of contagious."

Tests for the SOAR program are given between January and May. There are no open houses.

# PS 7
## 858 Jamaica Avenue
## Brooklyn, NY 11208
## (718) 647-3600

**Admissions:** neighborhood school    **Reading scores:** * * *
**Grade levels:** PK-4                 **Math scores:** * * * *
**Enrollment:** 977                    **Ethnicity:** 1%W 15%B 69%H 14%A
**Class size:** K: 20; 4: 30           **Free lunch:** 91%

As the train rounded the bend on the elevated tracks of the J line, we caught our first glimpse of PS 7. The school's clean façade, adorned with a brick mosaic of children jumping rope, stands out among the crowded, run-down buildings in its East New York neighborhood, adjacent to the el-tracks and across the street from a cemetery.

Erected in the late 1990s, the contemporary building boasts central air conditioning, elevators (used only by staff and physically challenged students), bathrooms in many of the classrooms, a dental clinic, a gym, a spacious library, a science lab, and an auditorium equipped with stadium seating. The school has a calm, nurturing environment, with much attention not only to the core curriculum, but also to little extras that soften the edge of a long day of learning and keep administrators in touch with classroom activities. Many of the classrooms have curtains and comfortable couches.

All students are encouraged to write letters to the principal about books they read, with the promise of a written reply. All along the well-lit corridors, bulletin boards show evidence of an impressive level of student writing. In 1999, barely 25% of the students tested met state standards for reading. By 2004, that number had jumped to 46%. The school's attention to math has also paid off. In 2004, 68% of 4th graders performed at or above grade level on the statewide math exam, a 15-percentage-point jump in results from the previous year's results and particularly impressive considering that 92% of the students are poor enough to qualify for free lunch. Some children from District 75, the district for severely disabled children, are integrated into regular classes. Admission is limited to children living in the zone, except for special education pupils.

# PS 89: Cypress Hills Community School

350 Linwood Street
Brooklyn, NY 11208
(718) 277-5044
*www.cypresshills.org*

**Admissions:** citywide
**Grade levels:** K–8
**Enrollment:** 260
**Class size:** 18–23

**Reading scores:** ***
**Math scores:** ***
**Ethnicity:** 0%W 27%B 72%H 1%A
**Free lunch:** 85%

PS 89 opened in 1997 with the help of the Manhattan education group, New Visions for Public Schools, as an alternative to the low-performing schools in District 19. Founded by parents in collaboration with Cypress Hills Local Development Corp., a community housing program, the school offers an unusual level of parent involvement, including visits to parents at home by staff, offering guidance and listening to parents' concerns and suggestions.

The dual-language school is designed to make both Spanish speakers and English speakers fluent in both languages. Ninety percent of the staff is bilingual in Spanish and English, and students learn all subjects in both languages in alternating 5-day cycles. Classrooms are equally divided into Spanish and English, with student work, grammar lessons, textbooks, and class libraries in both languages.

An open, supportive, and caring atmosphere flows throughout the school. Teachers lead one another in workshops, new ideas are welcomed, and students quickly help one another. Both children and staff pause for moments of laughter, yet everyone remains focused. Students learn through class discussions and reasoning, not lectures and memorization. One 3rd-grade math teacher sat on the floor with his students, teaching addition and multiplication by pulling a rubber band across plastic prongs creating different shapes. *"Dos por dos. Que figuro es?"* asked the teacher. *"Es un cuadro,"* said one student. They continued to create larger and larger squares and calculated the difference between the sizes.

The school accepts students from all five boroughs. Preference is given to Cypress HIlls and East New York residents.

# PS 185

**8601 Ridge Boulevard**
**Brooklyn, NY 11209**
**(718) 745-6615**

**Admissions:** neighborhood school/gifted program
**Grade levels:** K–5                    **Reading scores:** * * * * *
**Enrollment:** 760                      **Math scores:** * * * * *
**Class size:** K: 20; 5: 30             **Ethnicity:** 74%W 1%B 10%H 15%A
                                         **Free lunch:** 34%

PS 185 is a traditional school with strong art programs and a gifted program that accepts students from across the district. The school's test scores put it among the top elementary schools in the city. The old building has a brick façade and two symmetrical stairways —covered with children's artwork—in the entrance hall leading up to the office. A new science room and computer room have made the school more up-to-date.

The administration has long prided itself on the strict, controlled atmosphere and its high expectations. All classes participate in music—kindergartners and 1st graders learn the violin, 3rd graders play the recorder; others learn music history or sing in a chorus. Art and social studies are integrated. Children studying Asia, for example, created screens inspired by Japanese art and made origami kimonos. Older children wrote a poem using Chinese characters, and younger ones learned to write words such as "bird," "sky," "mountain," "man," and "water" in Chinese. Fifth graders performed *Anna and the King of Siam.*

Science classes "adopted" plots in the Amazon rain forest in conjunction with the Nature Conservancy. Parents volunteer in all classes, tutor in reading and math after school, help out at breakfast, and lead a folk dancing class. The school is overcrowded, with more than 700 children in a building designed for 500.

"It's a wonderful place with a lot of spirit," said a mother, adding that graduates frequently are accepted in the art specialty at the selective Mark Twain Middle School because of their strong training at PS 185.

Children may apply to be tested for the school's gifted, or Delta, program in January.

# PS 229

## 1400 Benson Avenue
## Brooklyn, NY 11228
## (718) 236-5447
### *http://schools.nycenet.edu/Region7/ps229*

**Admissions:** neighborhood school/gifted program
**Grade levels:** K–5      **Reading scores:** \* \* \* \* \*
**Enrollment:** 536      **Math scores:** \* \* \* \* \*
**Class size:** K: 22; 5: 32      **Ethnicity:** 56%W 1%B 8%H 35%A
     **Free lunch:** 38%

PS 229 is a small neighborhood school with a consistently strong and creative teaching staff, parents who are always ready to help out, and an administration that has created an *esprit de corps* among the staff. The test scores are among the highest in the city. The Delta, or gifted, program accepts a few children from outside the zone.

"The principal is the epitome of what a supervisor should be," a mother said. "The teachers are wonderful. My children love their school, their teachers, and their friends. What more can a mother ask for?"

This is a school where just about everyone does well—not just the high-achieving children, but also those who don't learn as easily. "Kids who come in with difficulties don't fall through the cracks here," said Principal James Harrigan. "I'm most proud of the fact that we're able to get the average and below-average child to succeed."

Art and music are integrated into the curriculum. For example, when 4th graders study slavery and the Civil War, they also learn hymns and freedom songs sung by the slaves. The school has an orchestra and band open to all 3rd, 4th, and 5th graders, and about half the children in these grades play an instrument.

One chronic problem is overcrowding, and there are plans to build an extension. However, many staff and parents fear the school would lose its cohesive feel if it became larger.

The school has an unusually active PTA, and mothers volunteer regularly in the classrooms, particularly in the lower grades. The Brooklyn Chinese-American Association offers an after-school program. Most of the children live in the neighborhood, and a few even go home for lunch.

Admission to the gifted program, called Delta, is based on a test administered by the district office.

# PS 247

**7000 21st Avenue
Brooklyn, NY 11204
(718) 236-4205**
*http://schools.nycenet.edu/Region7/ps247*

**Admissions:** neighborhood school
**Grade levels:** PK–5
**Enrollment:** 665
**Class size:** K: 22; 5: 28

**Reading scores:** * * * *
**Math scores:** * * * *
**Ethnicity:** 52%W 0%B 10%H 38%A
**Free lunch:** 72%

PS 247 combines the newest technology with old-fashioned fun. It's a happy, happening place where children hone their research skills on wireless laptop computers and compose music in a "music technology lab" made up of 16 computers, 16 Casio keyboards, and 32 headsets.

Some plugged-in 5th graders were "listening to the beat" while others were identifying which musical instrument was playing. Children study music theory, composing techniques, improvisation, instruments of the orchestra, and basic ear training. Teaching artists from the New York Philharmonic work with children to compose their own music, then at the end of the year students get to hear musicians actually play their compositions in a concert at Avery Fisher Hall.

Students continue to perform music the old-fashioned way as well. There is an after-school band and some students played recorders at Carnegie Hall. All kids have classes in movement and drama at least once a week, important in a school with no real gym or outdoor yard to speak of.

We saw kids using laptop computers in many classrooms. On the 100th school day, for example, kids found facts about what was happening 100 years ago. Some of their findings: Stamps cost 2 cents then and 37 cents now; Teddy Roosevelt was president then, George W. Bush now.

Principal Kathy LeDonni said small class size in the lower grades allows teachers to give individual attention and to challenge both high-achieving children and those who are struggling. Rather than take kids who need help learning English or who are struggling with academics out of the classroom for extra help, she brings extra teachers into the classroom. Children wear white or blue shirts with khaki or navy blue trousers or skirts. Some children come in from outside the neighborhood for prekindergarten and usually are allowed to stay if they wish to.

# PS 104: Fort Hamilton School
## 9115 5th Avenue
## Brooklyn, NY 11209
## (718) 836-4630
### *http://schools.nycenet.edu/Region7/ps104*

**Admissions:** neighborhood school/magnet
**Grade levels:** K–8  **Reading scores:** ****
**Enrollment:** 1,229  **Math scores:** ****
**Class size:** K: 20; 8: 27  **Ethnicity:** 61%W 2%B 19%H 18%A
 **Free lunch:** 52%

Even though it serves more than 1,200 students from kindergarten to 8th grade, PS/IS 104 still manages to feel cozy. The modern exterior is undistinguished, but a large stained-glass window casts a warm light inside. The school has two programs to attract children from outside the neighborhood: a gifted and talented program for high-achieving kids, and a magnet program, launched in 2005, for any child who is interested in the school's new theme of "Museum Studies."

Kids seem to get excited about learning. First graders, awaiting assignment to the classroom library or other activity "centers," cheered on receiving their marching orders. Throughout the school, students were attentive; the only bored kids we saw were those prepping for standardized tests.

This is a place where kids learn respect for others. In a music class we visited, students, not the teacher, shushed those who chatted when classmates performed the recorder. District 75, which handles special education, integrates children with multiple disabilities into regular classes with assistance from paraprofessionals.

Principal Marie DiBella, who has been at the school since 1989, operates a well-oiled machine and has a knack for making the most of her teachers' abilities. A gym teacher who studied in Spain doubles as the Spanish teacher. A math teacher offers classes in how to use photo and presentation software. Unfortunately, the school grapples with overcrowding. Kindergarten classes, unable to fit into the main school, take place in a district building three blocks away.

Applications for the Delta and magnet programs are available through the regional office. Call the school for tour dates.

# PS 204: Vince Lombardi School
## 8101 15th Avenue
## Brooklyn, NY 11228
## (718) 236-2906

**Admissions:** neighborhood school/gifted program
**Grade levels:** PK–5                    **Reading scores:** ★★★★
**Enrollment:** 1,023                     **Math scores:** ★★★★
**Class size:** K–2: 20; 5: 30            **Ethnicity:** 58%W 2%B 10%H 30%A
                                          **Free lunch:** 54%

From the office staff to administration, teachers, and parents, PS 204 exudes friendliness, retaining the feel of a small neighborhood school even with a population of more than 1,000 students. A new building addition opened in 2000, but because more students keep enrolling, PS 204 is stretched for space and no corner is unused.

The school houses a gifted program for kids from throughout the district and attracts many high-achieving students. But struggling kids get equal attention. In two impressive inclusion or collaborative team-teaching classes, general education students and kids receiving special education services worked together in the same classroom, overseen by two teachers who clearly wanted to be there.

The school has such an inclusive feel that a small program there for hearing-impaired kids chose to stay put even when it was offered bigger digs elsewhere. It is telling that students in this program participate in the life of PS 204: At assemblies, recognizing that deaf children cannot hear applause, all the children wave their hands in the air instead of clapping.

Classrooms are lively and attractive, and many have child-size rocking chairs and comfy beanbag chairs where kids settle in and read. Staff members meet at lunch to do their own professional development, and kids with good attendance dine with Principal Marie Reilly at special breakfasts. Parents raise money for everything from mundane items like vacuum cleaners to fun extras, such as a carnival for 5th graders. We saw moms working in and out of the classroom and helping out at lunchtime.

# PS 177

## 346 Avenue P
## Brooklyn, NY 11204
## (718) 375-9506

**Admissions:** neighborhood school
**Grade levels:** PK–5
**Enrollment:** 874
**Class size:** K: 25; 5: 30

**Reading scores:** ****
**Math scores:** ****
**Ethnicity:** 42%W 1%B 22%H 35%A
**Free lunch:** 73%

PS 177 is an unusually clean, spacious, and well-run school that more than meets the challenge of educating its many foreign-born students from Asia, Russia, and Mexico. Teachers from across the district visit PS 177 regularly to get ideas about the latest teaching techniques. Staffers constantly refine their skills and act as mentors to colleagues from neighboring schools.

You won't hear grown-ups raise their voices here—even in the cafeteria. The administration has created an atmosphere of collegiality and mutual respect that encourages teachers to do more than is required of them.

Pupils read several books by the same author and then use those texts to study other subject matter. For example, 1st graders read Eric Carle's *The Grouchy Ladybug* and linked it to a science study of insects. They used *The Very Hungry Caterpillar* as part of a lesson in counting and arithmetic. Later, in computer class, they created digital pictures of leaves and ladybugs.

The school has had considerable success in teaching those with learning problems and helping new immigrants learn English. There is one self-contained special education class and two collaborative team-teaching classes, in which two teachers lead a class comprising general education pupils and those with special needs. In addition, there is a small "literacy class" for 4th graders who need extra help.

There is a good relationship between parents and staff. Parents volunteer in the library, take part in parent–child workshops, and attend classes in English as a Second Language. On "Author Day," parents visit the school to hear children read aloud from their written work.

# PS 139

## 330 Rugby Road
## Brooklyn, NY 11226
## (718) 282-5254

**Admissions:** neighborhood school/gifted program
**Grade levels:** PK–5          **Reading scores:** ***
**Enrollment:** 1,100          **Math scores:** ***
**Class size:** K: 25; 5: 30   **Ethnicity:** 9%W 47%B 28%H 16%A
                               **Free lunch:** 83%

PS 139 is the site of an ambitious plan to break up a large building into intimate and manageable mini-schools and programs, each with its own personality and dedicated space. The plan has been so successful that PS 139 increasingly has become the school of choice for parents in the know—including teachers themselves. Test scores are on the rise, parents are enthusiastic, and the staff is energized.

"I would put my child in any one of these classrooms," said Principal Mary McDonald. The school is popular with families both inside and outside of Ditmas Park, a polyglot neighborhood of grand houses and modest apartments southeast of Prospect Park.

PS 139 has a drab exterior, but inside a giant aquarium dominates the lobby, along with bright, student-made paintings and murals. Walls are lined with writing projects and materials from math contests. The hallways are calm and clean. Even though PS 139 houses 1,100 pupils in a building designed to hold 900, the building doesn't feel terribly overcrowded because it has been divided into six smaller and manageable "mini-schools" and programs, each with its own turf within the building.

In one mini-school, the New Visions Flatbush Academy, children study the history of the neighborhood, its environment, and its many cultures. In another mini-school, the Brotherhood Institute, students explore different continents and learn to appreciate global diversity.

The Eagle, or gifted, program, for which kids are tested by the region, offers an accelerated and enriched curriculum. Kids are expected to do work that's at least one grade level ahead of their peers.

In the inclusion or collaborative team-teaching program, two teachers are assigned to each classroom. This program integrates children receiving special education services with their peers. Parents appreciate the rich student–teacher ratio, effectively half that of regular classes.

The fifth program in the building, the general education program, offers progressive teaching techniques, and children read from a wide range of literature and nonfiction rather than textbooks. And children whose first language isn't English—about 40% of the student body, with family ties to Pakistan, India, Mexico, the Middle East, Central Europe, and the Caribbean—often spend their early years in the sixth program with classes in English as a Second Language.

All of PS 139's students have science instruction once or twice a week and are exposed to art, music, and dance through the school's full-time art and music teachers, and partnerships with groups like the Brooklyn Academy of Music, the Brooklyn Philharmonic, and the youth drama group TADA!

With class sizes ranging from under 25 in kindergarten to 30 or more in the upper grades, classrooms feel a little crowded. Supplies are stretched tight—chipped desks, battered bookcases, weary carpets—but the children are engaged, active, and eager to participate. More than 20 students in the 4th-grade inclusion class volunteered when their teacher asked, "Who's brave enough to read this poem out loud?" And in a 1st-grade, mini-school classroom, students earnestly praised their classmate's "beautiful spaces and excellent word formation." Older students mentor their younger peers; 3rd graders typically help kindergartners with reading—but, teachers say, want their own playtime with the little kids' toys and games!

Although most of the children are poor enough to qualify for free lunch, the school has some professional families as well. Doctors, chemists, film producers, and lawyers—not to mention teachers—have chosen PS 139.

Parents say they are attracted by the creative curriculum, which is more progressive than in other District 22 schools; by the ultra-accessible administration; and by the atmosphere in which every child—from the newest immigrant struggling with English to the highest-achieving pupil—is treated with respect.

Parents are welcome in the classroom. They also organize after-school sports, participate in hiring new teachers, run bake sales and book fairs, and write grants to fund new programs. A middle school fair draws more than 200 parents of 5th graders.

The mini-schools and the Eagle program are most in demand. Siblings of current mini-school students and PS 139's two, half-day prekindergarten classes have mini-school priority, leaving up to 15 places open for new students, including families who live outside the school's zone. Mini-school students are chosen by lottery. Eagle applicants should contact the region for application and testing guidelines. School tours take place from February through June.

# PS 193

## 2515 Avenue L
## Brooklyn, NY 11210
## (718) 338-9011

**Admissions:** neighborhood school/gifted program
**Grade levels:** PK–5      **Reading scores:** ****
**Enrollment:** 895         **Math scores:** ****
**Class size:** K: 19; 5: 31    **Ethnicity:** 21%W 52%B 14%H 13%A
                            **Free lunch:** 67%

PS 193 is a large neighborhood school that houses a small, highly-selective, district-wide gifted program designed to give elementary school pupils academic challenges that most children don't have until middle school. Many kindergartners enter the program, called the Center for the Intellectually Gifted, or CIG, already knowing how to read and quickly progress to "chapter" books, while 5th graders read the *Odyssey* and study the Pythagorean theorem.

CIG (pronounced like the first syllable of cigar) is more selective than the Eagle programs in District 22's neighborhood schools. While PS 193 mostly serves black and Hispanic children from poor families, about 55% of the 130 children in the CIG program are white, and most come from middle-class families. They are more likely to work in groups or on independent projects and the approach is more progressive than in the rest of the school. Reading is taught with a mixture of textbooks and children's literature.

In one CIG class, a group of kids were sprawled on the floor looking at maps as part of a study of World War II, several others were checking out encyclopedia entries, while still others were writing imaginary letters to characters in books they were reading.

One mother said the program provided a rich, well-rounded education, while another called it "competitive" with a great deal of "pressure to perform." "They need to be taught skills about collaboration," the second mother said.

The school also houses an honors or Eagle program for children who score well on tests, but not as well as those in the CIG program. The Eagle kindergarten program is also very academic. Children practice reading and writing in the morning and complete math workbooks and phonics exercises in the afternoon.

There was a happy buzz in a 5th-grade Eagle class the day we visited. Children were sewing or stuffing pillowcases they had made featuring painted self-portraits and written descriptions of themselves. Others were reading *Julie of the Wolves,* a coming-of-age story about an Eskimo girl who runs away from home and is lost in the Alaskan tundra.

Children are grouped by ability. The "bottom" classes have fewer children, but also more discipline problems. The day of our visit, a bottom class of 5th graders was reading *Beezus and Ramona,* by Beverly Cleary—a book commonly read by somewhat younger children. The teacher, standing at the front of the class, was hard-pressed to keep the pupils interested and engaged. In another class of low-performers, children were struggling with a simple multiplication problem on the chalkboard.

Principal Frank Cimino says he stresses good citizenship as well as reading, writing, and arithmetic. The entry of the school has a "Hall of Respect" posting children's good deeds—everyday acts of kindness such as opening a door for a teacher or finding a dollar lost by a classmate. "We teach them: Be respectful, and be nice," Cimino said.

PS 193 is located in Midwood, a neighborhood that's increasingly Orthodox Jewish. Since most Orthodox Jewish families send their children to private religious schools, there is some room for children from outside the zone. Apply between March and May. Admission to the CIG and Eagle programs is based on a test given by the regional office. Children are tested in the spring and summer before kindergarten. Children also may enter the program in later years, up to 5th grade. Call the gifted coordinator at (718) 968-6100 for information. There are no open houses or tours for prospective parents.

# PS 195

## 131 Irwin Street
## Brooklyn, NY 11235
## (718) 648-9102

**Admissions:** neighborhood school/gifted program
**Grade levels:** PK–5                    **Reading scores:** * * * * *
**Enrollment:** 400                       **Math scores:** * * * * *
**Class size:** K: 25; 5: 34              **Ethnicity:** 85%W 7%B 6%H 2%A
                                          **Free lunch:** 23%

Housed in a charming building topped by a cupola in a well-to-do neighborhood overlooking Sheepshead Bay, PS 195 feels like a school in a small town. There's an *esprit de corps* among the teachers, and everyone in the school knows what's going on with every child. Test scores are consistently among the highest in the city.

PS 195 is strong in the visual and performing arts. Each class puts on a play, such as *Twelfth Night, A Midsummer's Night Dream, Lion King,* or a musical version of Maurice Sendak's *Really Rosie.* The children put on choral and band concerts

Classes are orderly and transitions from one activity to another are quiet. Classes with the best behavior in line receive American flags as incentives, and photographs of the child named "citizen of the month" are displayed prominently outside the principal's office. The child chosen from each class gets to read announcements over the loudspeaker.

Principal Arthur Forman says there are more class discussions and fewer teachers directing lessons from the front of the class than there were a few years ago. "We're teaching children not to give rote answers. We're teaching them how to think," he said.

The school emphasizes social as well as academic development, he said, offering, for example, ballroom dancing for 4th and 5th grades. "Children should learn how to relate to each other."

Children identified as gifted and talented are selected for the district's Eagle program. Kids of different ages sometimes are placed in the same class and stay with the same teacher for several years. They have a great degree of independence and usually work well above their grade level under the tutelage of fine teachers. A neighborhood school, PS 195 offers seats for the purpose of integration to a few children from Flatbush.

# WORTH WATCHING: BROOKLYN

Here are some Brooklyn schools that show promise for the future, as well as nice neighborhood schools that serve their students well—even if they don't attract a lot of attention outside their communities.

## Clinton Hill

**PS 56**, 170 Gates Avenue, Brooklyn, NY 11238, (718) 834-6900, part of District 13, is a well-run school in a gentrifying neighborhood. Test scores, still below average, have been inching up steadily. The school offers classes in dance, visual arts, band, and keyboard. Some art teachers start their day later so that the programs extend into the after-school hours. Children dress in uniforms of white tops and blue bottoms. Principal Deborah Clark-Johnson, a former biology teacher, is particularly proud of the fully stocked science lab, where, on the day of our visit, two gigantic gerbils were chomping away at huge carrots, a rabbit chewed contently in its cage, and a snake slithered from underneath its shelter to greet a visitor. There was even a tarantula, and a red-eared fiesta turtle was sunning himself on a rock in the terrarium. Each animal's habitat had a corresponding book, such as *Runaway Bunny* atop the bunny cage. PS 56 plays host to a weekly food co-op in "Le Cafe" (what the school affectionately dubs its cafeteria), which brings in neighborhood residents—many of them new to this quickly gentrifying corner of Brooklyn. Little by little, they'll no doubt begin to bring their children to the school as well.

## Bedford-Stuyvesant

An elementary school that encourages innovative teaching and student leadership, **PS 44: Marcus Garvey School**, 432 Monroe Street, Brooklyn, NY 11221, (718) 834-6939, helps many students meet its high expectations despite considerable obstacles. Many children in this District 13 school are poor, and parent involvement is limited, yet Principal Deborah Knight and her staff effectively use the progressive teaching methods that some skeptics deem inappropriate for low-income students. Housed in a 3-story brick building erected in 1951, the school has a somewhat gloomy interior that is brightened by bulletin boards with pictures of "animals we've been" in drama class or essays about "why rappers misspell words." Chalk pastels showing Henry Hudson's stormy sea voyage are accompanied by journals written by students as if they were sailors on the ship. On the day we toured, students in a 5th-grade class invited visitors to tour their writing "museum," in which their papers were grouped by theme on various tables, and Post-its were provided for guests' comments. All grades get some music, art, drama, or technology instruction in quarterly cycles.

# Williamsburg

Located in the heart of Williamsburg's old Puerto Rican neighborhood, which has become home to increasing numbers of Mexican and Dominican families, **PS 257**, 60 Cook Street, Brooklyn, NY 11206, (718) 384-7128, serves many children from the Williamsburg Houses, a mass of nearby housing projects. The school is a joyful place, where teachers seem happy to teach and kids are encouraged to treat one another with respect. "If I meet these kids in 20 years, I want to know that they are going to be nice people," says Brian Leavy DeVale, who became principal in 2002 and is popular among kids and teachers alike. Plus, he says, "School has to be fun!" Kids did, indeed, seem to be enjoying themselves at PS 257 when we visited a few days before Halloween. Classes were taking turns picking pumpkins from a small patch that teachers had set up in the schoolyard. "I want to hear you say, 'Hidey ho!'" bellowed DeVale to the students. "Hidey ho!" they shouted back eagerly. Teachers we met seemed unusually kind. On the day of our visit, the school's art teacher was tutoring a boy in math during the teacher's lunch period, and we heard several teachers complimenting students—and one another—as they passed by in the hallways. The school offers Spanish–English bilingual classes and has extensive special education services.

**PS 196: Ten Eyck School**, 207 Bushwick Avenue, Brooklyn, NY 11206, (718) 497-0139, sits on the edge of trendy Williamsburg, a neighborhood to which young professionals have been flocking in recent years. The school, part of District 14, has felt the reverberations of this Brooklyn-bound migration: Enrollment has shrunk by 200 students since 1999, as skyrocketing rents have forced many families to move. A number of the school's students live in Williamsburg Houses, a cluster of low-slung public housing complexes visible from the school's front entrance. There's a friendly atmosphere in the building, and most of the teachers, administrators, and kids seem happy. On the day of our visit, a handful of parents had gathered informally in the PTA room, saying they always felt welcome at the school. Classrooms are well decorated and bright, while colorful student work hangs in the hallways. We did hear one teacher yelling at a child, and one teacher said her class was hard to manage, but most of the teachers seemed solid and caring, and in most classrooms students were hard at work.

## Sunset Park

**The Magnet School for Early Childhood** in Sunset Park, at 411 46th Street, Brooklyn, NY 11220, (718) 330-9298, serves only children in prekindergarten—but it serves them unusually well. Open to children from across District 15, the school welcomes parent involvement and shapes its curriculum around children's interests and discoveries.

## Park Slope

"This school is a secret, it really is," says Karen Lane, a school librarian at **PS 124: Silas Dutcher School**, 515 4th Avenue, Brooklyn, NY 11215, (718) 330-9320. Located a few blocks from the Gowanus Canal, the school sits on 4th Avenue, a buzzing thoroughfare that is changing—a new restaurant here, a renovated building there—as Park Slope's middle-class residents move farther and farther south. Somehow, the school has remained under the radar of many parents, despite its pleasant atmosphere, solid teachers, well-stocked classrooms, and class sizes as small as 16. Classrooms have rugs, round tables, and plenty of books. Many teachers we observed seemed skilled at teaching math, a rarity in elementary schools. In several classrooms, students were using manipulatives—blocks and number cutouts—to learn how to add, subtract, multiply, or divide. In a 5th-grade classroom, two girls eagerly explained their assignment—they were learning about "arrays" by rolling dice, multiplying the resulting numbers, and graphing the results. Most of the students at PS 124 come from immigrant families, and a good number come from Spanish-speaking homes. The outdoor play space is small, and there is no jungle gym.

## Flatbush

Worth watching is **PS 249**, 18 Marlborough Road, Brooklyn, NY 11226, (718) 282-8828, a high-poverty school with nearly 900 children in grades K–3. Although test scores are below average, the administration has put in place a number of promising programs that may help boost achievement in coming years. Parents and "grandparent" volunteers (easily spotted in bright-red Department of Aging jackets) read to the children. Every Friday is devoted to hands-on science instruction. "When they leave on Fridays, they leave with a project, something they made, and in a calm, happy tone," says Principal Elisa

Brown. Children learn a second language through the Spanish–English dual-language program. The school has rich art, drama and African dance programs. The school serves mostly black and Hispanic children, 86% of whom are poor enough to qualify for free lunch. In recent years, PS 249, part of District 17, has had some seats available for children from outside the zone.

## Canarsie

A PK–8 school open to pupils zoned for overcrowded schools in District 18, **PS/IS 66**, 845 East 96th Street, Brooklyn, NY 11236, (718) 922-3505, treats all children as if they were in gifted classes. Teachers encourage independent thinking and an understanding of the "whys" of what they teach. Principal Joel Rubenfeld, who headed gifted programs for the district before the school opened in 2003, sometimes pops impromptu quizzes on students in the lunchroom. Students' emotional development also is nurtured. There are monthly award assemblies highlighting students not just for academic achievements, but for attendance and "random acts of kindness." Monthly, one student is chosen for the Principal's Club and becomes principal for a day. The student council meets with the principal monthly to propose and plan school activities such as a winter dance. The new building sprawls over a large lot that includes basketball and tennis courts as well as two playgrounds and a garden. The trade-off for space is the location—next to a heavy industrial area, bordered by heavily trafficked Rockaway Parkway. Because the school is new, Rubenfeld was able to handpick teachers and mold them to his philosophy of instruction. But the youth of the school also means that PS/IS 66 has many inexperienced instructors, 9 first-year teachers in 2004 alone. The dynamic parent coordinator, M. Anthony Baker, is of West Indian origin, as are most of the families at the school. A PTA president at PS 276 and a teacher in his home country of Jamaica, Baker shows up on students' home doorsteps when he cannot reach their parents on the phone.

## Ocean Hill-Brownsville

District 23, long a low-performing district in Ocean Hill-Brownsville, made some progress under the strong leadership of Kathleen Cashin, who was superintendent of the district for several years before being named superintendent of the new Region 5 in 2003. As regional superintendent, she is in charge of schools in District 23, District 27 in Queens, as well as District 19 in the East New York section of Brooklyn, where there seem to be flickers of hope in what have been some dismal schools.

**PS 137**, 121 Saratoga Avenue, Brooklyn, NY 11233, (718) 453-2926, is a disciplined, structured school whose teaching is based on the philosophy of E. D. Hirsch, the author of a series of books that argue that children need a solid, specific shared curriculum he calls "core knowledge." The school has a cheerful entryway painted taxicab yellow, contrasting with bright-blue tile floors. Teachers take pride in students' original writing, which is posted on clotheslines strung across the classrooms. No fill-in-the-blank worksheets are allowed here. The principal asks teachers to write substantive comments and not just scribble "good" on children's work. A jazz musician teaches music. Class size ranges from 18 to 28 and some classes have two teachers. In 1999, only 22% of the children tested met or exceeded state standards for reading. By 2004, that number had jumped to 49%. More than 95% of the school's 470 students qualify for free lunch.

## East New York

**PS 190**, 590 Sheffield Avenue, Brooklyn, NY 11207, (718) 346-8780, is so well regarded that children travel from outside District 19 to attend. Students are focused, productive, engaged, organized, and well behaved. Teachers work hard, often coming in on Saturdays or staying until late in the evening. The building is open until 7:30 p.m. during the week, and students may attend a "Saturday Academy" from 8:30 a.m. to 12:30 p.m. (which includes breakfast and lunch). Test scores, while still low, have improved dramatically in recent years, and the chancellor named PS 190 as one of the most improved schools in 2003. In 1999, only 13% of children tested met state standards for reading. By 2004, that number had jumped to 37%. That's a great achievement considering that 10% of PS 190 students live in homeless shelters, many parents lack a high school education, and abused children bring behavioral problems into the school.

Every month, 1st graders get a new theme to work into their studies. When we visited, the topic was bears, and the animals were integrated into all kinds of activities. Children counted bears, compared and contrasted grizzly bears with black bears, and made brown paper lunch-bag puppet bears. Teachers use plenty of phonics to help teach reading. In a 3rd-grade class, children sat on a carpet and enthusiastically said new rhyming words: "Sport, port short; Dirt, flirt, shirt, squirt." Fourth graders copied homophones from the board: "new, knew." A talented steel band practices during lunch, creating music that feels like you're on a sunny Caribbean beach. Parents receive free GED courses and are invited to attend workshops on such topics as stress management and parent–child communication. The school sponsors a father–child basketball day and family barbeques.

## Bushwick

Most the schools in District 32 have long had a dismal record of academic achievement. But **PS 384**, 242 Cooper Street, Brooklyn, NY 11207, (718) 574-0382, has high expectations for students, a strong sense of community, and test scores that have increased substantially in recent years—even though nearly every child is poor enough to qualify for free lunch and many are new immigrants learning English. In 1999, only 19% of children tested met state standards for reading and writing. By 2004, that number had increased to 48%. Students are engaged, polite, interested, and eager to share what they have learned. The school has several teaching fellows, second-career professionals in a program to become teachers, and they appear secure and effective in their classrooms, a contrast to the many city schools where teaching fellows quickly become overwhelmed because of lack of guidance and support. PS 384 has successfully tackled a problem facing a number of schools with large immigrant populations: disruption in the education of students when their parents pull them out of school for extended trips to their native countries. After her first year at the school in 2002, Principal Brunhilda Ortiz called in the parents and had a heart-to-heart with them about the impact of these absences on a child's education; the problem, we were told, diminished dramatically.

## Bay Ridge

The overall quality of schools in District 20, serving Bay Ridge, Bensonhurst, Fort Hamilton, and Borough Park, is very high, and we didn't have room to include entries for all the noteworthy neighborhood schools in this district. Check out *www.insideschools.org* for profiles of schools not listed here

**PS 69**, 63-02 9th Avenue Brooklyn, NY 11219, (718) 833-6710, has a new building filled with color, light, and interesting nooks and crannies. Opened in 2002 to ease overcrowding in three nearby schools, PS 69 is already overpopulated, and some of the oddly shaped classrooms seem small for the number of kids they house. Every room has sturdy tables and chairs where kids work together, but often the children are sprawled out on rugs, or sitting on comfy cushioned chairs. We saw math lessons taking place on the rugs, and kids frequently work either in the inviting atriums on every floor or just outside their classrooms. A 2nd grader, on her hands and knees in one of the sunny atrium spaces, was so happily engaged in her rainforest project that she didn't stop to talk to us. Art is woven into the curriculum. The school has hired a dynamic full-time artist as an art teacher and her room is equipped with a kiln and heaps of supplies. A kindergarten art gallery hangs in a corridor leading to an inviting outdoor playground, and the young children created "Rainbow Street in Brooklyn," complete with painted cardboard houses. We also saw 3rd graders making paper butterflies during a math lesson about symmetry.

The spotless assembly hall—with a hardwood floor—housed a ballroom dancing class, where 4th graders were learning to rumba. So enticing was the music wafting into the hallways that the principal tried out a few steps. The school was also the city's first to be equipped with a wireless computer system, and students are allowed to take laptop computers home for homework and research projects. The school, which borders on Brooklyn's growing Chinatown, has many students who are new immigrants.

**PS 102,** 211 72nd Street, Brooklyn, NY 11209, (718) 748-7404, is a large neighborhood school with a friendly atmosphere and a strong school spirit. It has a traditional tone: Children start the day by reciting *The Pledge of Allegiance* and singing *The Star Spangled Banner*. They wear white shirts and red ties on assembly days. But the school also has integrated the latest technology into the curriculum. Kids videotape their own assemblies and class plays. They use computers and digital cameras to publish their own school newspaper and yearbook. The school has a full-time art teacher. It has a large special education program. Classes for the vision-impaired have computers with extra-large letters on the keyboards and giant fonts on the screens. Long a Norwegian, Italian, and Irish neighborhood, Bay Ridge has become multiethnic in recent years. Children at PS 102 come from more than 50 nations. English-speaking parents say their children learn tolerance and respect for other cultures when, for example, a classmate fasts for Ramadan. "PS 102 is a large school and I thought my son would get lost," said a mother who transferred her child from a small private school. "But he has excelled in PS 102." The school has a gifted, or Delta, program for high-achieving children. Children are tested in January for admission to the gifted program.

At **PS 170**, 7109 6th Avenue Brooklyn, NY 11209, (718) 748-0333, teachers are encouraged to try new things, the school arts calendar is crammed with trips and events, and parents (as well as community members and retired people) drop by to tutor students, share books, or learn English. Although PS 170 qualifies for federal Title I funding, which goes to schools with large numbers of low-income students, its cultural programs and computer equipment rival those of more affluent schools, thanks to effective fund-raising and grant writing. The school's forward-thinking philosophy contrasts with the old-fashioned 5-story brick building, constructed in 1915, in which it is housed. The building is clean and freshly painted but overcrowded, so four classes are housed in trailers, and noise can rise to a din in the cramped lunchroom, half of which doubles as a gym. Still, class sizes are relatively small, children in upper grades fall silent and read during the last 10 minutes of lunch periods, and students track their cumulative exercise in the little gym on a map, imagining that they're jogging across America. The linoleum flooring is dreary, but imaginative student work and photos of school events brighten rooms and hallways. Each grade has one honors class, often slightly larger than other classes. There are two inclusion classes, in which special education and general education students learn side-by-side and are taught by two teachers. Three teachers of English as a Second Language serve the school's large number of immigrants, including children from China, Mexico, and Egypt. An enterprising parent coordinator, Maria Freedman, teaches English to a large group of parents.

## Fort Hamilton

**PS 105**, 1031 59th Street Brooklyn, NY 11219, (718) 438-3230, has more than 1,200 pupils, most of whom are of Chinese descent, many of them recent immigrants just beginning to learn English. We saw kindergartners, brows furrowed, intent on writing full sentences in their journals. In a bilingual class, a creative teacher engaged children with a cup of frozen water brought in from outside so they could feel the ice and learn to describe the sensations. "Cold!" they shouted. Many teachers are multilingual, but instruction is strictly in English in regular classes and mostly in English in the bilingual Chinese classes. The preferred choice for conversation among students remains Chinese.

In addition to art and music, students can take dance, including ballroom dancing. The school also offers a Gifted Learners of Bilingual Education (GLOBE) program, originally intended as accelerated classes for newcomers with limited English proficiency. Now the program offers enrichment in the Chinese language for all gifted students in the 1st through 5th grades. PS 105, part of District 20, helps kids stay connected to their native culture. Students begin celebrating Chinese New Year a week early with performances featuring a fusion of traditional song and dance, moral tales, and American arts, such as tap dancing. We saw rehearsals in the hallways before an assembly, and the rest of the day kids hummed their show tunes in class.

# Dyker Heights

Another nice school in District 20 is **PS 112**, 7115 15th Avenue, Brooklyn, NY 11228, (718) 232-0685, where the whole staff feels part of one community. The teachers carefully plan out each month's curriculum together and observe one another in action. The janitors are always on hand to make sure the floors shine, and the security guard welcomes visitors with a smile. Student projects about other cultures, families, and life-styles are proudly exhibited on tables that line the halls. One wall displayed written and visual responses to Roni Schotter's *Nothing Ever Happens on 90th Street*, the school's most recent "book of the month," an activity in which all students participate. It comes as no surprise that the children do well on city and state standardized exams. In the classrooms, the children can be found reading independently at their desks or sitting on a rug with journals in their laps. Everything is taught from a whiteboard on an easel amid the children on the carpet. According to Principal Louise Verdemare Alfano, "The kids are more focused with rug instruction." Indeed, excited little hands waved to volunteer sharing the beginnings of their fictional stories, or to give examples of how diseases are transmitted. The children could benefit from a bigger school building. Two 1st-grade classes are held in a trailer outside the school, and the auditorium has been modified into a multipurpose room of sorts with removable chairs. Two corners of the room have been cut away by a divider and designated for art classes. The class in session during our visit was busy creating "wycinanki" designs, a form of Polish folk art. For music, 1st graders can take violin classes, 2nd and 3rd graders study recorder, and older students can take chorus or band.

# Borough Park

**PS 192**, 4715 18th Avenue, Brooklyn, NY 11204, (718) 633-3061, a friendly school in the heart of the Orthodox Jewish community of Borough Park, has a rooftop garden filled with plants, tables, chairs, and benches that provides an oasis for children to read, to garden, and to work on art projects. The school's immaculate hallways are decorated with student artwork. The school, part of District 20, has many new immigrants from Pakistan, Egypt, Bangladesh, Russia, Mexico, and the Dominican Republic. "It's a small school and the teachers are all very caring," said a parent active in the PTA. The school was one of the first in the city to offer disabled children an inclusion program for special education—extra help that they need to stay in general education classes. The hallmark of the school is collaborative team teaching, in which two teachers work together in a class that combines general education children and those receiving special education services. The school also has a number of self-contained classes for students in special education. The special education program is successful, in large part because the staff is so committed to making it work. "We're not two separate programs," said Principal Basya Weinstein, the former special education supervisor. "We're one family." Children wear blue and white uniforms, and both boys and girls wear neckties. Parents are required to sign a "discipline policy."

**PS 176: Ovington School**, 1225 Bay Ridge Avenue, Brooklyn, NY 11219, (718) 236-7755, is a huge neighborhood school on the border between Borough Park and Dyker Heights. Teachers do not all use the same techniques: We saw one 5th-grade teacher giving a phonics lesson; in another 5th-grade class, a teacher seated in a rocking chair read aloud from Roald Dahl's *The Witches* to kids seated on the rug or at tables. In a kindergarten class, some kids were practicing handwriting, while the teacher supervised a few others making a "stone soup." First graders, many of them immigrants themselves, were able to describe pilgrims who came to America for the first Thanksgiving. The building is wheelchair accessible, and kids in wheelchairs sit at desks specially tailored to them. A child using a walker happily moved from one colored circle to the next during physical education in a makeshift gym that turns into a cafeteria at lunchtime. Trophies proudly displayed in the principal's office were earned by kids in physical education programs adapted to their needs. The school's population in this traditionally Italian neighborhood is becoming increasingly Asian. There are bilingual classes in all the lower grades. A sign at the school entrance is translated into Chinese, Spanish, Russian, Arabic, and English.

PS 176 is one of several District 20 elementary schools that have a gifted program, known as Delta. Children apply for its kindergarten classes in December and are tested in the winter. We saw especially creative projects in those classrooms: First graders decorated boxes with paper doll images of themselves, wrote about their favorite things, made family crests, and used the box to hold items they wanted to share with the class. Fifth graders were holding a mock trial, complete with plaintiff, defendant, and judge. Although there is a dress code—navy blue bottoms and yellow, light blue, or white tops—it is only loosely adhered to.

## Bensonhurst

**PS 48,** 6015 18th Avenue, Brooklyn, NY 11204, (718) 232-3873, in Bensonhurst is a school with many high-achieving students, but one where struggling children also get attention. Many of its students are recently arrived immigrants—most from Asia but also Latin America and the Middle East—who need English language instruction. PS 48, part of District 20, quickly moves them into the mainstream, and many test well in math even before mastering English. The fourth floor of this five-story building, erected in 1913, once had a large gym. It now houses "resource rooms," offices where students get remedial help, leaving the school without sufficient space for physical education. Instead of gym, some kids take health classes. The sole outdoor play area is a caged balcony open only in spring. Classrooms, however, have new furniture and are nicely decorated, with student papers on clotheslines and walls, and lists of educational tips scrolling from coat hangers.

Also in Bensonhurst is **PS 97**, 1855 Stillwell Avenue, Brooklyn, NY 11223, (718) 372-1800, a District 21 school that is so popular that some people buy homes in the zone just so they can send their children to it. Even though the school is overcrowded—860 children in a building designed to hold 625—Principal Gail Levine seems to know just about every child by name. Children clearly are used to seeing the principal every day when they arrive and frequently in the classrooms, and they come up to give her hugs. Kids also get a kick out of her amazing collection of stuffed animals that sing and dance. One dancing doll sang the Beatles tune "Do You Love Me" in honor of Valentine's Day. The school has a well-equipped television studio. Kids write scripts and shoot and edit documentaries with video cameras and a digital editing system. During our visit, children in a special education class were making a documentary about astronomy. There are large television screens in each room, and every Friday the president of the student council addresses the school on television. The school has a collaboration with the American Ballet Theatre for 4th and 5th graders. The art teacher took a 5th-grade class to the Frick Collection in Manhattan the day of our visit. Long an Italian-American neighborhood, more Asian families have been moving to Bensonhurst in recent years. The retired custodian comes once a week, just for the love of it, to work with 3rd graders in one of four portable classrooms. "I can't stay home," he says.

**PS 200**, 1940 Benson Avenue, Brooklyn, NY 11214, (718) 236-5466, between Bensonhurst and Bath Beach, is a big, old school in District 20, but it's also well kept and well run. It has a full-size gym—unchanged since Principal Sylvia La Cerra was a student here herself—an enviable auditorium with wonderful art on display, and a library/media center. The school has a bilingual gifted program for Russian-speaking children, called GLOBE, and an interesting mix of children from different countries. One spring morning, two women in traditional Egyptian garb waited with a woman in Pakistani dress, and a mother from Puerto Rico chatted with a mother from China outside the school. Inside, a group of 5th-grade girls—one Palestinian, one from Russia, one from Egypt, and another from Albania—made plans for graduation. "The best thing I did for my children was to bring them to this school," said a parent volunteer who was a teacher in her native Pakistan. A concert musician teaches violin to all children in kindergarten through 3rd grade. The school has collaborations with the Children's Musical Theatre and the Brooklyn Museum. The building has wireless Internet access, and children use laptop computers. The GLOBE gifted program accepts Russian-speaking students from across the district.

## Gravesend

When it comes to academics, **PS 215,** 415 Avenue S, Brooklyn, NY 11223, (718) 339-2464, is fairly traditional, with textbooks (rather than children's literature) in use in most classrooms. Lessons are substantial even in the youngest grades. The school's Sigma gifted program is notable for its high quality of teaching. We were particularly impressed with one class in which 4th and 5th graders were learning the history of musical theater. Gail Feuer, principal for 18 years, has made her office an inviting spot. The day we visited, her open-door policy had transformed her office into the school's Grand Central Terminal: The parents' association was holding a meeting there, and kids rushed in to drop off school supplies. The school, part of District 21, offers a strong instrumental music program, where students can learn to play violin starting in the 1st grade. One area of concern: We saw little student writing displayed in the school.

## Brighton Beach

Ask at **PS 225**, 1075 Oceanview Avenue, Brooklyn, NY 11235, (718) 743-9793, who was born in another country, and nearly every child raises his or her hand. You'll hear Russian and Urdu spoken as you walk down the hallways and see traditional dress worn during the "stepping up" ceremonies. Located in the heart of the Russian-immigrant community called "Odessa by the Sea," PS 225, in District 21, has an old-fashioned tone. Students wear white shirts and red ties on assembly day. Classrooms are orderly, and the style of teaching is mostly traditional, with teachers at the front of the class and plenty of textbooks and workbooks. But there are innovations as well. In the school's well-regarded writing program, every child writes and illustrates his or her own book for a school-wide celebration. About 250 parents attended one—a record turnout in this community where most parents work and attending school functions is not the norm in their culture. Third graders created their own websites, complete with sound, animation, photographs, and their own writing. Teachers take the children on as many trips as possible: to the zoo, parks, museums, even Broadway shows. There is a free after-school program. PS 225 was one of the first schools in the city to have an inclusion program—in which children receiving special education services are integrated into regular classes—and it still has one of the largest such programs in the city.

## Coney Island

**PS 100**, 2951 West Third Street, Brooklyn, NY 11224, (718) 266-9477, has a magnet grant designed to attract children from across District 21 as well as from other parts of the city. The theme of the magnet is "media arts and communication" and will include studies in the history of radio and television. A high-performing school serving a Russian-immigrant population, PS 100 was one of the 209 schools exempt from the citywide curriculum. Housed in an old, five story building with cramped classrooms, the school has had to make clever use of the building's quirky features to keep class size under control. The building's large bathroom lounges, like the kind found in old theaters, have been converted into offices and rooms for support services. The staff lounge is housed in a space once used as a custodian's apartment back when coal needed to be shoveled around the clock to heat the building. Nevertheless, the school is clean and cheerful. The hallways are painted in colorful hues and lined with bulletin boards filled with children's artwork and good writing, such as a display of 4th graders' essays entitled "If I Moved West in a Covered Wagon."

## Ditmas Park

District 22, which covers a large swath of Brooklyn from Ditmas Park to Bergen Beach, has some solid neighborhood schools, most of which are fairly traditional. Each school in the district has a gifted, or Eagle, program. **PS 217,** 1100 Newkirk Avenue, Brooklyn, NY 11230, (718) 434-6960, is a large school in the Ditmas Park section of Brooklyn, with a good racial balance among whites, blacks, Latinos, and Asians. The school is also economically mixed. Children walk to school from modest apartment buildings and grand Victorian houses. Recent immigrants include children from Ghana, Mexico, Pakistan, Poland, and the Ukraine. The renovated brick building has majestic marble columns flanking the entrance. Inside, the staff seems affectionate toward the children; a distracted student needed only a gentle touch on the head to become alert and attentive in class again. Parents say they love this school because they feel welcome. Some volunteer to help out in classrooms; one teaches a Spanish class with the teacher. A father helped to write a proposal that won the school a $1 million playground built by a non-profit organization called the Trust for Public Lands. The playground is also open to the neighborhood. The quality of teaching in the Eagle, or gifted, classes is particularly strong. In these, kindergartners write full sentences and talk about their writing with partners. Third graders hold book clubs in small groups, creating their own reading schedules and filling books with Post-it notes. Children in both gifted and regular classes enjoy the professional storyteller who offers catchy choruses and delightful gestures, and the science teacher has at least seven different animals in her room, including an iguana and a rabbit. PS 217 is a Project Arts model school.

## East Flatbush

Once the lower-grade annex of PS 269, **PS 361**, 3109 Newkirk Avenue, Brooklyn, NY 11226, (718) 856-0600, has been an autonomous K–2 school since 1998. The school has a young staff and dedicated principal who fosters a fun, attentive environment. Students are engaged in lessons, while displaying noticeable affection toward their teachers. About 85% of the children are black, and many come from immigrant families from the Caribbean; 92% are poor enough to qualify for free lunch. On our visit, children were well behaved and responsive. Faculty members are regularly asked to attend training sessions during their lunch and do so willingly. In return for their dedication to professional development, teachers at PS 361 find their requests are rarely refused. Classrooms are well furnished and well loved. Art, science, music, and dance teachers all have their own rooms. While there is no gym, students on our visit were doing plenty of movement in the dance room, and some teachers led short exercise sessions between lessons. The first-rate library is the heart of the school. Students may sign up for chorus, violin, or guitar, and the school provides the instruments. Unfortunately, sister school PS 269, where PS 361 students go upon graduation, doesn't offer these programs, and therefore budding musicians often give up the instruments. Each grade has a gifted Eagle class. Testing for the Eagle program is done by the regional office.

## Sheepshead Bay

**PS 255**, 1866 East 17th Street, Brooklyn, NY 11229, (718) 376-8494, is a traditional, neighborhood school. Many students are third-generation attendees; new immigrants are welcomed; and resources ranging from a dentist to computer labs work on behalf of children's success. Large, colorful billboards hang at the school's entrance, declaring: "Every child is a star . . . come watch us shine." And they do! Each morning, one student speaks into a microphone and leads the school in *The Pledge of Allegiance*. Names of students with perfect attendance gleam through a glass case, and recipients of student-of-the-month awards are honored with engraved pencils. Children are greeted in the morning and escorted to their classes, the cafeteria, recess, and the pre-lunch potty break. When an adult isn't present, children walk with their "buddy," never alone. Students seem supportive of one another. We were impressed to see kids applaud after a question was answered correctly, and offer help when it was not.

General education classes are organized according to academic levels, and students with high test scores and teacher recommendations are admitted into the Eagle program for gifted students. However, administrators say they may move a child who does not have high test scores into the Eagle program in special circumstances. When Principal Linda Singer arrived at PS 255 in 2001, for example, she found two emotionally disturbed and seemingly uncontrollable children in special education. Instead of transferring the children, however, Singer did the unexpected. "I placed them in the Eagle program," she said. Two years later, both children were excelling.

**PS 254**, 1801 Avenue Y, Brooklyn, NY 11235, (718) 743-0890, is a pleasant neighborhood school that serves African-American children whose families have lived in the neighborhood for generations, as well as Russians, Arabs, Chinese, and South Americans whose families have just arrived. "The teachers make you feel at home," said a graduate who is now in high school. "Three generations of my family have gone to this school. Every kid from my block has gone to this school and we all have or are going to graduate from PS 254." It's a school where newcomers learn English quickly. Its test scores are far above average compared with schools with similar demographics. Music and dance are an important part of the school. Children learn English as they memorize lyrics for, say, a class production of *The Sound of Music*. Dance teaches them English in an active way. When the teacher says, "Step to the left, step to the right," children pick up the meaning very quickly. PS 254 limits admission to children who live in the zone.

## Marine Park

Yellow ribbons in support of American troops adorn the fence outside **PS 207**, 4011 Fillmore Avenue, Brooklyn, NY 11234, (718) 645-8667, a proud, patriotic school in District 22. The lawn in front of the sturdy brick building boasts a rock garden in the shapes and colors of an American flag, made by a school custodian in tribute to police officers and firefighters who died on 9/11. Children regularly write to soldiers in Iraq—"thank you for keeping our country safe," read one letter—and participate in a "patriotic day," marching around the school carrying the flag. Marine Park is a solidly middle-class neighborhood, mostly Italian- and Irish-American, that is attracting an increasing number of immigrants. This traditional neighborhood school, which has "high" and "low" gifted (Eagle) classes as well as students grouped by ability in the upper grades, also has generally high test scores and supportive parents.

Recently, the school began embracing the Writer's Workshop method, developed at Teachers College, Columbia University, in which children write multiple drafts of their papers, offer editing suggestions to one another, then "publish" their essays for their classmates and parents to read. We saw lots of student writing in all the classrooms. Third graders read us poems they were submitting to the *National Anthology of Poetry*, a book of children's poems, and shared memoirs they were writing. The staff—including the principal—prides itself on knowing each child's strengths and weaknesses and using whatever it takes to make the child successful in school and on tests. Early-grade teachers actually take the 4th-grade standardized exams to learn how to best prepare their students. We saw several teachers work one-on-one with struggling readers, some using the Wilson method—a special phonics approach. A 4th grader sounded out simple sentences more suited to 1st-grade readers but took pride in her success.

At **PS 222**, 3301 Quentin Road, Brooklyn, NY 11234, (718) 998-4298, every classroom has a rug, and many have little nooks and playhouses that children can crawl into and read undisturbed. While the teacher concentrates on reading with a few children, the others work happily on their own. Teachers write their own stories or letters to the kids, and offer them as models of different kinds of writing, good spelling, and punctuation. The children keep journals and even kindergartners have spelling tests. The frequent practice gives kids both enthusiasm and proficiency. "I used to be happy if at the end of kindergarten they could write two sentences," said one kindergarten teacher, who said her pupils prefer reading and writing to playing with blocks. "Now I'm seeing five pages." Children are tracked, or grouped by ability, beginning in 1st grade. The school is wheelchair accessible and about 30% of the students receive special education services. The most severely disabled are placed in self-contained, or segregated, classrooms, but many children with learning disabilities, emotional problems, or physical disabilities are placed in general education classes. In these so-called inclusion classes, two teachers (one of whom is licensed in special education) work as a team. "The key to the success of the inclusion program is that teachers want to work together and usually have a personal relationship as well," an administrator said. "It's like a marriage. We really integrate all students here. Everyone is included." Very few children from outside the zone are admitted. Tours are given on request.

Tucked away in a small peninsula between Marine Park's salt marshes and Shell Bank Creek, **PS 277: Gerritsen Beach School,** 2529 Gerritsen Avenue, Brooklyn, NY 11229, (718) 743-6689, makes the most of its location: It offers courses in marine biology. The program was started in the early 1990s by then science teacher Jeanne Fish, currently the school's principal, and it remains her biggest pride. It features a large room with large fresh- and saltwater tanks filled with locally caught wildlife, including horseshoe crabs and puffer fish. During our visit, a kindergarten class sang along and used hand gestures to illustrate the three stages of the water cycle—precipitation, evaporation, and condensation.

This cohesive community of single-family homes is surrounded by water on three sides, and everyone in the community, heavily populated with civil servants, seems to know everyone else. "When I leave the school, there's always someone going by who beeps the horn to say hi," said Fish. The school has a certified dance teacher, a resourceful and enthusiastic music teacher, a 4th-grade chorus, and a 5th-grade drama program. Most staff members have more than 10 years of experience and are obviously comfortable in the classroom. Gerritsen Beach Cares, a local environmental group, regularly gives recognition to children in the school for their community work. With the exception of three buses that come from Flatbush, the vast majority of students are from the immediate neighborhood. Some kids even get to go home for lunch. A small, intimate community and an experienced staff make PS 277 a stable, cheerful neighborhood school with the bonus of a special program tuned in to its location and history.

## Mill Basin

**PS 236**, 9302 Avenue U, Brooklyn, NY 11234, (718) 444-6969, is a well-run, well-equipped school in a neighborhood with lots of stay-at-home mothers and one- and two-family homes with manicured lawns. Fifth graders lead *The Pledge of Allegiance* and sing *The Star Spangled Banner* over the public address system each morning. Classes are tracked, with children placed in groups according to their abilities. Homework is heavy. "They start homework at 4:00 in the afternoon and don't finish until after dinner," one parent said. "This breeds discipline and will pay off down the road." Even kindergartners have homework assignments, such as filling out a phonics worksheet from a workbook. The school has an inviting library with classical music playing, plants, dioramas made by the kids, and big windows that overlook a playground. Students in all grades perform and stage musical plays. PS 236, a District 22 school, has teaching artists from Puppetry in Practice, who help children make puppets and put on shows connected to the social studies curriculum, such as Native American music and dance. The school has two gifted programs, the district-wide Eagle program and a school-based Scholar's Academy, designed for children in grades 2–5 to integrate social studies and reading. Children receiving special education services are integrated into regular classes and receive extra help from a second teacher for part of the day. The school is overcrowded and there isn't much room for children from outside the zone. Tours are given by appointment.

## Bergen Beach

On a spring day you can smell the ocean outside **PS 312**, 7103 Avenue T, Brooklyn, NY 11234, (718) 763-4015, in Bergen Beach, a remote Brooklyn neighborhood with a small-town feel. The school is next door to District 22's Environmental Study Center, where students from PS 312 and other schools care for plants and animals in habitats ranging from a simulated Amazon rain forest to a salt-water marsh. Principal Linda Beale-Benigno, a reading specialist and former New York University professor, has invigorated the staff with new ways to teach reading and writing. Kids are more likely to read picture books and novels they choose themselves and less likely to read textbooks assigned by the teachers.

PS 312 has an unusually successful inclusion program in which children in special education are placed in classes with general education pupils and team taught by two teachers, one of whom specializes in kids with special needs. Teachers are proud of the way children use laptop computers to do research on topics such as the civil rights movement. "It gave them, besides knowledge of civil rights, a sense of how to write concisely and to use visuals and sound in their presentations," a teacher said. Art is integrated with social studies and science projects. Children studying Mexico designed paper-mache plates and created clay vessels based on Mexican art. Students studying volcanoes created a "volcano dance" for a school performance and tie-dyed T-shirts depicting volcanic eruptions.

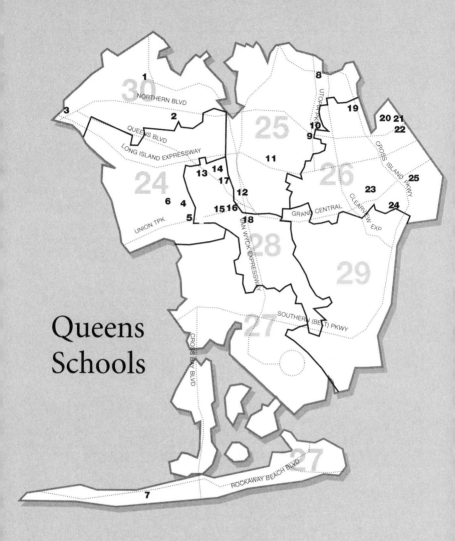

# Queens
# Schools

**District 30**
1  PS 122
2  Renaissance Charter
3  PS 78: Robert F. Wagner Jr.

**District 24**
4  PS 87
5  PS 113: Isaac Chauncey
6  PS 128

**District 27**
7  PS 114: Belle Harbor

**District 25**
8  PS 209
9  PS 107
10  PS 130
11  PS 165
12  PS 164: Queens Valley

**District 28**
13  PS 139
14  PS 175
15  PS 144
16  PS 101: School in the Gardens
17  PS 196
18  PS 99: Kew Gardens School

**District 26**
19  PS 41
20  PS 98
21  PS 94: Davis Porter
22  PS 221: North Hills
23  PS 188
24  PS 18
25  PS/IS 266

# QUEENS

Queens was once a place of scattered villages set amid farmland. Today, the farmland is gone, but the identity of the old villages remains. Ask people where they live, and they're likely to say Richmond Hill or Woodside or Douglaston rather than Queens.

Some neighborhoods have the distinctive feel of one ethnic group. You're just as likely to hear Greek as English spoken on the busy streets of Astoria, where the music from bouzoikis fills the air late into the night. In Little India in Jackson Heights, there are more women dressed in saris than in blue jeans, and the perfume of curry spices wafts through the streets. Other neighborhoods are polyglot, where you'll see newsstands with papers in a dozen different languages. More than 100 languages are spoken in the borough today.

Much of Queens was rural until World War II, and the borough still has many suburban neighborhoods with single-family homes and large lawns. The population boomed in the 1980s and 1990s with newcomers from all over the world, particularly from Asia. Single-family homes were divided into many small apartments, often in violation of zoning regulations. School construction didn't keep pace with immigration, and many of the schools are badly overcrowded. Some have new annexes. Many others have portable classrooms on the playground, built in the early 1990s as temporary spaces to house the overflow of students. Now these portable classrooms are seemingly permanent fixtures across the borough.

In many schools, these additions put serious burdens on the building's common spaces, because the cafeterias and gymnasiums weren't designed to accommodate so many children. Although the temporary spaces are snug and cheerful at some schools, many have flimsy walls that can't support bookshelves, poor heating, and no Internet access. More important, as the schools' enrollments grow, principals become more involved with the mechanics of crowd control and the details of administration and less involved with developing the curriculum and supervising teachers. Plus, as enrollment has climbed at many schools, class size often has followed.

Immigration brings great challenges to public education in Queens. In some schools, more than 40 languages are spoken and it's a struggle to teach the newcomers English. But immigration also has enriched the schools. Children learn about customs and holidays around the world, whether it's through a lion dance in celebration of Chinese New Year or an international dinner sponsored by the PTA.

The schools tend to be more traditional than those in Manhattan, and Queens was the one borough in which hundreds of teachers actively rebelled against the mayor's move to introduce progressive teaching techniques. In early 2005, 800 teachers demonstrated in front of the Region 4 offices at Queens Plaza to protest what they called "micromanagement" by the regional offices. At least in some schools, the new curriculum seems to have been introduced clumsily by administrators who gave minute-by-minute lesson plans to teachers rather than broad guidelines of good teaching practice.

The schools in Queens vary tremendously in quality. The schools in District 26, which includes Little Neck and Bayside, have consistently ranked at the very top of the Department of Education's annual ratings. The District 26 schools are well equipped and beautifully maintained. They have incorporated the latest teaching techniques while maintaining a traditional tone, with rituals such as reciting *The Pledge of Allegiance*. Other schools, including some of those in southeast Queens, rank near the bottom. Most of the schools limit enrollment to children living in their zone, and school choice is very limited.

Still, there are a few opportunities for parents to shop around for schools in the borough. A few schools listed here accept children from anywhere in their district or even from anywhere in the borough. A few neighborhood schools have room for out-of-district children. In some cases children from outside a school's zone are admitted through the federal No Child Left Behind law, which allows children at "failing" schools to transfer to better schools outside of their immediate neighborhood. And some schools have gifted programs that admit children according to their scores on tests, not their address.

## Region 4 (Districts 30 and 24, and parts of Brooklyn)

Region 4 encompasses the old Districts 30 and 24, as well as parts of Brooklyn. The regional offices are located at 28-11 Queens Plaza North, (718) 391-8300. The gifted and talented program coordinator is Sheryl Quatrano, (718) 397-5472.

The Queens neighborhoods closest to Manhattan—Long Island City, Astoria, Sunnyside, and Jackson Heights—make up **District 30**. A traditional district, its schools are large and many have far more children than they were designed to accommodate. The district has a mix of longtime residents of the Greek-American community of Astoria, recent refugees from Manhattan's sky-high real estate prices who live in artists' colonies in Long Island City, and new immigrants from Mexico and Latin America. In years past, many of the most prosperous and educated parents sought seats for their children in the progressive schools of Manhattan's District 2; as schools throughout the city are granting fewer and fewer variances, however, parents are forced to look closer to home for options. Luckily, a few new schools have opened in District 30 and some of them are quite promising.

The district doesn't encourage shopping around, and most children go to their neighborhood school. However, there are two district-wide gifted programs in the elementary schools. The program at **PS 122** begins in 2nd grade; the program at **PS 150** begins in 1st grade. Teachers recommend children for the gifted program in January and children then are tested for admission. Our World Neighborhood Charter School and the Renaissance Charter School admit students by lottery and are open to children in all five boroughs.

To the southwest of District 30 is **District 24**, which serves Elmhurst, Middle Village, Maspeth, Corona, and Glendale, and has long been one of the most overcrowded school districts in the city. The neighborhoods of District 24 historically have had large numbers of Irish- and Italian-Americans. In recent years, they have become home to increasing numbers of new immigrants from Latin America and Central Europe. School construction fell far short of what was needed to accommodate immigration of the 1980s and 1990s, and school choice is next to impossible because of lack of space. A few exceptions: District 24 offers a test at kindergarten registration for the district gifted magnet programs at **PS 153** and **PS 16**. Entrance in later grades is possible if there are openings.

## Region 5 (District 27 and parts of Brooklyn)

Region 5 comprises the former **District 27**, as well as parts of Brooklyn. Its offices are at 8201 Rockaway Blvd., Ozone Park, (718) 642-5800. Kathleen Cashin, named the region's superintendent in 2003, is well regarded for her work reviving schools in the Ocean Hill-Brownsville section of Brooklyn and is well liked by principals. For District 27, a beleaguered district with serious overcrowding and mediocre-to-poor test scores, strong leadership is something that many of the schools sorely need. There is little opportunity for school choice within the district because of overcrowding. The gifted and talented coordinator is Rita Giaramita, who may be reached at (718) 642-5844.

District 27 encompasses the neighborhoods of southeast Queens near JFK Airport—Howard Beach, Ozone Park, Richmond Hill, and the Rockaway Peninsula. It has a district-wide gifted program called Astre, for students in kindergarten through 5th grade. Testing for admission to Astre is conducted in late winter and is administered through the Region 5 office. Call Sherry Copeland at (718) 642-5871 for testing information.

## Region 3 (Districts 25, 26, 28, and 29)

Region 3 is home to the top-scoring district in the city—District 26 in Northeastern Queens—as well as Districts 25, 28, and 29, which also boast many very good neighborhood schools. Region 3 has two offices: 90-27 Sutphin Boulevard, Jamaica, NY 11435, (718) 557-2600 and 30-48 Linden Place, Jamaica, NY 11354, (718) 281-7575.

Districts 25 and 26 have district-wide gifted and talented programs. In the past, Districts 28 and 29 have not had district-wide gifted programs, but some schools in those districts have enrichment programs or accelerated classes, and may add more-formal gifted programs. For information on gifted and talented or accelerated classes, call one of the Region 3 offices, listed above, or your district's parent support officer: for District 25, Regina Schroeter, (718) 281-7625; for District 28, Cheryl Goode, (718) 557-2804; for District 29, Wanda Gaines, (718) 341-8280, ext. 1120. For District 26, call the district office, (718) 631-6982.

**District 25** includes very diverse neighborhoods in north-central Queens, from Flushing's bustling Chinatown to Whitestone's quiet residential streets. Many immigrants from Korea, India, and China have moved to the district in recent years. The southern part of the district feels very much a part of the city, with busy commercial streets and apartment buildings and a fast connection to Manhattan via the number 7 train. The northern part has a suburban feel, with big trees and single-family houses and stops on the Long Island Railroad. Schools tend to be smaller and less crowded in the northern end of the district.

Many parents are satisfied with their neighborhood schools. Although the district is too crowded to accept children from outside its boundaries, there is some shopping around within the district. Two schools in the district, **PS 209** in Whitestone and **PS 165** in Kew Gardens Hills, have gifted programs, called Alpha, for high-achieving children. Most schools offer tours for prospective parents in the winter; call individual schools for dates.

Every single school in **District 26** in northeast Queens, long the highest-achieving district in the city, has test scores that are well above the citywide average in both reading and math. The schools are mostly cheerful and well equipped, with experienced teachers, effective principals, and parents who help out in any way they can. The district's schools are so successful that almost all were on the original list of 209 schools exempt from the standardized curriculum that Chancellor Joel Klein mandated in all but the top-scoring schools beginning in 2003.

One of the great benefits of District 26 schools is their small size. Elsewhere in Queens, you'll find gigantic schools with 1,000 or even

1,500 children, but many District 26 schools have 300 or 400 children, and few are larger than 800.

District 26 has had effective leadership and a senior teaching staff for many years. Many schools work closely with the Reading and Writing Project at Teachers College, Columbia University, and many teachers have trained with writing guru Lucy Calkins. Teachers use children's literature to teach reading, rather than the basal readers of the past.

The teaching of math has evolved as well. Basic arithmetic skills of addition, subtraction, multiplication, and division are still taught. But children are now expected to explain in words how they got their answers to problems. They learn elements of geometry and algebra along with arithmetic.

The district is known for its staff development. Teachers keep up-to-date with current practices and hone their skills with summer courses, after-school seminars, and regular visits to other schools.

The neighborhoods that make up District 26 have a suburban feel, with single-family houses, large yards, and big shade trees, particularly in the areas closest to the Nassau County border. But, unlike Nassau just over the city line, this section of Queens hasn't succumbed totally to car culture and shopping malls. The old villages of Bayside, Little Neck, and Douglaston retain their pre-automobile charm, and it's possible to get a quart of milk without getting into a car. Many families own only one car, and the adults commute to Manhattan on the Long Island Railroad. Many immigrants from Korea, China, and Japan have moved to the district in recent years, attracted by the reputation of the schools. Although a few District 26 schools offer variances, and some out-of-zone children are admitted to the district's schools through the federal No Child Left Behind law, in most cases it has become nearly impossible to gain admission from outside a school's zone.

Kindergarten registration begins in March for neighborhood children. Register early. If you wait until September, you risk having your child bused to another school.

District 26 has two gifted and talented programs, at **PS 18** in Queens Village and **PS 188** in Bayside. Parents or teachers may recommend children for the program, which begins in 1st grade. About 400 kindergarten children are tested beginning in March. The top 50 are offered seats. Because the quality of the neighborhood schools is so good, some parents of high-achieving children forgo the gifted program to keep their children close to home.

**District 28** stretches from the bustling immigrant neighborhoods of Rego Park to the posh houses and quiet tree-lined streets of Forest

Hills to the modest bungalows of south Jamaica. The district has long been divided by race and class. Parents in the poor, mostly black and Hispanic southern section of the district have long complained that their schools are neglected. Parents in the prosperous, mostly white northern section, meanwhile, claim that the southern schools fail to make good use of the extra federal money they receive because of their high poverty rates. The schools in the southern end of the district are mostly low-performing, while those in the north are mostly high-performing.

The district as a whole is overcrowded, and parents are encouraged to send their children to their neighborhood school. Many schools have enrichment classes. Variances rarely are granted, usually only when a parent can demonstrate a need based on a children's health or safety. If, say, dust from construction at the neighborhood school is causing asthma attacks, such special permission may be granted. In a few schools, there is occasionally room for a few children from outside the zone; pick up an application for a variance either at the individual school or at the regional office in May.

**District 29**, which includes the middle-class, mostly African-American communities of St. Albans, Hollis, and Springfield Gardens and the ethnically mixed neighborhoods of Holliswood and Queens Village, has long suffered a brain drain. For years, some of its best students went to private schools or applied for variances to attend public schools in the adjoining District 26. That has changed as District 26, facing a population boom and stricter variance policies from the central Department of Education, has restricted the number of out-of-district children it admits.

District 29 has seen the arrival of many immigrants in recent years. School enrollments have increased, and there has been a lot of illegal development, with single-family houses converted into small apartments in violation of zoning regulations. Most of the schools are very large, some with more than 1,500 pupils, and some have a factory feel to them.

In the past few years there has been construction in the district to alleviate some of the most overcrowded schools. As a result, there are several new, promising, district-wide K-8 programs in District 29, all housed in beautiful, new facilities. Students are admitted via a lottery for kindergarten for PS 251, PS/IS 268, PS/IS 270, and PS/IS 208. You can find profiles of these schools in the Queens "worth watching" section. The lottery is held in February and is open to District 29 residents only. Students rank the schools in order of choice. Applications are available at the District 29 office at 233-15 Merrick Boulevard, Rosedale, or at the Region 3 office at 90-27 Sutphin Boulevard, Jamaica.

# PS 122

## 21-21 Ditmars Boulevard
## Long Island City, NY 11105
## (718) 721-6410

**Admissions:** neighborhood school/selective program
**Grade levels:** PK–8
**Enrollment:** 1,300
**Class size:** K: 25; 8: 29
**Reading scores:** ****
**Math scores:** *****
**Ethnicity:** 34%W 6%B 32%H 28%A
**Free lunch:** 79%

PS 122 is an extremely large, traditional, very high-performing elementary school with a district-wide gifted program and a selective middle school called the Academy. The school uses a Core Knowledge curriculum, based on the philosophy of E. D. Hirsch, author of *Cultural Literacy: What Every American Needs to Know.*

Hirsch offers a grade-by-grade list of what children should learn. First graders, for example, learn a smattering of ancient Egyptian history and read excerpts from *Winnie the Pooh.* Fifth graders learn the date of the French Revolution and read excerpts from Homer's *Iliad* and *Odyssey.*

Despite its fairly traditional philosophy, the school recently has introduced some new, progressive teaching techniques. In 2003, PS 122 elected to adopt the new standardized math and reading curriculum along with the rest of the city, even though it was given a waiver because of its sky-high scores. "There is always room for improvement," explained Principal Mary Kojes. "Change is good."

In recent years, teachers have worked to expand classroom libraries and incorporate more novels, biographies, and nonfiction science discovery books into lessons. The school uses the Teachers College Workshop approach to writing, in which students write multiple drafts of each paper and edit one another's work.

All students keep a writer's notebook, and students write multiple drafts and then "publish" their work—presenting it at a "celebration" attended by parents. There are two science labs. The school's pretty, red-brick building is very clean and pleasant. The building has two gyms and two computer labs

A district-wide gifted program begins in 2nd grade. First-grade teachers recommend children in January, who then are tested by the district office. Each year, PS 122 sends 10 to 12 children to the super-selective Hunter College High School. Nearly all 8th graders graduating from the Academy are admitted to super-selective high schools such as Stuyvesant, Bronx Science, and Townsend Harris.

# Renaissance Charter School
## 35-59 81st Street
## Jackson Heights, NY 11372
## (718) 803-0060
### *www.trcs.org*

**Admissions:** lottery; citywide
**Grade levels:** K–12
**Enrollment:** 500
**Class size:** 25

**Reading scores:** ***
**Math scores:** ***
**Ethnicity:** 21%W 21%B 42%H 15%A
**Free lunch:** 56%

This progressive, experimental school has the feel of a small-town school, with kids from kindergarten through 12th grade under the same roof. Housed in a former department store, the school has an unusual architectural design that gives it a homey feel and encourages children of different ages to mix.

Kindergarten and 1st-grade classrooms on the ground floor open on a central indoor playroom equipped with playground equipment. It serves as a gathering place for parents at the end of the day, and for teachers to meet informally between classes. Upstairs, classrooms open on a central lounge with sofas and carpeted areas—places for students to chat with teachers or one another.

Founded in 1993 by a group of teachers who wanted a school that was run jointly by staff and parents, the Renaissance Charter School has attracted super-involved parents and hard-working, talented teachers. Half a dozen parents work at the school; others volunteer on a regular basis. Children call grown-ups by their first names. Children with disabilities are integrated into regular classes.

It's sometimes noisy and a bit disorganized, and the teachers spend a fair amount of time cajoling children to settle down and behave. But it has a joyous, liberating atmosphere, test scores are respectable, and parents are enthusiastic.

"My son is very shy, and he would have been lost in regular public school," one mother said. "I don't think he would have been called on. Here, he gets the attention he needs. The children have room to explore and there's more interaction among the kids."

Classrooms have sofas and tables—not desks. Tables are moved around according to whether children are working in small groups or meeting together as a class.

Principal Montee Joffee said he has been influenced by the philosophy of the Rudolph Steiner Schools, also called Waldorf Schools. Like those private schools, Renaissance has continuity from kindergarten through high school, and teachers attempt to present material in ways that speak to a child's own experience and to address children's feelings as well as their intellect.

Whenever possible, activities reinforce lessons from books. In a 5th-grade math and science class, children studied the reaction times of astronauts and learned to calculate a "mean" by dropping strips of paper and calculating how long it took them to catch the paper with either hand. Sixth graders studying China made Chinese robes from brown paper and learned to write Chinese characters.

Renaissance became a charter school in 2000. Children are admitted by lottery. Applications are due in February. There is one tour in late September and additional tours in January and February. In recent years, there have been 100 applications for 14 kindergarten seats. Siblings of current students are given priority. Children from anywhere in New York City may apply.

# PS 78: The Robert F. Wagner Jr. School
## 48-09 Center Boulevard
## Long Island City, NY 11109
## (718) 392-5402
### *http://ps78qpta.org*

**Admissions:** neighborhood school    **Reading scores:** ***
**Grade levels:** PK–5                          **Math scores:** ****
**Enrollment:** 216                             **Ethnicity:** 22%W 9%B 52%H 17%A
**Class size:** K: 14; 5: 22                   **Free lunch:** 72%

At PS 78, 4th and 5th graders tend to the oyster bed they are maintaining in the East River, and learn about marine life from the plant and fish-filled aquariums in their classrooms. As part of a collaboration with the South Street Seaport, students get plenty of opportunities to learn about marine ecology and oceanography. In one 4th-grade class, an oceanographer from the South Street Seaport brought in various types of live crabs to show and discuss with students. The school carries this marine theme into other parts of the curriculum as well. One class studied poems about the sea; another painted a large watercolor of sea scenes that hangs at the entrance to the school.

Located at the base of the City Lights apartment building on the shore of the East River in Long Island City, PS 78 offers a spectacular panorama of Manhattan from its front entrance. The school's neighborhood, just a 10-minute subway ride from midtown Manhattan, has changed dramatically in recent years, as artists and young professionals looking to escape Manhattan's rising rents have moved in.

Parents are involved in the school. A father who is a photographer took children to his studio to learn about photography. The school has an intimate, collaborative feel, and with just over 200 students, parents say their children get a lot of individual attention.

Lessons encourage kids to learn by doing—and by getting their hands dirty once in a while. In a 2nd-grade class, for example, students learned about botany and the lifecycle of plants by digging in a marigold garden in front of the school. And teachers frequently integrate the arts into their lessons. In a 5th-grade class we visited, students researched particular New York City bridges, wrote about them, and depicted them in artwork. One 4th-grade class had erected a multicentury timeline in the hallway, then created artistic and literary pieces representing historical events and tied them to dates on the timeline.

# PS 49

## 79-15 Penelope Avenue
## Middle Village, NY 11379
## (718) 326-2111

**Admissions:** neighborhood school
**Grade levels:** K–5
**Enrollment:** 469
**Class size:** 25–30

**Reading scores:** ****
**Math scores:** *****
**Ethnicity:** 52%W 2%B 25%H 21%A
**Free lunch:** 30%

PS 49 is a happy place, where daisies grow just outside the front door in warm weather, and students study art and music to better understand their social studies or reading lessons. There's a big emphasis on the arts—a subject that grown-ups at the school seem just as passionate about as the kids. The school's longtime principal, Anthony Lombardi, majored in poetry in college and has portraits of Frank Sinatra prominently displayed in his office.

Thanks to PS 49 alumnus and businessman Tom Petrosino, every classroom has stereo equipment to listen to music. Students study song lyrics and other works of art to make connections to the curriculum. Fourth graders might listen to "I've Got Plenty of Nothing," while studying the Great Depression, or might learn about math concepts by creating Picasso-inspired Cubist shapes. The school library has been turned into an art room.

Academics at the school are also strong, something that Lombardi attributes to a strict emphasis on teaching, reflected in his decision to hire extra teachers for each grade rather than an assistant principal. And Lombardi has high expectations for teachers at the school. Lessons encourage kids to edit each other's work, and teachers use the progressive teaching methods developed by Columbia University's Teachers College. When we visited, we saw kids sprawled on the floor, writing notes on sticky papers, chatting over books, or reading quietly. One benefit of this curriculum according to teacher Mary Shannon, is that kids are "writing a lot better."

Students speak a host of languages, including Chinese and Polish. Lombardi has an affinity for these students (he spoke only Italian as a child) and says he was always in trouble for questioning rules. As a result, his goal is to "teach kids to think rather than telling them what to think."

# PS 113: Isaac Chauncey School

## 87-21 79th Avenue
## Glendale, NY 11385
## (718) 847-0724

**Admissions:** neighborhood school   **Reading scores:** *****
**Grade levels:** K–5                **Math scores:** *****
**Enrollment:** 541                  **Ethnicity:** 75%W 2%B 17%H 6%A
**Class size:** 24–28                **Free lunch:** 55%

PS 113 is a traditional, orderly school that consistently ranks among the top 5% of schools in the city in reading and math scores. There is an extraordinarily active Parents' Association that raises as much as $18,000 a year.

Parents say longtime Principal Anthony Pranzo is a good administrator, and they praise the attention paid to safety. "Teachers walk the children everywhere," said one parent.

The school has some of the feel of a parochial school, and parents fondly call the principal "Brother Anthony." "He runs it like a Catholic school," said one parent. "All that's missing is the saint's statue in the corner." The neighborhood, which was formerly home to mostly Irish- and Italian-American families, has undergone a dramatic demographic shift in recent years. There are now many more Spanish-speaking families at the school. Parents are proud of the values taught at the school and say that students' families share the same values at home. "It's mostly the same type of child from the same type of family," said one mother. "You don't have to keep up with the Joneses."

Some parents complain that the school has limited special education services. One parent put it this way: "I agree it is a wonderful school, but not if your child has special needs." Another parent said that while academics, safety, and discipline at the school are top-notch, she'd like more emphasis on arts and music. Still, she adds, the school is a great place, and she'd opt for it over any other school in the neighborhood, public or private.

# PS 128

## 69-26 65th Drive
## Middle Village, NY 11379
## (718) 894-8385

**Admissions:** neighborhood school
**Grade levels:** K–5
**Enrollment:** 350
**Class size:** K: 25; 5: 29

**Reading scores:** *****
**Math scores:** *****
**Ethnicity:** 88%W 2%B 6%H 4%A
**Free lunch:** 22%

In the close-knit community of Middle Village, PS 128 serves families who have lived in the neighborhood for generations, as well as many recent immigrants from Eastern Europe.

Children wear navy blue and white uniforms. When longtime Principal John Lavelle walks into a classroom, students stop what they are doing to say, "Good morning, Mr. Lavelle!" PS 128 is consistently among the top 5% of schools in the city in reading and math scores.

Nightly homework begins in kindergarten, with children typically given a reading and writing assignment. A 2nd grader might have reading, math, and spelling homework.

Each class performs a play for the entire school once a year. Children read poems and stories they've written. Parents, grandparents, aunts, and uncles flock to the daytime performances. The principal has an open-door policy. "You can go in and see him anytime," one mother said.

Because of overcrowding, children in grades 3–5 attend classes in a converted factory building across the street. The main building houses kindergarten through 2nd grade. The main cafeteria doubles as a gym and auditorium.

Parents who attended Catholic schools themselves as children now send their offspring to PS 128.

# PS 114: Belle Harbor School
## Beach 135th Street & Cronston Avenue
## Belle Harbor, NY 11694
## (718) 634-3382

**Admissions:** neighborhood school/selective
**Grade levels:** PK–8
**Enrollment:** 877
**Class size:** K: 20; 5: 28

**Reading scores:** *****
**Math scores:** *****
**Ethnicity:** 86%W 5%B 5%H 4%A
**Free lunch:** 21%

PS 114 is located in the idyllic seaside community of Belle Harbor, a "village" perched on a tiny strip of land just blocks away from the Atlantic Ocean. The school has a nice, small-town feel: There are girls in Brownie uniforms, and bicycles in racks out front. The neighborhood is home to many firefighters and police officers, and has tight-knit Irish- and Italian-American communities.

Long the highest performing school in the district, the school was buffeted by a revolving door of administrators until Brian O'Connell was named principal in April 2003. O'Connell, who grew up in the neighborhood, says that some students at the school are the sons and daughters of children he went to school with. "I had sand in my diapers," he said. "Growing up here, I know everybody."

While the school still has a traditional feel, it also has changed quite a bit over the past few years. When O'Connell arrived he found a school that "was 1952 in every respect," with "piles of white chalk next to the blackboards and desks in rows. "

Now, classrooms are more likely to have white boards than black, and markers rather than chalk. Kids sit at tables so they can work together. For example, in a 1st-grade classroom where desks might have been in rows a few years ago, some kids were seated on the floor with the teacher, others were at computer centers, and still others were writing, on individual white boards, "tricky" words they encountered in books they were reading. Other kids were working with a parent volunteer to learn about rhyming words.

The kindergarten program is academic—too academic for some parents who mourn the loss of time when kids can just "play." We saw students doing show and tell. They brought in objects from home that began with the letter "e," such as stuffed elephants or envelopes, and then the class charted which objects were brought in the most.

The cafeteria is small, but there is a nice-sized gym.

# PS 209

## 16-10 Utopia Parkway
## Whitestone, NY 11357
## (718) 352-3939

**Admissions:** neighborhood school/selective program
**Grade levels:** K–6          **Reading scores:** * * * * *
**Enrollment:** 613            **Math scores:** * * * * *
**Class size:** K: 25; 6: 32   **Ethnicity:** 51%W 2%B 8%H 39%A
                               **Free lunch:** 13%

PS 209, in a stable middle-class community between the Throgs Neck and Whitestone Bridges, is home to the district's gifted program and ranks among the top 5% of schools in the city on both reading and math tests. This Italian, Jewish, and increasingly Korean neighborhood of one-family houses and garden apartments has a great sense of community.

Classrooms are organized so that students can work in groups and independently, and lessons are increasingly collaborative. The school uses the "workshop" model approach, during which teachers give mini-lessons to the class and then students explore topics in small groups or independently.

The school's principal, Mary McDonnell, says she is focused on making sure the school identifies students' strengths and weaknesses early. "If we assist the students in their early years, they have a much better chance of success," she said.

There is a school band and a chorus, as well as a basketball and cheerleading squad. The building is clean and attractive, with a beautiful auditorium decorated with colorful murals painted by students. Parents are enthusiastic. One mother was thrilled that teachers spotted her son's learning problem early—and got him the help he needed. "The kids are very happy," said another mother. "They feel like this is home."

The school admits children to the gifted program, called Alpha, from across the district. Applications are available at the regional office. Children are tested for Alpha in January.

# PS 107

### 167-02 45th Avenue
### Flushing, NY 11358
### (718) 762-5995

**Admissions:** neighborhood school  **Reading scores:** ****
**Grade levels:** PK–6                **Math scores:** ****
**Enrollment:** 1,135                 **Ethnicity:** 28%W 2%B 25%H 45%A
**Class size:** K: 21; 6: 32          **Free lunch:** 42%

PS 107 is an unusually warm and gentle school, perhaps because it has a long history of integrating disabled children in regular classes, with extra help. It gives severely disabled and chronically ill children—those who might have stayed in hospitals or institutions in another era—the simple pleasures of school life: the chance to go on class trips, to take part in school assemblies, and to enjoy a carnival put on by the Parents' Association.

It gives average and high-achieving children an unusual sense of compassion and tolerance—along with a solid education. Go to the 6th-grade dance, and you might see able-bodied children ask children in wheelchairs to dance. Look outside and you'll see trees planted in memory of a few children who died. A child who needs physical therapy might invite her able-bodied friends along just for fun. "The kids are more accepting," one mother said. "They don't see the wheelchairs or the helmets or the crutches—they just see the kid."

Parents praise the leadership of Principal Jim Phair and say that teachers work well together. They say the school feels small—even though it has more than 1,100 children. The school has a strong art program and has collaborations with Carnegie Hall and the Brooklyn Conservatory of Music. The school has a large population of new immigrants and a history of teaching them English well.

In grades 4–6, there is one class designated as the Intellectually Gifted Class, or IGC. One 6th-grade IGC class took part in the "Living Museum" project at a local PBS station as part of their study of ancient Egypt. Dressed in homemade costumes, the students played the role of ancient Egyptians and answered questions such as, "What rights are there for women?" or "What do you do about pollution?"

The school has a spacious occupational and physical therapy room—equipped with swings, mats, and big rubber balls. There are some classes for learning disabled and developmentally delayed children, as well as extra help in reading and math for those who need it.

# PS 130
## 200-01 42nd Avenue
## Bayside, NY 11361
## (718) 357-6606

**Admissions:** District 25
**Grade levels:** K–3
**Enrollment:** 275
**Class size:** K: 25; 3: 20

**Reading scores:** * * * * *
**Math scores:** * * * * *
**Ethnicity:** 24%W 4%B 13%H 59%A
**Free lunch:** 22%

PS 130 is one of the most sought-after schools in Queens, and if you visit it you'll see why. Small and enchanting, with strong leadership and a talented staff, PS 130 is a schools that's both academically challenging and fun for kids. Small class size, beautiful books and equipment, and lots of extra grown-ups (student teachers and paraprofessionals) in the classroom make the school especially appealing.

The school takes the curiosity that all small children have about their world and uses it as the foundation for formal education. Teachers build the curriculum around children's interests. Kids' everyday experiences are linked to knowledge available in books to answer questions the children pose themselves.

For example, they might learn to predict the weather from cloud formations, using a reference book on the weather in their school library. They might capture the gas released when baking powder combines with water by mixing the two in a bottle, attaching a balloon to the bottle neck, and watching it inflate—an idea from a children's book on chemistry in the school library.

Children learn to read from works of literature, study math using coins and blocks, and learn how to write by making up their own stories. Children are encouraged to use their own spelling in kindergarten and 1st grade; in 2nd grade, teachers begin to edit their work and encourage conventional spelling.

Children work independently or in groups at tables and on rugs, while the teachers move from child to child, giving help and advice. Sometimes the children gather together and the teacher reads to them as a group. The atmosphere is homey, "almost an extension of nursery school," one mother said. The school is orderly and the children are attentive, moving smoothly from one activity to another.

PS 130 is open to children who live in District 25. Open houses are held in January, and applications are due in February. Notification is in May. Applications are available at the regional office.

# PS 165
## 70-35 150th Street
## Flushing, NY 11367
## (718) 263-4004

**Admissions:** neighborhood school/selective program
**Grade levels:** PK–6          **Reading scores:** \*\*\*\*
**Enrollment:** 750            **Math scores:** \*\*\*\*
**Class size:** K: 20; 6: 32   **Ethnicity:** 23%W 16%B 21%H 40%A
                               **Free lunch:** 58%

At PS 165, older children act as "dance mentors" to younger ones, teaching them moves and even choreographing dances based on their interests. If 2nd graders are curious about whales, for example, older children will read books about whales, learn songs about whales, and then make up a dance—about whales.

The dance program helps build friendships among children of different ages and begins to create a community out of the disparate groups that make up PS 165: from gifted children in the Alpha program to children receiving special education services, from native-born children to new immigrants from Afghanistan.

Children go on educational trips to the New Victory Theater, the Metropolitan Museum of Art, the Tenement Museum, and the Brooklyn Botanic Garden. There is an inclusion class for special education that mixes disabled children and those in general education, with two teachers, one of whom is trained in special education, and a teacher's aide or paraprofessional.

The school has one Alpha, or gifted, class per grade in 1st through 6th grades. In the past, parents complained of division between the Alpha program and the rest of the school. But the principal has made a good start at forging bonds in the school. The staff is cohesive, morale is high, and the children are happy. "Kids really want to come to school," a mother said.

There is a full-day SuperStart prekindergarten program that is composed half of students with special education needs, and half of students from the neighborhood.

Admission to the Alpha program is based on a test administered by the regional office. While class size in the general classes ranges from 20–24 students, Alpha classes are as large as 32. Kids in the Alpha program do projects such as studying Picasso: viewing slides of his work, reading his biography, and making self-portraits in his style.

# PS 164: Queens Valley School
## 138-01 77th Avenue
## Flushing, NY 11367
## (718) 544-1083

**Admissions:** neighborhood school
**Grade levels:** PK–6
**Enrollment:** 450
**Class size:** K: 20; 5: 30

**Reading scores:** ****
**Math scores:** ****
**Ethnicity:** 28%W 12%B 32%H 28%A
**Free lunch:** 73%

At PS 164, students can twirl in the dance studio, practice in the drama room, or tinker with their films in the video production studio. The school (which, incidentally, was attended by singer-songwriter Paul Simon as a child) has a strong emphasis on the arts. Kindergartners and 1st graders learn to play piano in "Music and the Brain," a 2-year course designed to enhance academic achievement through music. Third and 4th graders rotate through instrumental music, vocal music, dance, visual arts, and video production electives. In grades 5 and 6, students focus in on one of the arts disciplines.

Teachers take pains to integrate literacy into all subjects, including the arts. In one dance class, for example, the teacher encouraged students to stretch and mediate by referring to themes contained in *A Quiet Place*, PS 164's book of the month, the story of a boy's search for peace and solitude.

Students say their teachers are friendly, hardworking, and supportive. One student praised her teacher for staying at school long after school hours to give her extra help. At the same time, parent involvement could be stronger. One member of the PTA called the schools' parents "commitment-phobic," something that might result from cultural and language barriers between parents and the school. Almost 70% of the school's families do not speak English at home. To address this and increase parent involvement, the school is working to supply interpreters at parent meetings.

The school's enrollment has declined in recent years, not because it is undesirable, but because it has been overlooked. Nestled in an affluent, predominantly Orthodox Jewish neighborhood, the school imports most of its children from outside the immediate area, because many local families send their kids to private religious schools. As a result, the school has had room to welcome special education students from outside the immediate area. It offers several self-contained classes exclusively for students with special needs, as well as team-taught inclusion classes for both general education students and students with special needs.

# PS 139: Rego Park School
## 93-06 63rd Drive
## Rego Park, NY 11374
## (718) 459-1044

**Admissions:** neighborhood school   **Reading scores:** ****
**Grade levels:** K–6                **Math scores:** ****
**Enrollment:** 800                  **Ethnicity:** 33%W 3%B 29%H 35%A
**Class size:** K: 24; 6: 28         **Free lunch:** 51%

PS 139 is a friendly, well-equipped school that prepares its students—including many new immigrants from Latin America, Israel, China, Korea, and Russia—for demanding middle schools and high schools. The school has two in-house gifted programs—one called Kappa, for the school's highest scorers, and the other, TAG.

Students from different backgrounds learn to work together. The Glee Club sings songs in Tagalog, Yiddish, Korean, and Russian. "I like the diversity, I like that culturally there's no one focus on any one culture, but they are all respected," one American-born mother said.

Housed in a red-brick building in the heart of bustling Rego Park, PS 139 has a new, spotless, air-conditioned addition, with a library, a science lab, and early childhood classrooms. There is a mini-lunchroom for the kindergartners; all the kindergarten classes are outfitted with reading lofts, and there are colorful tiles on the floor. Upstairs is a beautifully equipped science room.

Computer class activities are integrated with what the children are learning in science or social studies. For example, 4th graders studying Native Americans made graphic pictures of long houses on the computer. Children graduate having learned to do a spreadsheet, create a database, and do word processing.

A 6th-grade math class made "tessellations" to create gift wrap, repeating arrangements of shapes that lock into each other. The object is to bring real life into math, said their teacher. Other students were learning about unit pricing by creating their own cereal boxes, including math games on the back of the box as well as nutrition facts, and learning about fractions.

School achievement is high; in an average year a few 6th graders gain entrance to the competitive Hunter College High School. One year, three of the four who were admitted to Hunter started out at PS 139 not speaking English.

The school has a collaboration with the American Ballroom Theatre. A resident teacher works with 5th graders, and students recently won a silver medal in a ballroom dancing competition.

Parents are welcome, and are active in the school every day. They sponsor a monthly ice cream party. "There are very high expectations from everybody right across the board," said one parent. "There is an open dialogue between parents, teachers, and administrators. Parents' concerns are taken very seriously and that's a big plus."

The school's talented and gifted program is partly a "pull-out" program in which students see a specialist for research-oriented lessons for certain periods of a day, and partly a "push-in" program in which the special teacher works with children in their regular classroom. Students are selected for the program by teacher recommendation, classwork, and test scores. The school zone includes a few neighborhoods in Corona and East Elmhurst, located in another district, for integration purposes.

# PS 175

## 64-35 102nd Street
## Rego Park, NY 11374
## (718) 897-8600

**Admissions:** neighborhood school  **Reading scores:** ****
**Grade levels:** PK–5                **Math scores:** ****
**Enrollment:** 661                   **Ethnicity:** 60%W 4%B 17%H 19%A
**Class size:** K: 20; 5: 25          **Free lunch:** 70%

With a Native American feast for 4th graders, a circus coming to perform, and a Shakespeare festival, PS 175 is a happening place. Parents are an integral part of the school—and its biggest boosters.

Principal Linda Green believes in giving teachers freedom "to stand on their own and cooperate with each other." Classrooms vary in set-up: Some teachers favor desks in rows, while others prefer rugs and child-size beanbag chairs where kids sprawl out to read.

PS 175 has an interesting mix of families. It's a Title I school, which means that it has a high number of kids eligible for free lunch and is, therefore, entitled to special federal funding. It also has a large number of new immigrant students from Russia and, increasingly, China. While the school has found it a challenge to reach out to the many newcomer parents who work long hours, it has been able to enlist parents who are professionals with flexible schedules to volunteer at the school daily. They publish a bimonthly, 36-page newsletter, run an after-school program, and provide funds for a sophisticated, school-based weather station.

Kids at PS 175 seem comfortable working together in groups and reading in pairs, and the school has a good science program. In a 5th-grade science class, students confidently defined "biomes" to visitors and comfortably explained a "Venn diagram" they made comparing and contrasting biomes in Alaska and Florida. PS 175, the reporting school for a local television channel, has a weather station on its roof, connected to a computer in the science lab, and monitored by the children. The science lab also boasts Chinese fighting fish in tanks kept crystal clean by students. Scientists from Cold Spring Harbor work with older students on studies of genetics.

The school has a gifted and talented coordinator who takes children out of the classroom for special projects and goes into the classroom to work with all students.

# PS 144

**93-02 69th Avenue
Forest Hills, NY 11375
(718) 268-2775**

**Admissions:** neighborhood school
**Grade levels:** PK–6
**Enrollment:** 700
**Class size:** K: 25; 5: 28

**Reading scores:** ****
**Math scores:** ****
**Ethnicity:** 36%W 9%B 17%H 38%A
**Free lunch:** 25%

Arts and technology play a big role at PS 144, where kids often use computers to research projects and are encouraged to find creative ways of expressing what they've learned. After studying how electricity is created, for example, upper-grade students designed working Tiffany lamps, which are displayed on a web page the school has created through its partnership with the Queens Museum of Art.

PS 144 has been aggressive in applying for grants for performing and visual arts residencies. Its large and active parents' association raised funds to purchase 3rd-grade dance and 1st-grade puppetry residencies. Performers- and artists-in-residence typically meet with each class for 6 to 10 weeks. After seeing the Broadway musical *42nd Street*, 6th graders were taught songs and dances from the musical by a choreographer and piano accompanist. Fourth graders were taught Flamenco dancing after seeing a performance at City Center.

Parents say that teachers care about shaping well-rounded students—not just good test takers. Teachers say the school is a collaborative place where parents, teachers, and kids are all involved. "The parents are terrific," said the computer lab teacher. "Whenever we need them, they're here. We [teachers] are like a big family. It crosses all ages and experience levels. We're close in school and out of school."

Test scores are well above the city average. There is a gifted and talented program for children in grades 2–6. Participants in the program meet with teachers both in and out of their homerooms and are guided through enrichment projects based on what they have been studying in their regular classes. For example, 5th graders designed fictional cultures using criteria—such as religion, currency, and clothing—discussed in their social studies classes.

There are eight self-contained special education classes, as well as a 1st-grade inclusion class that mixes special education and regular education children.

# PS 101: School in the Gardens
## 2 Russell Place
## Forest Hills, NY 11375
## (718) 268-7231
### *www.schoolinthegardens.org*

**Admissions:** neighborhood school   **Reading scores:** * * * *
**Grade levels:** PK–6                **Math scores:** * * * * *
**Enrollment:** 615                   **Ethnicity:** 48%W 8%B 15%H 29%A
**Class size:** K: 22; 5: 25          **Free lunch:** 18%

Long one of the highest scoring schools in the city, PS 101 has a small-town feel. Nestled in the heart of Forest Hills Gardens, the school is surrounded by winding streets, large shade trees, and million-dollar homes.

The school draws on a stable group of educated parents, many of whom are doctors and lawyers. Some choose PS 101 over private schools because they want their children exposed to others of different races and social classes.

Long a traditional school, PS 101 gradually is introducing some progressive elements into its teaching methods. Ronnie Feder, who became principal in January 2005, got to work de-cluttering the building right away: Students and teachers discarded outdated textbooks, readers, and unused reference materials to make space for classroom libraries comprising children's literature. Teachers are beginning to rely less on textbooks and more on fun-to-read picture books.

Despite this period of transition, the school is humming along smoothly. Not all tried-and-true techniques are being abandoned. Children are tested on vocabulary and spelling and use text- and workbooks for math. The school has its own talented and gifted program. Some children, based on test scores and teacher recommendations, are selected to participate in academic enrichment activities.

The school has a large chorus, and 4th, 5th, and 6th graders perform musicals such as *Grease* and *Guys and Dolls*. There are two self-contained special education classes and two collaborative team teaching (CTT) classes.

There are monthly tours. The district office occasionally grants variances to children who live outside the zone. Pick up an application in May.

# PS 196

## 71-25 113th Street
## Forest Hills, NY 11375
## (718) 263-9770

**Admissions:** neighborhood school
**Grade levels:** PK–5
**Enrollment:** 633
**Class size:** K: 24; 5: 30

**Reading scores:** * * * * *
**Math scores:** * * * * *
**Ethnicity:** 45%W 4%B 14%H 37%A
**Free lunch:** 15%

With a longtime reputation as a top-notch school, PS 196 attracts demanding, educated parents who move to the neighborhood to send their children there. Academics are fast-paced and kids are pushed to excel.

Some parents complain there is too much emphasis on standardized tests, teachers pile on the homework, and the atmosphere fosters unhealthy competition. But many parents say that the school's recent focus on music and arts programs has brought more joy into the building. "It was always a high-performing school but now it's a happy school," said a teacher.

Throughout the school, kids are sprawled on the floor reading, or sitting on chairs writing in their writer's notebooks. Fifth graders and their science teacher built ecosystems in bottles. In the corner of the room were tufts of grass and bags of soil and seeds.

A 5th-grade class read *The Cay*, a story of a white boy and a black man shipwrecked in the Caribbean during World War II. Rather than write traditional book reports, students wrote essays about how the conflicts that these characters faced related to their own lives. They learned a Calypso song and studied the Caribbean plants and animals described in the book—a lesson that integrated science and music with the reading lesson. Classes mix kids with different abilities.

Forty years ago, the neighborhood was made up mostly of upper-middle-class Jewish families who were prevented by discrimination from buying houses in nearby Forest Hills Gardens. Since the early 1980s, many newcomers have arrived from India, Pakistan, China, Korea, Japan, Iran, and, more recently, the former Soviet Union. The fierce overcrowding of the late 1990s has been alleviated by portable classrooms built on part of the playground.

# PS 99: Kew Gardens School
## 82-37 Kew Gardens Road
## Kew Gardens, NY 11415
## (718) 544-4343

**Admissions:** neighborhood school    **Reading scores:** ****
**Grade levels:** K–6                   **Math scores:** ****
**Enrollment:** 850                     **Ethnicity:** 24%W 11%B 38%H 27%A
**Class size:** K: 25; 6: 31            **Free lunch:** 58%

"Fair is foul and foul is fair," cackled the 4th-grade witches, reading aloud from Shakespeare's *Macbeth*. At PS 99, students put on live performances and puppet shows of plays such as *A Midsummer Night's Dream* and *Taming of the Shrew*. Or, they might join the school's student government and offer their two cents worth about school policies.

PS 99 is a top-notch school that balances academic subjects with the arts. Parents in this mostly middle-class but very international neighborhood are generous with their time and money, helping to pay for "extras" as well as the basics.

A talented and gifted (TAG) program, based on the "Renzulli" philosophy, which pulls students out of their classroom for enrichment activities, begins in 3rd grade. Children are taken out of their regular classes several times a week. The TAG teacher also provides enrichment in all classes.

The school is not tracked, and lessons encourage students to work together in groups. Children learn to read using children's literature, rather than the trade books of the past. Younger students might use rods and blocks, or other hands-on objects, to learn mathematics concepts. In a 1st-grade math lesson, children brought in toy cars, held races to see how far they could go, then measured the distance.

The school has a strong sense of community, and students are taught to think about values and the moral implications behind what they might read in a story, for example. Students are given a say in their school: There's a student council and a peer mediation program. "It's a way for children to solve their disputes with their peers and not get punished," said one student of the peer mediation program. Of the student council, he added, "it's a fair and democratic way to choose our leaders."

# PS 41

## 214-43 35th Avenue
## Bayside, NY 11361
## (718) 423-8333

**Admissions:** neighborhood school
**Grade levels:** K–5
**Enrollment:** 412
**Class size:** K: 20; 4: 34

**Reading scores:** * * * * *
**Math scores:** * * * * *
**Ethnicity:** 36%W 6%B 14%H 44%A
**Free lunch:** 18%

Surrounded by Little League fields and city parks, the old-fashioned building that houses PS 41 has a cozy neighborhood feel. The principal gives children hugs and "high-fives." One child stopped the principal to boast about an essay she had written. "Bring it to me!" the principal said.

Teachers place an emphasis on creativity, discovery, and debate. In a science experiment to see how plants make food, children soaked green leaves in Borax and hot water, laid them on a sheet of paper, and banged them with toothbrushes. Then they soaked them in hot water and learned how to take out the green plant cells. They were left with a graphic representation of the vascular system of the green cell.

Teachers receive training from staffers from the Teachers College Reading and Writing Project, and children learn to express their ideas in imaginative ways. Parents are active in the school and help to bring extracurricular activities into the building. There's an international night, a carnival, and a movie night—all organized by parents.

The school has a partnership with Young Audiences, which brings a resident artist into the school to give musical theater workshops. Eventually, the children get to put on a culminating performance, and show off their musical and dramatic skills.

One father who moved back to the city from Long Island said the exposure to different cultures makes PS 41 special. His son's 3rd-grade teacher, a native of China, taught Chinese history to the students. "That's something you wouldn't see on Long Island," he said.

Classes include children of all abilities.

# PS 98

### 40-20 235th Street
### Douglaston, NY 11363
### (718) 423-8535

**Admissions:** neighborhood school    **Reading scores:** * * * * *
**Grade levels:** K–5    **Math scores:** * * * * *
**Enrollment:** 311    **Ethnicity:** 56%W 12%B 7%H 25%A
**Class size:** K: 25; 5: 26    **Free lunch:** 11%

Lush, large maple trees, an immaculately trimmed lawn, groomed shrubs, and colorful flower beds surround PS 98, a clean, red-brick building with a Palladian window over open front doors. Birds chirp and bells from a nearby church chime "What a Friend We Have in Jesus." Mothers pushing strollers greet their children as the school day ends and walk them home the through quiet, tree-lined streets of Douglaston Manor. Is this really a public school? Are we still in New York City?

Situated on a small peninsula on the north shore of Long Island not far from the Nassau County border, PS 98 is in one of the richest neighborhoods in the city. The tiny school has long been one of the highest scoring in the city. Classes are small, the atmosphere is friendly, and the teachers are capable and imaginative. Parents buy houses in the neighborhood just so their children can attend.

Principal Sheila Huggins has a good rapport with the staff and jokes with everyone from the school safety officer to the cafeteria workers. It's a quiet and peaceful school, and teachers have developed techniques to keep classrooms peaceful. For example, children wear earphones in the computer lab, and the teacher instructs them to put a stuffed doll on top of their monitors when they need help—instead of clamoring loudly for the teacher's attention. Parents are grateful for the individual attention children receive when they have problems. One mother said the school "worked wonders" for her daughter, who was diagnosed with attention deficit disorder.

The school has an in-house postal service called "Wee Deliver." The idea is to help kids improve their writing by encouraging them to send letters to one another at school. Art and music also are emphasized. Students learn to play the guitar or recorder, and the school has a partnership with Midori and Friends, a group that provides kids with music education classes.

# PS 94: David Porter School

## 41-77 Little Neck Parkway
## Little Neck, NY 11363
## (718) 423-8491

**Admissions:** neighborhood school  
**Grade levels:** K–5  
**Enrollment:** 419  
**Class size:** K: 25; 5: 35  

**Reading scores:** * * * * *  
**Math scores:** * * * * *  
**Ethnicity:** 42%W 4%B 11%H 43%A  
**Free lunch:** 9%  

Eggs were hatching and foot fungus was growing in the 5th-grade classrooms at PS 94, a school that retains its old-fashioned, small-town charm even as it embraces creative teaching methods.

Teachers use the Writing Process, the technique for teaching writing pioneered by Lucy Calkins at Teachers College, Columbia University. Math lessons draw on children's curiosity about the world around them rather than rote memorization. Second and 3rd graders, for example, learn elements of geometry along with arithmetic facts by charting the number of blocks they walk or ride on their way to school. Teachers constantly are going back to school themselves to hone their skills.

Fifth graders have their very own business endeavor, the Cozy Comfort Company, which manufactures originally designed pillows and sewn-by-students "critters" that are filled with shredded papers collected throughout the school during recycling efforts. Some students, part of the Cozy Comfort dancers, work with the school's resident dance and physical education teacher to choreograph original dance routines and commercials to advertise the Cozy Comfort project.

The school has a full-time graphic artist, who teaches kids how to produce and enhance artwork, and gives them a background in art history. Students in all grades can participate in the school's Suzuki violin program. Carnegie Hall performers come to the school and pupils go to Carnegie Hall to hear concerts else.

Located in the northeast corner of Queens just west of the Nassau border, PS 94's yellow stucco building was constructed in 1913 and is vaguely reminiscent of the Alamo. It's surrounded by large trees, manicured lawns, and single-family houses. Inside, there are high ceilings and dark-wood paneling. There's a pot of coffee and a plate of coffee cake in the office, and anyone who stops by is made to feel welcome. With 420 pupils and two or three classes in each grade, everyone knows everyone else.

Principal JoAnn Barbeosch encourages teachers to create imaginative projects that are exciting for the children. Fifth graders grew foot fungus as a science project, swabbing their own feet with Q-tips and watching the fungus grow in petri dishes. (The hypothesis was that boys would have more fungus than girls.) Some teachers, including the principal, also tested their feet. (The fastest growing appear to be the fungi of the principal's husband, she noted.) Students even took a fungus sample from Lilly, the school's resident guide dog, who accompanies the school's social worker, Linda Paul.

A science area, tucked in the corner of the cafeteria because of lack of space, has colorful posters and aquariums with mealworms, snails, and guinea pigs. Science lessons spill over into the gymnasium next door. Third graders studying simple machines—and potential and kinetic energy—were in the gymnasium enthusiastically catapulting cotton balls from plastic spoons taped to wooden blocks.

Even in the youngest grades, students write original stories and edit their own work. "My fiction story is that everything is upside down except for a man," a 1st grader told his classmates. "Even the balloons are upside down." The other children applauded. Second graders were "book shopping" in their classroom libraries, putting their choices in clear plastic bags to take home. There were no workbooks in sight for math or literature.

Many classrooms have student teachers getting their master's degrees from Queens College. When there's an opening on the teaching staff, Barbeosch handpicks some of the best of them. Unlike many other schools in the district, PS 94 hasn't lost many teachers to nearby Nassau County. "I try to make my teachers' life as good as possible," she said. "I feed them a lot. I try very hard to keep them here."

Parents' main complaint is overcrowding. In addition to science, special literature classes are taught in the lunchroom. There is rarely room for children from outside the school zone.

# PS 221: North Hills School
## 57-40 Marathon Parkway
## Little Neck, NY 11362
## (718) 423-8825

**Admissions:** neighborhood school  
**Grade levels:** PK–5  
**Enrollment:** 670  
**Class size:** K: 20; 5: 32  

**Reading scores:** * * * * *  
**Math scores:** * * * * *  
**Ethnicity:** 32%W 3%B 9%H 56%A  
**Free lunch:** 14%  

PS 221 is a calm school, with a well-deserved reputation for high academic performance. "I love showing off the school," Principal Sheelia Twomey repeated several times during our visit to PS 221. Indeed the bulletin boards and classroom activities reflect rigorous lessons and hard-working, often-precocious students. "How do you spell *onomatopoeia*?" one 2nd grader asked Assistant Principal Stephen Leo.

Erected in the 1950s, the building is fairly standard for a school, save one small detail—it is built into the side of a hill. The bottom story of the building overlooks the roof of the adjacent public library, while the top floor offers a panoramic view of Queens and beyond. Inside, the hallways are quiet and spotless. The maintenance staff routinely walk the school with a towel under foot to remove scuff marks from the floor.

At PS 221 children learn to read by selecting their own books from well-stocked classrooms. They hone their writing skills through a lot of drafting and revision of work. "When you work on an 'all about' book," instructed one teacher to her kindergarten class, "you are an expert on that topic." Every month students in all grades read and craft written responses to the school's book of the month. Children in the younger grades may write letters to the main character, while older children discuss the author's purpose or how changes in the main character relate to the message of the story.

In math, students learn to compute and solve problems with the use of manipulatives (such as blocks, tiles, or coins) and use words as well as numbers to explain their reasoning.

The school does not have a gifted and talented program, but offers enrichment activities to high-achieving students. PS 221 rarely has room for children from outside the zone.

# PS 188
## 218-12 Hartland Avenue
## Bayside, NY 11364
## (718) 464-5768
*http://schools.nycenet.edu/Region3/ps188*

**Admissions:** neighborhood school/gifted program
**Grade levels:** K–5                    **Reading scores:** \* \* \* \* \*
**Enrollment:** 480                      **Math scores:** \* \* \* \* \*
**Class size:** K: 20; 5: 25             **Ethnicity:** 38%W 10%B 11%H 41%A
                                         **Free lunch:** 10%

PS 188 is home to a district gifted program, but every class in the building might be mistaken for a gifted one, since students throughout the building perform at such a high level. The school's strong leadership, a creative staff, and an active parent body have made it one of the best regarded in the city.

Housed in a pleasant three-story, red-brick building, PS 188 is shaded by large oak trees and surrounded by clipped lawns and shrubs on a quiet residential street. It has a library with books grouped by "levels" so children can easily make selections that are just right for them.

Throughout the building teachers speak with gentle, encouraging voices and often refer to their students as "writers" and "readers." "Okay, readers," posed one teacher to her class, "why was the main character scared?"

Every classroom that we visited offered evidence of creative lessons, an accelerated pace of learning, and an engaged student body. For instance, in a science class, 3rd graders were busy manipulating pieces of tin foil to study how altering the shape of matter affects its density. Since few, if any, students are "struggling" within the context of state- and citywide standards, the school can hone in on the nitty-gritty details of students' strengths and weaknesses. "Everything is in place," said Principal Janet Caraisco who took on leadership of the school in 2004. "Instead of correcting things, we can go to the next level."

In the upper grades many classroom libraries are stocked with books normally reserved for a middle school curriculum. In band, children are pulled out of their music class for small-group instruction in their chosen instrument. Even inclement weather is an opportunity to stretch the mind—children play board games in the gym rather than watching movies as is done in many schools.

In mathematics, students use words as well as numbers to explain their reasoning. Children discover numerical relationships through activities and games, using blocks, tiles, and coins. A 5th-grade class investigated the total number of eyelets (shoelace holes) found in shoes and sneakers worn by the students in the class. Their inquiry involved several steps, including estimation as well as strategies to compute the precise answer—all accompanied by explanations presented in well-written prose. The math program yields impressive results. On the 2003 and 2004 statewide standardized math exams, 100% of 4th graders performed at or above grade level.

Admission to the gifted program is determined by District 26 and not by the school administration. In every other respect the school guides the learning of all its students. The same curriculum is used in all classes, and all students have the opportunity to participate in extracurricular programs such as school plays, student council, and the basketball league. "It's more like a school with a top class than a separate program" said Caraisco. The only difference, she said, is that the gifted class moves a bit faster than the other classes.

There is rarely room for children from outside the immediate zone, except in the gifted program. Children are tested for the gifted class in March of their kindergarten year.

# PS 18

## 86-35 235th Court
## Queens Village, NY 11427
## (718) 464-4167

**Admissions:** neighborhood school/gifted program
**Grade levels:** K–5                    **Reading scores:** *****
**Enrollment:** 460                      **Math scores:** *****
**Class size:** K: 19; 5: 32             **Ethnicity:** 19%W 9%B 12%H 60%A
                                          **Free lunch:** 23%

PS 18, which houses a district-wide gifted program, is a warm, homey school in a neighborhood with single-family homes, garden apartments, and lots of stay-at-home moms. Principal Joy Hammer greets children outside as they arrive in the morning. Parent volunteers whisk open car doors and escort children inside—so parents don't have to search for parking or hold up traffic by double parking.

Hammer makes parents welcome. A large room behind the auditorium has been refurbished as a "parent room." There are monthly workshops to keep parents up-to-date on what's going on in the classroom. "She's very open, very accessible," said one mother.

Nearly all classrooms have rugs for a meeting space and comfy chairs for reading. Most classrooms are richly decorated with samples of children's writing and art. Children also get to see their work "in print" in classroom newsletters published by students or parents.

The Teachers College Reading and Writing Project model is in use in most classrooms. Students have monthly writing celebrations and display their work on classroom walls. Students are encouraged to take books home from their classroom libraries so they can read at home each night.

Some parents complain there is little mingling between children in the gifted program and the neighborhood children. Technology has not been a priority, and not all classrooms are well equipped with computers. But overall parents are enthusiastic and use words like "phenomenal" and "terrific" to describe the quality of teaching and the school leadership.

Most children come from the school's zone. Children from across the district are tested in kindergarten for entrance to the gifted program. An after-school program is available and includes activities such as chess, drama, soccer, and yoga.

# PS/IS 266
## 74-10 Commonwealth Boulevard
## Bellerose, NY 11426
## (718) 479-3920

**Admissions:** lottery
**Grade levels:** PK–8
**Enrollment:** 667
**Class size:** K: 20; 5: 33

**Reading scores:** ****
**Math scores:** *****
**Ethnicity:** 40%W 15%B 13%H 32%A
**Free lunch:** 11%

Newest and shiniest of the jewels in District 26's crown, PS/IS 266 opened in September 2003 with a teaching staff culled from a pool of eager applicants, a PTA already organized, and a principal, Kenneth Morris, with 8 years of experience as assistant principal of much-admired MS 67. A school with progressive teaching methods and high standards, PS/IS 266 seems destined for academic distinction.

It may have a harder time, however, establishing a sense of community. The school's airport-like setting—children are taken by bus or car to "drop-off points" at the end of an access road—deters casual encounters among families. But enrollment is small, parent involvement is high, and Morris immediately established a student government. "We're looking to groom our students as leaders," he says.

Part of a three-school complex on 32 acres, formerly part of the Creedmore Psychiatric Center, PS/IS 266 shares a campus in the Glen Oaks area with District 29's **PS/IS 208** and the High School of Teaching, Liberal Arts and Sciences. (Graduates of both primary-intermediate schools get priority in admission to the high school.) An attractive brick building with brown-and-tan tiled halls and sunlit classrooms, the school is free of the crowding typical of Queens schools and hopes to cap enrollment at 680. Kindergarten rooms are vast, computers abound, science labs gleam, and there are kilns in the art studio. It is not quite paradise: Lacking a classroom, the music teacher holds classes on the auditorium stage. There's a playground for young children and a courtyard at the entrance for older ones, but no athletic fields: An access road and parking lot, where motorists battle for spaces, occupy much of the campus.

Like the building, teaching here is state-of-the art, with lots of groupwork and meaningful projects. As we toured, a 2nd-grade teacher worked with one group while another read independently, marking challenging words with Post-its. Kindergarten children recorded numbers in "math notebooks" as a teacher gave a lesson. For a "then and now" social studies project, young children interviewed adult relatives about their childhood homes and hobbies, then wrote and illustrated books contrasting past and present. Math is emphasized, and the curriculum is rigorous: Kindergartners are expected to write, and, as we toured, an 8th-grade English teacher gently chided students who hadn't completed creative but demanding homework.

Children in 7th and 8th grades are tracked by standardized test scores; the top honors group studies Regents math and science. Beginning in 3rd grade, all children take at least one period of Spanish a week. Middle school students get three "talent" periods a week in art, music, or computers. Children aren't likely to fall through the cracks here. As we toured, the guidance counselor informed the principal that a child's drawing had alarmed a teacher. Morris directed the counselor to call in a therapist; she said it was already done.

The school serves a cross-section of the district, which, according to Morris, includes some "less affluent" families, if not many poor ones. The school has some inclusion classes, where children with special needs and general education students learn side by side. Admission is limited to children living in District 26 and is by lottery. Contact the school for details.

# GOOD NEIGHBORHOOD SCHOOLS: QUEENS

Every single school in District 26 has scores that are well above the city average. Most of the district is composed of neighborhood schools, and students typically come directly from the school's zone—very few schools accept variances. The schools vary in personality, but all are good, and many are exemplary. Below are thumbnails of the district's neighborhood schools. For additional information, parent comments, and maps that show each school's zone, visit *www.insideschools.org*.

## Bayside

**PS 31**, 211-45 46th Road, Bayside, NY 11361, (718) 423-8288, is a school where parents praise the lessons as "well-rounded," and the academics are very strong. The school's enrollment grew rapidly in the late 1990s, and the school's library is still converted into a make-shift classroom as a result. Now, bookshelves line the hallways, and children have painted charming portraits of their favorite characters—Harry Potter, Amber Brown, and Matidla—overhead and between classroom doorways. Parents say that teachers are warm and caring, and teachers say the building is a collegial place. "There's a lot of heart and caring in this school," said one teacher. Another teacher said: "It's an interesting, financially diverse neighborhood . . . the community functions nicely within the school."

The school's principal, Terri Graybow, began in 2003 and is described by her staff as thoughtful, intelligent, and cooperative. The school has guest artists who visit to paint murals or make books with the students. Guest storytellers visit the school to tell fairy tales and lead the children in circle stories. Parents are very involved and raise money to buy books and fund school trips. Some parents complain that the school's classes are too large in the older grades, with as many as 35 students per class. The school has a notable after-school program. Students can rent instruments and rehearse for winter and spring concerts. For a fee, children may participate in weekly classes in dance, physical fitness, and karaoke.

**PS 203: Oakland Gardens School**, 53-11 Springfield Boulevard, Bayside, NY 11364, (718) 423-8652, is an unusually welcoming place, where students are engaged in their work, happy to be in class, and even sorry when school ends. "Whenever I'm on vacation, I miss school and wish it would start again," a 5th-grade boy said.

Colorful artwork and murals cover the walls and spill into the general office, where even the desks are decorated. Principal Carole Nussbaum greets every student by name as she walks through the halls. A table in her office is covered with bins of cookies and candy for children who come to visit.

Each classroom has a carpeted reading area with bins of books. Potted plants and art and science projects—such as painted and shellacked papier-mâché volcanoes with green moss—cover the tables and shelves. Every kindergarten classroom has a raised wooden loft where children can read or play. The school has a notable drama program: Children put on a 2-hour musical, and some have become so proficient they were finalists in auditions for Broadway plays such as *The Lion King*. Clubs and special classes include Suzuki violin, gardening, photography, and "Constitution Works," in which 5th graders play-act U.S. Supreme Court cases.

There are several programs designed to challenge high-achieving children. In grades 1–5 there is one "top" class. In the WINGS and STAR programs, children are taken from their classes once a week for special programs in architecture, design, or computers. There are well-equipped, pleasant self-contained special education classes.

**PS 46**, 64-45 218th Street, Bayside, NY 11364, (718) 423-8395, is a calm and nurturing school with a strong record of achievement. The school is accessible to children in wheelchairs and with other physical disabilities and accommodates a substantial special education population. Many of the school's classes are inclusion, meaning that special education and general education students share their classrooms. Kids learn how to be tolerant of one another's differences. "Special education is woven into the fabric of the school," said Principal Marsha Goldberg, who previously served as the District 26 supervisor for special education.

PS 46 is high-performing and lessons are purposeful and interesting. Children always have a book close at hand so that if they finish a test or task early they spend their down time reading. Classroom routines are well established and transitions between lesson blocks are smooth and quick.

To foster a sense of community, PS 46 organizes events to draw parents into the school, such as the international festival, during which parents are invited into the classrooms to share dances, stories, and food from their heritage. In one class a mother and daughter wore traditional African garb and shared stories of their cultural celebrations with the students. Elsewhere a child recited the Hamotzi, the Jewish prayer for bread and meals; another mother told a Chinese version of a Mother Goose story. The school occasionally has room for a few children from outside the zone.

**PS 205**, 75-25 Bell Boulevard, Bayside, NY 11364, (718) 464-5773, is a small, cozy school defined not only by its academic achievements, but also by the focus the principal and staff place on building a sense of community. Everyone calls the principal, Susan Sherer, "Mama Sherer," and parents say the school feels like a big family. Many of the parents went to the school themselves as children.

The school encourages staffers to learn new techniques for teaching reading, writing, and social studies. Children read historical fiction and nonfiction, even in the early grades. For example, as part of a study of American history, children read *Orphan Train Rider: One Boy's True Story,* the biography of a destitute New York City boy sent to live in Texas in 1926. They watched a video that dramatized the "orphan train," an early form of foster care that sent homeless children from cities to farms between 1854 and 1930, then did their own research and writing under the tutelage of educators from Queens College.

**PS 162: John Golden School**, 201-02 53rd Avenue, Bayside, NY 11364, (718) 423-8621, is a school where the fine quality of instruction is literally written on the walls. Classrooms and hallways feature well-written essays, challenging math projects, and other evidence of good, creative lessons. One hallway displayed the results of 5th graders' efforts to measure the dimensions of the school, while another hallway offered up the dioramas that emerged from children's studies of Mexican culture.

The school is relatively big and has more students enrolled than ideal. Still, it feels snug, not overcrowded, and kids get plenty of individual attention. Teaching is strong. In one class, an energetic kindergarten teacher read her students the story "There Was an Old Lady Who Swallowed a Fly" and had them come up with their own versions of what the old lady might have swallowed. Second graders grappled with the hard questions suggested by a book entitled *Tight Times*: Why do people lose their jobs? What happens afterwards? "The teachers bring out things in your child you didn't even know they had," said one parent. Her daughter's 5th-grade teacher, she said, saw to it that the students entered poetry, book writing, and essay contests.

A significant percentage of students at PS 162 are immigrants and do not speak English at home. While parent involvement in the school is generally high, the school struggles to boost participation of immigrant parents. The school has no self-contained special education classes. Special education services are offered both inside and outside regular classrooms.

**PS 159**, 205-01 33rd Avenue, Bayside, NY 11361, (718) 423-8553, is a kindergarten through 6th-grade school housed in a boxy, three-story brick building located in a quiet residential neighborhood. The outside calm hints at what goes on inside, where student work is displayed on neat bulletin boards. Even the cafeteria—typically rowdy and deafening even at the best schools—has a controlled feel.

A "Students of the Month" bulletin board greets visitors in the front hallway. Each child at the school is featured on it at least once before graduation, says Principal Marlene Zucker. The emphasis on giving every student a public pat on the back also says something about the school's approach to teaching. "Our educational philosophy focuses on differentiating instruction for each student," says Zucker, who has led the school for over a decade. The school also offers strong art and music programs and a smaller drama program. There is ample space at the school, which even has an outdoor reading garden, and a class-size reduction grant has allowed the school to keep younger classes small. Unfortunately, beginning in 4th grade, classes push the upper limit, with 30 students per class. The school has one separate special education class. Other special education students are enrolled in general education classes, but receive special services every day. PS 159 is the only elementary school in District 26 with a 6th grade, and most students continue on to IS 25, in District 25, which begins in 7th grade.

Situated next to Alley Pond Park in a quiet suburban neighborhood, **PS 213: Carl Ullman School**, 231-02 67th Avenue, Bayside, NY 11364, (718) 423-8747, is a tranquil place. Kids are extraordinarily well behaved, if their seamless transitions between activities are any indication. In some classes, kids line up at a clap of the teacher's hands.

Students do a lot of groupwork. In a 4th-grade math class we saw, students were exploring geometry by sorting shapes and explaining their answers. Hallways are well decorated with lively student artwork, everything from paper owls perched on a bulletin board tree to dinosaurs that help students to learn math. This may be the result of a well-established art program. For 12 years, Studio-in-a-School, which is funded by a grant, has enlisted the talents of an artist who works with kids to integrate art into academic subjects. Students paint their own renderings of facial expressions to help them better learn vocabulary about emotions, for example.

PS 213 has six self-contained classes, mostly for children with learning disabilities. The school is wheelchair accessible and shares the building with a District 75 school. (District 75 is a citywide district that runs programs and schools for severely disabled students.) Most graduates go on to MS 74, their neighborhood middle school.

## Fresh Meadows

**PS 173**, 174-10 67th Avenue, Flushing, NY 11365, (718) 358-2243, is a high-performing school that takes fun seriously. Whether the children are planning a birthday party for a teacher, or learning to write a "narrative" description by watching their teacher put on makeup, this school shows that learning doesn't have to be drudgery.

Test scores in both reading and math put PS 173 among the very best schools citywide—a great achievement, especially considering the fact that many children come from homes where English isn't spoken.

It's clear the children learn the basics well. But there is also a warmth and friendliness that seem to include everyone in the school. Once a month, grown-ups and children all read the same book and write "responses" to it. Even the school safety officer and custodian participate.

The school facilities are basic. The cafeteria, built in the 1950s when most children walked home for lunch, is tiny. The school has very few computers.

**PS 26: Rufus King School**, 195-02 69th Avenue, Flushing, NY 11365, (718) 464-4505, is a diverse school where children of different cultures as well as those with different abilities and disabilities are welcomed. The school shares its building with PS 224, a District 75 school for emotionally and physically disabled kids. The two schools share activities, and an inclusion program allows students from PS 224 to participate in some general education classes. Principal Dina Koski is committed to the inclusion program, which she says teaches students tolerance. The school is welcoming to parents. The day we visited, a group of parents met in the library to plan a book fair, then moved to a nook off the gymnasium where they run the school store.

Teaching is consistently solid, and there is an easy rapport among the students, teachers, and principal. Drama and music are particularly strong at PS 26: Two full-time teachers focus on drama and music, one for the upper grades and the other for the younger students. On our visit, the drama program was gearing up for a production of *Beauty and the Beast* and, as with many of the activities at the school, both PS 26 and PS 224 students were participating. Although students with special education needs may receive services both in and out of their regular classes, the building is not wheelchair accessible. Class size is 25 in the younger grades, 32 in 5th grade.

## Floral Park

**PS 191**, 85-15 258th Street, Floral Park, NY 11001, (718) 831-4032, is located just a few blocks from the Nassau County border, in a community that traditionally sent its children to parochial and private schools. Increasingly, parents are enrolling their children at PS 191—attracted by a good art program, active parents, and some of the top reading scores in the city.

The hallways are lined with children's artwork. Third graders displayed "The Many Faces of Vincent Van Gogh," with paintings in four different styles: Cubism, Realism, Surrealism, and Impressionism.

Teachers are collegial. The school has a large multicultural population and holds school-wide events, such as cultural dance performances, where kids are encouraged to share their backgrounds with their peers. Parents are very involved. They run a school store in the morning and an after-school program taught by the school's teachers, with such offerings as drama, quilting, arts and crafts, and soccer.

Space is tight. One year, a 3rd-grade class had 36 children (with two teachers). But most classes are smaller. In recent years, five to ten children have been admitted from outside the zone.

## Jamaica Estates

**PS 178: Holliswood School**, 189-10 Radnor Road, Jamaica Estates, NY 11423, (718) 464-5763, is a small school nestled in a neighborhood of suburban-looking homes and well-groomed lawns. While the school's size is part of what makes it work, it owes the bulk of its success to its teachers, who are energetic, creative, and just plain good at what they do. Lessons have a lot of substance, both in the school's general education classes and in its four separate special education classes. For example, in a special education kindergarten class, after learning about Van Gogh and his paintings, students worked on their own renditions of "Starry Night."

The strength in teaching was replicated in all of the classrooms we visited; even in a classroom where the teacher was strict and edgy, the kids were learning. Lessons in the upper grades are sophisticated. Fourth graders discussed the power loom and its effects on society, and 5th graders read a story about World War II and discussed how war affected daily life. ("Dig deeper," the 5th-grade teacher prodded her class.)

## Bellerose

**PS 133**, 248-05 86th Avenue, Bellerose, NY 11426, (718) 831-4016, is a friendly school with an informal style. It's place where kids can be kids. The day of our visit, for example, students zoomed freely around the science fair, which was set up in the gymnasium. At the same time, the children apparently respect the freedoms that they are given; the school has few discipline problems. Students do a lot of writing. Kindergartners might draft "how to" paragraphs, 3rd graders create realistic fiction stories, and 4th graders compose letters to pen pals upstate. The school's technology program is strong and offers some good art programs. It has a partnership with Carnegie Hall that culminates in a springtime student performance at the famous concert venue. PS 133 has four self-contained special education classes, but it is also the only school in the district with classes that integrate special education and general education students in the lower grades. There is a Super-Start Plus prekindergarten program, made up half of students with special education needs and half of students in the neighborhood. Twice a week PS 133 is home to an adult, daytime English language learner program, which welcomes parents, grandparents, as well as other community members. The school is open only to children who live in its zone.

# Glen Oaks

**PS 115: Glen Oaks School**, 80-51 261st Street, Floral Park, NY 11004, (718) 831-4010, is an old-fashioned school that successfully serves a very modern-day student body. It houses a special education program for hearing-impaired students and also has many new immigrants from the neighborhood's burgeoning South Asian community. A visitor can expect to see students with hearing aids learning alongside students with Indian turbans, all in a place with old-fashioned structure and style. The school has a weekly assembly of 3rd, 4th, and 5th graders, where kids wear black-and-white assembly dress, march into the auditorium, and recite of *The Pledge of Allegiance*. Other throwbacks include a student council (elected after formal campaign speeches) and an "honor society."

Teachers encourage students to talk about the books they read—to make sure they understand what they've read. PS 115 has five self-contained classes for its students with special education needs. In addition, there are separate classes for hearing-impaired students from District 75. Class size in kindergarten through 2nd grade is less than 22. Fifth-grade classes have 30 students. In recent years, the school has had some room for children from outside the zone.

**PS 186: Castlewood School**, 252-12 72nd Avenue, Bellerose, NY 11426, (718) 831-4021. Most Queens schools are filled to the brim, but PS 186 is an anomaly—an excellent school with a relatively small population. Enrollment at the school, in an area that many families see as a stepping-stone to the suburbs, has declined in recent years, and as a result Principal Dolores Troy-Quinn encourages teachers in younger grades to use Debbie Miller's book *Reading for Meaning*, which teaches kids to make connections and inferences while they read. We saw one or two less-than-inspiring classes, but on the whole, teaching was excellent. An enthusiastic technology teacher showed kindergartners how to follow directions and sequence while using the KidPix software program. Also notable was a 5th-grade class where students were engrossed in a seminar-style discussion of a question drawn from Plato's *Republic*: "Are people good because they want to be good, or because they are afraid of the consequences of being bad?" Fifth-grade classes are larger than others in the school, because underenrollment has led the district to collapse smaller classes in upper grades. While the early grades have classes in the low 20s, 4th grade has 33 and 5th grade has 26.

PS 186 is a friendly place, and everyone, including the security guard and custodial staff, spoke about it fondly. The large schoolyard abuts Little Neck Farm, a sprawling, 18th-century working farm filled with cows and sheep.

# WORTH WATCHING: QUEENS

Included here are some nice neighborhood schools outside of District 26; some schools that accept children from across Queens (or across a district); and some new schools that show promise.

## Sunnyside

**PS 150**, 40-01 43rd Avenue, Long Island City, NY 11104, (718) 784-2252, is a gigantic, sprawling school that serves 1,400 children—new immigrants from Ecuador, Mexico, and Kosovo, as well as children of middle-class professionals who live in the pleasant townhouses of Sunnyside Community Gardens. Test scores put PS 150 in the top 15% of schools citywide—a remarkable achievement given the large number of children learning English as a Second Language. It has a district-wide gifted program and an unusual bilingual special education inclusion program for Spanish-speaking children. The huge, red-brick building has a sparkling new early childhood wing, decorated in primary colors. Children sit and read or plant flowers in an attractive gazebo in the front yard. Parents take English lessons and learn skills, such as how to get a library card, at the "family center" in the school's old cafeteria. PS 150's kindergarten classes are housed in cramped quarters upstairs from a billiard parlor on Queens Boulevard. There is no outdoor play area—kindergartners watch videos instead of going outside for recess. The main building has a playground. It's an orderly, well-run school with a strong art program, a roller-blading physical education teacher, and a dance teacher who was once a professional clown. Children in the gifted program are automatically admitted to the Academy, a selective middle school at PS 122. There is no room for children from outside the zone, except in the gifted program.

Located in an area of Queens once known as Irishtown, in the past **PS 199: Maurice A. Fitzgerald School**, 39-20 48th Avenue, Long Island City, NY 11104, (718) 784-3431, lost many neighborhood students to nearby Catholic schools. Now, with an influx of immigrants from Turkey, Poland, and the Middle East, many of those Catholic schools are closing due to underenrollment, and PS 199 is bursting at the seams. In fact, several of PS 199's kindergarten and 1st-grade classes are housed in rooms rented in nearby Catholic schools.

Despite its space problems, PS 199 is a calm and happy place. Teachers and students take academics seriously, and the school's principal, Anthony Inzerillo, leads the school with an effective, gentle style. Inzerillo, a former longtime 3rd-grade teacher at the school, is popular among parents, teachers, and students. Parent involvement is strong: PTA meetings regularly draw about 150 parents.

Classrooms display lots of quality student work, and lessons encourage kids to work together and collaborate on projects. Teachers often visit one another's classrooms for ideas and share teaching strategies with one another. About 420 students receive assistance learning English, and there are six Spanish bilingual classes spread across the grades. There are no self-contained classes for students who receive special education services. There is an after-school program run by Sunnyside Community Center that offers homework help and activities like karate, art, and basketball.

## Astoria

**Our World Neighborhood Charter School**, 36-12 35th Avenue, Astoria, NY 11106, (718) 392-3405, a new school that serves children in kindergarten through 8th grade, accepts children by lottery from all five boroughs. Located in a landmark building in the "Hollywood East" section of Astoria, directly across the street from the Museum of the Moving Image and right beside K.A. Studios, Our World Neighborhood Charter School looks as though its classrooms might have been plucked from a movie set. The school's interior is sparkling new and neat, with white hallways, bright lights, and colorful decorations adorning classroom walls. The school opened in Fall 2002 in partnership with Mosaica Inc., a for-profit company that provides the school with much of its curriculum as well as with teacher training and support. Begun as a K–5 school, it added a 6th grade in 2003, a 7th grade in 2004, and an 8th grade in 2005. The principal, Brian Ferguson, seems to have a warm relationship with students (although he is more formal with adults). Kids are allowed to work independently and stretch their legs in the hallways and classrooms; many classrooms we visited were set up with "stations," where kids were working in groups at different tasks. The teaching is strong and the kids seem happy and engaged. Another plus: The student body is racially diverse. Call the school or visit *www.owncs.org* for information about admission.

Housed in a brand-new building, **PS 234**, 30-15 29th Street, Astoria, NY 11102, (718) 932-5650, opened in Fall 2003. Parents describe the school as "warm" and "welcoming," and say that its young, assertive principal, Thea Pallos, returns phone calls promptly and really seems to care what parents have to say. The school does a good job of incorporating arts into the curriculum, and reading is encouraged everywhere in the building. There's a book of the month club, and classrooms display lots of books written by children. Third graders might write books describing their favorite fictional characters, and 2nd graders might write about their grandparents or parents, and then learn about the cultural backgrounds of their classmates by reading one another's books.

Teachers try to bring art into as many lessons as possible. In one 2nd-grade science class, for example, students researched butterflies and used artwork to demonstrate their findings. The school has a partnership with Studio-in-a-School, an arts organization that brings professional artists into the classroom. As part of a project organized by City Lore, a cultural organization that promotes New York City history and folklore, 3rd graders who were learning about foreign countries in social studies class created postcards from the countries they had studied. On the postcards, they wrote messages to their families about what they had "seen in their travels."

PS 234 has three self-contained classes for children with special needs, as well as extra help for kids who need it. The school offers an after-school program that includes academic assistance, science and art activities, as well as English language instruction for parents.

## Long Island City

A large school serving more than 1,150 pupils, **PS 166**, 33-09 35th Avenue, Long Island City, NY 11106, (718) 786-6703, has an immigrant population so large that two-thirds of kindergartners and 1st graders receive English as a Second Language instruction. Happily, they do so well that by 3rd grade more than three quarters meet the state standards for reading—a number that is far above average for schools of similar demographics. On our tour, we saw many teachers and other staff members working with children individually or in small groups. In a number of classes for English as a Second Language, we saw kids with an impressive command of the language, even though, we were told, they had spoken little or no English only 6 months before. Throughout the school, teachers were confident and capable and students were well-behaved. The school places more emphasis on phonics instruction than is typical in city schools and uses textbooks to supplement the children's literature that most schools now use to teach reading. The school also uses a more traditional approach to math, including more drilling in basic skills. Parents' association meetings draw more than 100 people. The school has an open-door policy and encourages parents to visit classes. Students are supposed to wear uniforms—navy pants and skirts, white shirts and blouses. However, the dress code is enforced flexibly.

# Jackson Heights

Kindergartners at **PS 222: Early Childhood Magnet School of Exploration**, 86-15 37th Avenue, Jackson Heights, NY 11372, (718) 429-2563, may still be learning to read, but that doesn't stop them from exploring the Internet. Indeed, there are two computers in every classroom at this sparkling, new pre-K–2nd-grade center. The modern facilities, as well as an enthusiastic staff and dedicated principal, make PS 222 a promising school. The four-floor building opened in September 2002 and by 2003 the school reached its full size of 320 children. Writing is practiced every day, and teachers try to integrate language and literature into as many daily activities as possible. Although the school is in its infancy, its principal, Maria Ciccone, has almost 30 years experience in Queens public schools, including 4 years as an assistant principal in District 28. The building is bright, spotless, and modern, with hallways and classrooms color-coded by grade. The atmosphere is creative, but orderly. Children's artwork and writing decorate the cafeteria and line the hallways. Described as "a dream" by an early childhood teacher who visited the school, PS 222 offers ample-sized classrooms with plenty of books and toys for active learning. Apart from one self-contained class, special education students are integrated into general classes, including a handful of kids from District 75, the citywide administrative district for severely disabled children.

Housed in a brand-new building on a pleasant, residential street, **PS 212**, 34-25 82nd Street, Jackson Heights, NY 11374, (718) 898-6973, opened its doors in September 2000. The school has warm, gifted teachers and active parents. It's a dynamic, welcoming place. PS 212's physical plant is exceptionally well maintained, and the climate of the building is happy and cheerful. Lots of student writing is posted on walls and in hallways. PS 212 uses the reading and writing "workshop" model, which encourages kids to write several drafts of their work and to edit their classmates' writing. Lessons encourage students to work in pairs and share their ideas with one another. Teachers we observed had different styles—some were less structured and more free-flowing than others. Overall, the school has a strong teaching staff. Its principal, John Bernardino, has an open-minded and kind manner, and is well liked by kids and parents alike. Parents and teachers say the principal has an open-door policy and really takes the time to listen to them.

"Write this in big letters: THEY CARE," one mother said. "Parents here have a voice, and you can see that the administration cares."

Parents and teachers describe the school as tight-knit and inviting. There are three self-contained classes for children receiving special education. The school is barrier-free. PS 212 offers an after-school program for students in grades 2–5.

# Rego Park

Housed in a two-story, red-brick building that's surrounded by neat, single-family brick homes, **PS 174**, 65-10 Dieterle Crescent, Rego Park, NY 11374, (718) 897-7006, is a serious, orderly school that attracts children of educated newcomers from Russia and Asia who move to the neighborhood because of the school's reputation. The curriculum is demanding. One mother said the 6th-grade literature discussions are as sophisticated as you might find in college.

In one 1st-grade class, with 27 children from 21 different countries, pupils each wrote and illustrated a report on their home country, using *National Geographic*, the encyclopedia, and maps as research tools. The same class researched animals in the rain forest. A writing sample: "Butterflies are really insects. The butterfly sleeps during the winter. Some fly to warmer areas."

The school has stable leadership in Principal William Bet, who says staff development training can invigorate both the junior and the senior teachers. Teachers are trained in the Writing Process by Teachers College writing guru Lucy Calkins. The staff learned ways to integrate art into the curriculum in another program at Columbia University.

# Flushing

After five years of being housed in portable trailers on the Queens College campus, **PS 499: Queens College School for Math, Science, and Technology,** 148-20 Reeves Avenue, Flushing, NY 11367, (718) 461-7462, a K–8 lab school that draws students from all across the borough, finally got a permanent home in 2004 in an award-winning building adjacent to the campus playing fields. It also received a permanent principal, the seventh in the school's short life, which should bring some stability to a school that had its share of growing pains. The new concrete building has a gray and coral color scheme. Soothing light enters walls of windows with panoramic views of Flushing. The school has art rooms with kilns and an attractive library. Lower-grade classrooms each have their own sink and bathroom attached. A dance room has a sprung floor. Kids sprawl on the floor to work on projects in airy atriums outside of classrooms. A science room is stocked with birds, beetles, a rabbit, and other animals.

Sadly, budget constraints make it hard to use all the facilities: "I have wonderful space and a beautiful art studio but I can't afford an art teacher," said Principal Anastasia Schneider, a graduate of the Leadership Academy, a new city initiative to train new principals. Some concerns: Parents wish busing were provided and would like an after-school program. Although Queens College sends student teachers to the school and holds monthly meetings with the school's staff, some parents say they'd like to see more collaboration with professors from Queens College. There was tension between the principal and some PTA leaders when we visited. But the quality of the teaching is good, particularly in science. In one lesson, kids researched how to ensure their sea monkeys would hatch. In another, kids traced one another's bodies on huge sheets of paper as part of a study of anatomy and bone structure. Students wear white and navy blue uniforms. Applications are available in February and due in March. Students are selected by lottery from all the districts in Queens. There are typically 1,000 applications for 40 kindergarten seats.

## South Ozone Park

**PS 124**, 129-15 150th Avenue, South Ozone Park, NY 11420, (718) 529-2580, is a school that uses Core Knowledge, a curriculum based on the work of E.D. Hirsch, who wrote *Cultural Literacy: What Every American Needs to Know.* Hirsch, an educational reformer, believes all Americans must have a shared body of knowledge, and he offers a specific, grade-by-grade list of what children should learn. First graders, for example, should learn a smattering of ancient Egyptian history; understand the basic tenets of the world's major religions; and read Aesop's fables, fairy tales such as "Hansel and Gretel," and excerpts from *Winnie-the-Pooh*. Fifth graders, he maintains, should know the date of the French Revolution and the importance of the Italian Renaissance. They should read Lincoln's Gettysburg Address and excerpts from Homer's *Iliad* and *Odyssey*.

The school, within walking distance of JFK Airport, is a lively place. Children, dressed in bright yellow shirts and plaid skirts or navy blue trousers, are exuberant. Many projects are interdisciplinary. A 1st-grade class, for example, focused on Germany. They studied the origin of the Christmas tree, learned about Martin Luther, and read "Hansel and Gretel." They baked gingerbread cookies and made holiday ornaments with glitter and glue.

A new addition to the school was opened in September 2002 and has helped to alleviate overcrowding by adding 10 new classrooms and a cafeteria. Only neighborhood children may attend the school. There is one gifted (Astre) class in each grade, kindergarten through 6th. Children are tested by the region in the spring of their prekindergarten year. There is also a "#1 class" for top students in each grade. Other classes mix children of differing abilities. Children who need extra help are placed in smaller classes of 17 pupils and provided with academic intervention services, or extra help.

# Howard Beach

With its veteran faculty, mentor principal, and gifted and talented program, **PS 232: Walter Ward School**, 153-23 83rd Street, Howard Beach, NY 11414, (718) 848-9247, is a place where children feel safe and encouraged to excel. Principal Norann McManus says she is determined to make the school feel like a home away from home for kids. The school aims to teach kids how to be good citizens as well as good learners, and to that end students are encouraged to participate in volunteer projects. A student organization, "Kids Who Care," meets weekly to organize community service projects, such as collecting clothing for mothers in need, hosting barbecues for the homeless, and sending gift boxes to soldiers in Iraq.

The school boasts a veteran staff of skilled teachers, and a good number of student teachers from Queens College use the school as their training ground. One mother, who said her daughter never had a teacher with less than a decade of experience, praised teachers for being expert at their craft. "They really know what they're doing," she said.

Students from surrounding neighborhoods attend the school and may test into its gifted and talented program, called Astre. Some parents say the school does well with struggling students as well. According to one parent, her child received little extra help when she was falling behind in Catholic school. She transferred to PS 232. "They give a lot of extra help to students here," the parent said.

# Richmond Hill

At **PS 62**, 97-25 108th Street, Richmond Hill, NY 11419, (718) 849-0992, teachers try to give all children the kind of education generally reserved for gifted classes at other schools. Here, everyone gets to read fun books, go on lots of class trips, and discuss esoteric topics such as the industrialization of rural China.

Long a mostly Irish and Italian neighborhood, Richmond Hill began changing rapidly in the 1980s as various new immigrant groups moved in. Now the school serves a diverse group of children, including ethnic Indians from Guyana and Punjabs and Sikhs from India.

All subject areas are woven into a theme. For example, children read novels and folktales set in China, learn Chinese dances and songs, and make paper lions for Lunar New Year. They go to Chinatown in Manhattan, eat at a Chinese restaurant, tour a Buddhist temple, and visit a school where Chinese is spoken. Even math is part of the theme: They learn to use abacuses and make pictures with "tangrams," geometric shapes that form a puzzle.

While class size is big, children at PS 62 get lots of individual attention. The school's principal, Angela O'Dowd, started in July 2003. She is an immigrant herself and says she understands the stresses that many parents face when they move to New York.

**PS 66: Jacqueline Kennedy Onassis School**, 85-11 102nd Street, Richmond Hill, NY 11418, (718) 849-0184, is housed in a 19th-century building called the "Little Red Schoolhouse," which recently was restored and given landmark status. The building may be old, but it is equipped with the latest technology, and the school has integrated computers into its curriculum more than is usual in public schools. Computers are right in the classrooms—not in a lab. At some schools, computers are used as a kind of electronic workbook to drill kids in arithmetic facts or spelling, but here children use computers to research, write, and draw. Children learn to write on computers starting in kindergarten, even before they can read or write letters with a pencil, and older children use computers, for example, to compete in the Stock Market Game, research documents for history projects, and illustrate their work.

The school has a well-equipped library, and children's literature is used to supplement textbooks in reading. An art teacher works with children on painting, working with clay, and making collages. A large immigrant population is aided by an English language learner specialist, who trains classroom teachers in ways to help non-English-speaking students. English-speaking classmates also help tutor these children.

## Laurelton

There is a culture of mutual respect at **PS/IS 270**, 233-15 Merrick Boulevard, Laurelton, NY 11413, (718) 341-8280, where each day begins with an assembly led by the principal or assistant principal in which students learn about the day's activities and have the opportunity to share their "random acts of kindness." Each child gets many accolades and much affirmation: "You are the future leaders," the principal tells the children at this new K–8 school open to children from across District 29. A vertical building on a corner of a busy commercial street, PS/IS 270 has a cascade of spheres resembling bowling balls in the welcoming entryway. The principal's office is just past the security desk, and you get the feeling Principal Eleanor Andrew, former principal of PS 132, is easily accessible—if you can catch her. She doesn't spend much time in the office but meets frequently with parents and spends lots of time in classrooms. (She says she has her own chair in each room, and in fact we saw one with her name on it.) The building has rotundas on each floor offering attractive benches where kids can gather and work. Artwork and student projects spill over from the bulletin boards and are plastered on the walls. Some concerns: School aides in the cafeteria barked at children who were misbehaving and forced them to put their heads down or stand against the wall. The schoolyard is small, so children don't always go out to play. But the tone of the building is mostly respectful, and both teachers and students speak kindly to one another. Admission is by lottery. Applications are due in February.

## Jamaica

Long the highest scoring school in District 29, **PS 131**, 172nd Street & 84th Avenue, Jamaica, NY 11432, (718) 739-4229, succeeds admirably in difficult circumstances.

Portable classrooms on the playground have about 30 fifth graders each. There is no art studio and no gymnasium. Still, the school has strong teachers, and its principal, Randolph Ford, who took the helm 2003, says that he is committed to making sure kids develop social skills and become good citizens, in addition to learning how to succeed in academics.

The school no longer has scripted school days with lessons on grammar, punctuation, vocabulary, and spelling, as it did in the past. Now, teachers use the Teachers College writing program, which teaches kids to write from their own experiences and edit one another's work. Teachers manage creative projects: One autumn day, 1st graders took a walk and collected leaves, seeds, and nuts, which they sorted and classified as a science lesson. Parents praise "the excellent music program" in which students learn violin, guitar, and flute recorder.

Racially and ethnically mixed, the school has immigrants from South America, China, India, Pakistan, and Bangladesh. Many students speak a language other than English at home. Parents say the different ethnic groups get along well—both the children and the parents in the PTA. Native-born children don't mind helping newcomers with English.

Another plus: Because of the vagaries of Department of Education zoning, PS 131 sends some of its graduates to a well-regarded junior high school in District 26, George Ryan.

Lime-green windows pop out in the new building that houses **PS 268**, 97-02 175th Street, Jamaica, NY 11433, (718) 206-3240, a new school serving children in kindergarten through 6th grade that's open to all children in District 29. Yellow, orange, and blue hallways, and red staircases make it seem more like a Lego construction than a school. It is a space conducive to displaying art, with sunlight filtering in through large glass panels and a main staircase overlooking the lobby. Mosaics with concise messages for the children—such as "poeTRY"—were created as part of the construction of the school and adorn the walls alongside student art projects. In addition to art classes, every student is exposed to science, multicultural social studies, dance, and gym. The school has a dance studio complete with ballet barre and "word wall," vocabulary words posted for the children to learn. Outside the studio, student reports about ballet techniques hang on the nearest bulletin board. In the multicultural social studies classroom, "artifacts" from different cultures sit on desks and shelves. Richly illustrated books about these cultures, such as *Sundiata: Lion King of Mali* and *One Grain of Rice: A Mathematical Folktale*, are displayed along low counters. Mobiles hang from the ceiling. The teacher introduced a class to the room and their first lesson by asking them to explore the room and its "primary sources" and talk with a classmate about what they liked most.

The school opened in September 2003 to help relieve overcrowding in District 29. Children from all over the district may apply to the school by participating in a lottery, and many of the current students are bused to the school.

## Queens Village

No elementary school should be this large, but the teachers and administrators manage to do a good job at **PS 33**, 91-37 222nd Street, Queens Village, NY 11428, (718) 465-6283, despite serious overcrowding. Reading teachers have carved-out classrooms in storage closets and tutor children in odd corners. A gymnasium is used as an art studio and as a science room. Children paint in the hallways to free up classroom space.

The arts are a priority. On one visit, we saw a large mural that featured children's self-portraits holding hands with one another. PS 33 boasts a large music program, including a school chorus. Some students' poetry is left out on tables in the entrance for visitors and students to peruse and make written comments about.

There is a gifted class starting in 1st grade. Otherwise, students of different ability levels share their classrooms. There is one self-contained class for students with special education needs only. Two other classes are inclusion, meaning that general education and special education students share a classroom. PS 33 is a school-based option school, which means the administration, staff, and parents are able to interview and choose their own teachers.

Many of the school's families now live in what were formerly single-family homes in Middle Village, including many immigrants from Bangladesh, India, and Afghanistan. One staff member praised the student body for being particularly well behaved and said students embrace one anothers' diverse cultures.

"We have no cliques in PS 33," said one parent. "Everybody just wants what's best for the children." Tours are available on request.

## Springfield Gardens

Open to all children in District 29, **PS 251: Early Childhood Magnet School**, 144-51 Arthur Street, Springfield Gardens, NY 11413, (718) 276-2745, is designed with very small children in mind. Kids are encouraged to explore their own interests and to move around their classroom from one activity to another. Children may sit on a rug, listening to a teacher read a story; observe a live snake in the science corner; or study early math concepts with blocks.

Trips are an important part of the curriculum: Children go to the Queens Botanical Garden, the Bronx Zoo, the American Museum of Natural History, the New York Aquarium in Coney Island, the Alley Pond Environmental Center in Queens, and a working farm on Long Island.

Parents describe the principal, Jacqueline Jones, as "very receptive." The school has an open house for parents once a year. Parents may pick up an application in January. A lottery is conducted in February. The school serves children in kindergarten through 3rd grade.

## Bellerose

**PS/IS 208**, 74-30 Commonwealth Boulevard, Bellerose, NY 11426, (718) 468-6420, is a K–8 school open to students in District 29, most of whom come by bus. Built to alleviate overcrowding in District 29, the school shares a spacious, sparkling campus with two other schools, PS/IS 266 and the High School of Teaching and Liberal Arts. The campus features a well-equipped playground and pleasant walkways. The school has many students of South Asian and African descent, with a sprinkling of whites.

We saw many creative teachers, as well as some more accustomed to schools where teachers teach from the front of the room and desks are placed in rows. We saw a "publishing party" where 5th graders read their writings—informative, and funny, nonfiction books. "Do you think the life of a lizard is easy? Do you?" asked a boy, in a grabbing opening statement about his book on iguanas. He then pointed out that these lizards shed their skin 20 times a week. His fellow students clapped and commented about what they had learned from his "book."

A District 75 school serving children with severe disabilities shares the building, and its principal gave PS/IS 208 high praise. "This is the most exceptional group of administrators I've ever met," she said. Admission to PS/IS 208 is by lottery.

## Middle Village

**PS 87**, 67-54 80th Street, Middle Village, NY 11379, (718) 326-8243, has long been known as a good neighborhood school with a particularly strong special education program. Seven of the school's classrooms are designated as "inclusion" classes. Children with speech and language problems or learning disabilities are integrated into regular classes with extra teachers to help out.

The school is a bustling, happy place and staffers have been trained in the Teachers College Reading and Writing Project. Every child writes for at least 40 minutes a day. Teachers make the rounds, conferring with children on their work. "You have an awful lot of information in one sentence," a 1st-grade teacher tells a boy. "Can you break it down into two or three sentences?" Children "publish" their work—present it to the rest of the class to read—at least 10 times a year in 1st grade and even more in the older grades.

PS 87 is housed in standard-looking, boxy brick building, and has struggled with some space issues as it has added middle school grades in recent years—there is a small lunchroom and no real gym. Still, inside, the school is a pleasant place, with rooms that are well thought-out and organized.

# Staten Island
# Schools

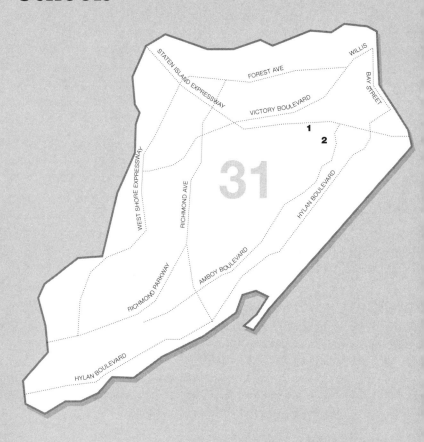

**District 31**
1  PS 80: Michael J. Petrides
2  PS 48: William Wilcox

# STATEN ISLAND

Staten Island is a world apart from the rest of New York. Sleepy, suburban, even rural in parts, the island attracts people who are looking for quiet neighborhoods, nice backyards, and reasonably priced housing. Lots of Staten Islanders work on the island rather than face the long commute by ferry to Manhattan or the traffic jams on the Verrazano-Narrows Bridge to Brooklyn.

Politically conservative, Staten Island has long been a Republican stronghold in a predominantly Democratic city. For many years, Staten Island was home to mainly white, Italian- and Irish-American families with stay-at-home moms and dads who worked in construction or as firefighters or police officers. Those families still make up a large part of the island's population, but they have been joined by African-Americans and immigrants from the Caribbean, Central America, India, and Korea—particularly in the northern, more urban parts of the island.

**District 31**, which includes all the schools on the island, has long been a stable, traditional district. For years, the schools offered children a meat-and-potatoes kind of education: Most schools taught the basics adequately, but without a lot of innovation or imagination. In recent years, that's been changing and many schools have blossomed with the introduction of livelier teaching techniques. Regional Superintendent Michelle Fratti, who worked in Manhattan's successful and innovative District 2 and who was superintendent of the well-regarded District 25 in Queens, has encouraged schools to rely less on textbooks and more on children's literature, to ask children to spend more time writing from their own experience and less time copying from the chalkboard, and to introduce math lessons that involve more conceptual understanding and less drill.

The schools are served by Region 7, which covers Staten Island and Districts 20 and 21 in Brooklyn. The regional offices are at 715 Ocean Terrace, Staten Island, NY 10301, (718) 556-8350.

The north shore schools are crowded, and housing development on the south shore has led to overcrowding as well, but some mid-island schools occasionally have room for children from outside their immediate zone.

The district has announced plans to open gifted and talented programs in six neighborhood schools. See *www.insideschools.org* for updates on gifted programs as well as profiles of schools not listed here.

# PS 80: Michael J. Petrides School
## 715 Ocean Terrace, Building B
## Staten Island, NY 10301
## (718) 815-0186
### *www.petrides.com*

**Admissions:** lottery
**Grade levels:** K–12
**Enrollment:** 1,210
**Class size:** K: 25; 8: 33

**Reading scores:** ****
**Math scores:** ****
**Ethnicity:** 66%W 14%B 12%H 8%A
**Free lunch:** 19%

The Michael J. Petrides School, open to all Staten Island residents, is a laboratory school designed to develop new teaching techniques and share them with other schools. With children in kindergarten through 12th grade, Petrides is a place where high school students tutor elementary school pupils, teachers of children of different ages learn tips from one another, and teachers and children get to know one another well.

A lavishly equipped school set on 43 acres on the former campus of Staten Island College, Petrides looks like a private school set in a country club. Surrounded by tennis courts and playing fields, the school has a huge gym, a science lab, a large auditorium, and an outdoor track.

In the elementary school, some teachers take a progressive approach, with kids sprawled on rugs on the floor working independently on projects. Others have a more traditional style, offering instruction to the whole class while kids are seated around a large table. Elementary classrooms are homey and appealing—some with white picket fences outside and curtains hanging from the windows. Kindergarten, 1st-, and 2nd-grade classrooms have "reading lofts" so students can work upstairs or underneath them.

A lottery for kindergarten admission is held in June. About 1,000 children apply for 75 kindergarten seats. There are a few openings in 4th grade and occasionally in other grades. Call the school in January for information.

# PS 48: William Wilcox School
### 1055 Targee Street
### Staten Island, NY 10304
### (718) 447-8323

**Admissions:** neighborhood
**Grade levels:** PK–5
**Enrollment:** 377
**Class size:** K: 19; 5: 28

**Reading scores:** ✶✶✶✶✶
**Math scores:** ✶✶✶✶
**Ethnicity:** 58%W 11%B 13%H 18%A
**Free lunch:** 31%

PS 48 is a neighborhood school with skyrocketing test scores and an enrichment program designed to give all children opportunities generally reserved for gifted classes. A small school, PS 48 has a strong sense of community. We visited on the Friday before Valentine's Day, and the principal, staff, teachers, and students were all excited about the handmade valentines children had made to recognize the people in the school who had made a difference in their lives. While the active, engaging principal, Jacqueline Mammolito, seemed to be getting plenty of thanks and good wishes, many other staff and students also were represented in the valentine distribution, including the friendly and welcoming security guard.

Popular programs include "Family Arts Night," lunchtime and after-school clubs, musical instrument instruction for 3rd and 4th graders, a "tranquility garden," an early childhood playground, volunteer reading instruction offered by Staten Island Mental Health and Learning Leaders, and an initiative that put five laptops in every 2nd- to 5th-grade classroom. The school has a partnership with the Guggenheim Museum to integrate the arts with social studies and literacy. Classes make trips to the museum, and teachers receive professional development at the museum as well as in the school.

Students in all grades seemed to be engaged and interested in their classes, and not at all fazed by the presence of a visitor. The rooms are generally large, clean, well lit, and full of children's work, which spills into the halls. PS 48 uses the Teachers College reading and writing workshop model, and students are encouraged to write a lot and to edit one another's work. There is continuity among the teachers at each grade level and classes are grouped heterogeneously. The principal's rapport with and respect for all students was evident, even those who had been sent to the office for misbehaving. As she said, "If kids are treated with respect, you get the respect right back."

# WORTH WATCHING: STATEN ISLAND

## Port Richmond

**PS 19: Curtis School**, 780 Post Avenue, Staten Island, NY 10310, (718) 442-3860, has an intensive writing program for young students, classical music and jazz in the hallways, and a science room that's full of imaginative and exciting projects. On the north shore of the island, PS 19 serves a mix of middle-class and poor children. More than 70% qualify for free lunch. One quarter are white, one quarter are black, and about half are Hispanic. Under the leadership of Principal Mary Petrone, PS 19 has assembled a team of enthusiastic teachers and staffers who make education exciting. The school's limited space has been used creatively. The science room and a number of offices have been fashioned out of old, out-of-the-way storage areas, for example. The school's test scores have increased significantly in recent years, but that is not the only indicator of its success. In the classrooms we visited, there was an air of excitement, and it was clear that the students, while often right, were not afraid to be wrong either. Apparently they have learned that error, too, is important to education. One 2nd-grade teacher fashioned a group of art, music, reading, and writing lessons around Van Gogh's "Starry Night." A 5th-grade teacher used a trip to the Bergen County Science Center to devise math and writing lessons based on calculating the trajectory necessary for a space capsule to catch Halley's comet. Hallways and classrooms are filled of impressive student work, and the school works hard to involve parents in their children's education.

## Clove Valley

**PS 35: The Clove Valley School**, 60 Foote Avenue, Staten Island, NY 10301, (718) 442-3037, is a school with high test scores and about 350 pupils on Staten Island's north shore. "Every day when I arrive at school, I feel like Mister Rogers," says Timothy Behr, principal since September 2002, and his enthusiasm is contagious. The school combines progressive and traditional teaching techniques, so you will see the "workshop" approach to writing (in which children make several drafts, edit, and "publish" their work) alongside more traditional readers. In a 4th-grade class we visited, students used various geometric figures to indicate multiples on a number line and were learning about equivalent liquid measures. In addition to reading and writing and mathematics, the school also emphasizes effective use of technology. Several classes had read a book on Ruby Bridges, the child who first integrated schools in Louisiana. Afterwards they learned how to format a letter on a computer, so they could correspond with Bridges. The students also used a sort of junior version of the PowerPoint presentation software to construct Venn diagrams showing the similarities and differences between their lives and Bridges' life. Another class visited a virtual Ellis Island on the Internet, using the material they found to write about the immigrant experience. The school embraces the arts. Reproductions of famous works of art decorate hallways, where music is played. (Beatles songs were featured the week we visited to commemorate the 40th anniversary of John, Paul, George and Ringo's arrival in the United States.) A local folk singer visits regularly, and a 2nd-grade class we visited painted Cubist-style watercolors of animal figures, after having studied Picasso and principles of Cubism. The school's dress code of blue, gray, and white clothing is in effect Mondays through Thursdays. There is a student newspaper, and the playground in front of the school has tables and benches where the students can read or play chess when the weather is good. Another plus: PS 35 has its own solarium.

## Graniteville

Parents at **PS 22: Graniteville School**, 1860 Forest Avenue, Staten Island, NY 10303, (718) 442-2219, say their children love the school: one mother said her daughter never wanted to leave. Serving more than 1,100 children, PS 22 is racially diverse, with white, black, Hispanic, and Asian children each making up about one-quarter of the population. Test scores are only average for the city, but as you tour PS 22, you see both teachers' enthusiasm for their jobs and the caring attitude they bring into the classroom. Kids are polite and respectful, but enthusiastic. One 3rd-grade class we visited was busy reading about the Renaissance (the school theme for the year), enjoying not only what they were learning about Florence but the bit of Italian they were picking up in the process. A science teacher conducted a lively discussion with a group of 4th graders about water displacement, using getting in and out of the bathtub as an example. In one writing class, students were sprawled on the floor intently drafting outlines of their next project. The visual arts teacher, wheeling her supply cart around, was eager to tell us about her Renaissance-related art instruction plans. Students put together an award-winning "rock" musical that incorporated performance, science class, and community service at the nearby Graniteville quarry. The students learned about geology and cleaned up the quarry, a local recreational site. The musical used what the students learned about the characteristics of the minerals in the quarry to promote the value of respecting the differences of people in the community.

## Tottenville

**PS 6**, 555 Page Avenue, Staten Island, NY 10307, (718) 356-4789, offers strong academics and a great sense of community in a modern facility opened in 2000. The building, which houses more than 800 children, most of whom are white, has curving hallways, floor-by-floor color themes, and a multistoried atrium at the entrance. Next door there is a wonderful park with fairy tale character sculptures and an amphitheater where some classes are held during mild weather. PS 6 promotes technology and science, housing a computer and two applied science labs, one for older kids, one for younger. When we visited the lower-school lab, where clever displays used Humpty Dumpty and Jack and Jill to teach gravity, a 1st-grade class was working enthusiastically on a project about astronauts' space suits. In the other lab, students learned about heat absorption by observing changes in black paper left on a window sill. The school has three self-contained classes for children with special needs, and ten team-taught classes, where special needs and general education kids learn side-by-side.

## Eltingville

Kathleen Schultz, principal of **PS 55: Henry Boehm School**, 54 Osborne Street, Staten Island, NY 10312, (718) 356-2211, combines a caring manner with a commitment to the arts. A 5th-grade unit on jazz combined lessons in music, literacy, and social studies. The students then shared what they had learned with a 1st-grade class. Students take music at least once a week. The physical education teacher gives dance and yoga classes, while the teacher heading the school's multicultural programs (offering such activities as a skit on Martin Luther King, Jr., in celebration of Black History month) puts on impressive performances. The school unfortunately lacks a science lab and therefore science classes are conducted from an equipment-filled cart transported from room to room. The school offers both self-contained special education classes and collaborative team-teaching classes, which have both a general education and a special education teacher, and mix children with special needs and those in general education. The school plays host to an interscholastic volleyball tournament and an interscholastic dance festival in which teams from participating schools include general and special education students. The school's test scores place it in the top 15% of schools citywide. It serves nearly 700 students, most of whom are white.

**PS 42**, 380 Genesee Avenue, Staten Island, NY 10312, (718) 984-3800, combines a warm atmosphere with a strong academic program. Principal Janice Lopresti and her staff set a tone that says: "We're going to learn here, but we're going to enjoy doing it." Teachers combine progressive and traditional techniques, and both students and teachers seem enthusiastic. The principal has made the arts a priority. A dancer teaches a movement class that boys and girls are equally excited about. Fifth graders created works in the Impressionist and Pointillist styles. Several classes watched shadow puppet shows, in a program sponsored by the Staten Island Children's Museum. First and 2nd graders sang a moving rendition of Neil Diamond's "Coming to America" during their lunchtime sing-along. The school has a literary magazine, and a children's author discussed writing with the kids the day of our visit. The school has five self-contained special education classes and three inclusion classes that mix disabled children and their mainstream peers.

## Rossville

Kids aren't the only ones receiving an education at **PS 56**, 250 Kramer Avenue, Staten Island, NY 10309, (718) 605-1189. Teachers also benefit from training opportunities emphasized by Principal Eileen Greenspun, who arrived at the school in 2003. And parents come to monthly meetings to learn about the curriculum. Test scores are high, and children are happy and engaged. The modern, welcoming building houses nearly 800 kids, the vast majority of whom are white. The day we visited was cold and icy, so a pre-K class was learning how rock salt melts ice. Kindergartners performed skits based on a book they had read and created picture books about transportation. Second graders were studying ants. And 5th graders studying decimals worked literary forms like idioms and similes into the discussion. PS 56 has a strong sense of history. Discovery of Lenape Indian artifacts when the school was constructed led to a presentation to the kids by a Lenape chief. A ceramic mural with Lenape themes was designed in part by students. On the horizon are projects involving Sandy Ground, one of the area's oldest African-American communities, and a tinsmith shop in nearby historic Richmondtown.

# QUICK REFERENCE GUIDE

## K–12 SCHOOLS
Renaissance Charter School
NEST+M
Petrides School

## K–8 SCHOOLS

### Manhattan
Talented and Gifted School
Special Music School of America
PS 187
Amistad Dual Language Academy
Harbor Science and Arts Charter
    School
Washington Heights Academy
Manhattan School for Children
PS 126
Ella Baker

### Bronx
PS 315
PS 175

### Brooklyn
Cypress Hills Community School
Beginning with Children Charter
    School
PS 132
PS 308
PS/IS 66

### Queens
Our World Neighborhood Charter
    School
PS/IS 270Q
PS124
PS/IS 268
PS/IS 251
PS/IS 208
PS 122
PS/IS 266Q

## CHARTER SCHOOLS (CITY-WIDE ADMISSIONS)
Renaissance Charter School
Our World Neighborhood Charter
    School
Future Leaders Institute
Harbor Science and Arts Charter
    School
Harlem Children's Zone Promise
    Academy Charter School
Bronx Charter School for the Arts

## OTHER CITY-WIDE ADMISSIONS
NEST+M
Ella Baker
Hunter College (Manhattan only)
Central Park East
CPE II
River East
Talented and Gifted School
Special Music School of America
Anderson Program at PS 9
Bronx Little School
Cypress Hills Community School
PS 499: Queens College (Queens
    only)
PS 251 (Queens)

## DISTRICT-WIDE ADMISSIONS

### Manhattan
The Children's Workshop School
    (District 1)
Earth School (District 1)
Neighborhood School (District 1)
Tribeca Learning Center (District 2)
Midtown West (District 2)
Bilingual Bicultural Mini-School
    (District 4)

Amistad Dual Language Academy
(District 6)
Hamilton Heights Academy
(District 6)

**Bronx**
Bronx New School (District 10)
PS 304 (District 10)

**Brooklyn**
The Children's School (District 15)
Brooklyn New School (Region 8)

**Queens**
PS 130 (District 25)
PS/IS 266 (District 26)
PS/IS 270 (District 29)
PS 267 (District 29)
PS 208 (District 29)
PS 268 (District 29)

**Staten Island**
Petrides School

## MAGNET PROGRAMS
PS 8 (Brooklyn)
PS 31 (Brooklyn)
PS 154 (Brooklyn)
PS 172 (Brooklyn)
PS 104 (Brooklyn)

## DUAL-LANGUAGE PROGRAMS

**Manhattan**
Shuang Wen Academy
Bilingual Bilcultural Mini-School
PS 87
PS 163
PS 75
Amistad Dual Language Academy
PS 178

**Brooklyn**
Cypress Hills Community School

## GIFTED AND TALENTED PROGRAMS

**Manhattan**
Hunter College Elementary School
PS 124
PS 130
PS 116

Lower Lab School for Gifted
Education
PS 171
Talented and Gifted School
Anderson Program at PS 9
PS 9 G&T
PS 166
PS 163
PS 178

**Brooklyn**
PS 193
PS 122
PS 104
PS 206
PS 299
PS 185
PS 235
PS 308
PS 230

**Queens**
PS 122
PS 150
PS 209
PS 165
PS 188
PS 18
PS 150
PS 232

## NOTEWORTHY SPECIAL EDUCATION

**Manhattan**
PS 158
PS 199
Manhattan School for Children
PS 75

**Bronx**
PS 153

**Brooklyn**
PS 10
PS 29
PS 372
PS 321

**Queens**
PS 107
PS 46

# INDEX

# ABOUT THE AUTHOR

**Clara Hemphill** is the founding editor of *Insideschools.org*, a website sponsored by Advocates for Children of New York. She is the primary author of *New York City's Best Public Middle Schools* and *New York City's Best Public High Schools*.

She was a foreign correspondent for The Associated Press, a producer for *CBS News* in Rome, and a reporter and editorial writer for *New York Newsday*, where she shared the 1991 Pulitzer Prize for local reporting. Her work has appeared in the *New York Times*, the *New York Daily News*, and *Newsday*.

She lives in Manhattan with her husband and two children, who attend public school.

**Deborah Apsel** visits and reviews schools for *Insideschools.org* and edits readers' comments on the site. Co-author of *New York City's Best Public Middle Schools*, her work has appeared in the *New York Daily News*, *Newsday*, and the *Gotham Gazette*. A graduate of Brown University, she was also an editor at *Facts on File* News Service.

**Catherine Man** visits and reviews schools for *Insideschools.org* and assists the technical director with website development. She attended PS 124 and The Lab School for Collaborative Studies in Manhattan and graduated from Barnard College. She began her work with Advocates for Children as an Americorps Vista volunteer. Her work has appeared in *Newsday*.

**Pamela Wheaton** is deputy director of *Insideschools.org* and co-author of *New York City's Best Public High Schools*. She advises parents on school choice for Advocates for Children. She was a reporter and editor at the *Buenos Aires Herald* and a public television producer. She lives in Brooklyn with her husband and a daughter who attends public school. Another daughter, now in college, is a public school graduate.